Corporate Rivalry and Market Power

Tourism, Retailing and Consumption series

Edited by:
Professor Gareth Shaw, University of Exeter
Professor Dimitri Ioannides, Missouri State University

Consumption has become an important theme in geography and the social sciences and within this broad debate two key areas of concern are tourism and retailing. To date there is no series that brings together these closely related topics under a unifying perspective. *Tourism, Retailing and Consumption* provides such a perspective.

   The scope of the series is wide-ranging, covering both contemporary and historical debates in tourism, retailing and consumption, and includes core texts for students of geography and related disciplines at first-degree level together with a number of more specialised texts suited to postgraduate study.

Books already published in the series:

Tourism in Transition:
Economic Change in Central Europe
Allan M. Williams & Vladimir Balaz

Understanding Urban Tourism:
Image, Culture and Experience
Martin Selby

Tourism in the New South Africa:
Social Responsibility and the Tourist Experience
Garth Allen & Frank Brennan

Corporate Rivalry and Market Power

Competition Issues in the Tourism Industry

Edited by
Andreas Papatheodorou

I.B. TAURIS
LONDON · NEW YORK

Published in 2006 by I.B. Tauris & Co. Ltd
6 Salem Road, London W2 4BU
175 Fifth Avenue, New York NY 10010
www.ibtauris.com

In the United States and Canada distributed by Palgrave Macmillan,
a division of St Martin's Press, 175 Fifth Avenue, New York NY 10010

HB ISBN 10: 1 84511 155 9
HB ISBN 13: 978 1 84511 155 7
PB ISBN 10: 1 84511 156 7
PB ISBN 13: 978 1 84511 156 4

A full CIP record for this book is available from the British Library
A full CIP record for this book is available from the Library of Congress

Library of Congress catalog card: available

Typeset in by Keystroke, Jacaranda Lodge, Wolverhampton
Printed and bound in Great Britain by TJ International Ltd, Padstow, Cornwall

Contents

List of figures   vii
List of tables   ix
List of contributors   xi
Preface   xv

Chapter 1
Corporate rivalry, market power and competition issues in tourism: an
introduction   1
Andreas Papatheodorou

Chapter 2
The theoretical pillars of industrial organisation in tourism   20
Zheng Lei

Chapter 3
Quantitative techniques for tourism competition analysis   35
Gang Li and Haiyan Song

Chapter 4
Corporate rivalry and competition issues in the airline industry   54
John F. O'Connell

Chapter 5
Competition in airports   76
Anne Graham

Chapter 6
The market influence of tour operators on the hospitality industry   94
Dimitris Koutoulas

Chapter 7
Competition in the travel distribution system: the US travel retail sector   124
Dimitri Ioannides and Evangelia Petridou Daughtrey

Chapter 8
The impact of information technology on tourism competition   143
Dimitrios Buhalis

Chapter 9
Competition in visitor attractions   172
Stephen Wanhill

Chapter 10
Market definition in the tourism industry   187
Gunnar Niels and Reinder van Dijk

Chapter 11
Conclusion: the need for constructive policymaking   201
Andreas Papatheodorou

Index   206

Figures

1.1	The characteristics model in tourism	10
1.2	Short-run tourism flows	12
1.3	Long-run tourism flows	12
2.1	The structure–conduct–performance paradigm	22
2.2	Decision tree for the sequential capacity expansion game	29
4.1	World air transport growth airlines (domestic and international)	55
4.2	Yield decline of world airlines (scheduled)	56
4.3	Industry operating profit and margin	57
6.1	The relationship between cost, price and demand in tourism	100
7.1	Travel distribution channels	126
7.2	Commission cut timeline	135
8.1	Internet impacts on the tourism industry	152
9.1	The attraction product	173
9.2	Monopolistic competition	176
9.3	Oligopolistic competition	180
9.4	Pricing rules by ownership	182

Tables

2.1 Vertical integration and consolidation in the UK charter industry, 2000   26
2.2 Price war game   27
2.3 Capacity expansion game   29
2.4 Entry deterrence game   30
3.1 The top tour operators in Germany and Italy   36
3.2 HHIs of Taiwanese international tourist accommodation markets   37
3.3 The average fares per passenger kilometre in London   40
3.4 Paired-samples test for fare differences   40
3.5 UK local bus fare indices   41
3.6 Correlations between UK local bus fare levels in different regions 42
3.7 Correlations between UK local bus fare changes in different regions 43
3.8 Long-run compensated price elasticities of UK tourism demand in key European destinations   49
4.1 Airline models formed since 2002   58
4.2 Changes in hub-and-spoke market shares   61
4.3 Eleven major characteristics of Open Skies   71
6.1 International tourist arrivals and total hotel bed capacity in Greece and in selected Mediterranean countries   95
6.2 Market share of Germany's and the UK's five largest tour operators, 2003   97
6.3 Tourist arrivals in Greece, 2003: TUI customers and overall market 103
6.4 Size, category and location of hotels participating in the survey 106
6.5 Business mix of hotels participating in the survey for the year 2004 107
6.6 Main nationalities of hotel guests for the year 2004   109
6.7 Occupancy and average room rates for the year 2004   110
6.8 Variations of tour operator-generated business over the last three years   112
6.9 Expectations regarding tour operator-generated business and requirements of tour operators towards hotels   113
6.10 Tour operators contributing most customers   114

6.11 Positive and negative aspects of working with tour operators as seen
      from the hotels' point of view   116
6.12 Financial results for the year 2004   117
7.1   US travel agencies with sales more than $1 billion   131
7.2   Cendant Holdings   132
8.1   Competition levels, tourism challenges and ICT solutions   146
8.2   How the Internet influences industry structure   148
8.3   Typologies of incremental revenues in airline CRSs   157
8.4   GDS worldwide bookings comparison   159
8.5   GDS profiles   160
8.6   Online majors travel bookings revenue   166
9.1   The variety of imagescapes   174
10.1 Percentage critical sales losses   193
10.2 Alternative options considered by holiday park customers after
      10% price increase   196

Contributors

Dimitrios Buhalis is Course Leader MSc in Tourism Marketing and Leader of eTourism Research at the School of Management University of Surrey. Dimitrios is also Adjunct Professor at the MBA in Hospitality Management at the Institut de Management Hotelier International (Cornell University–École Supérieure des Sciences Économiques et Commerciales ESSEC) in Paris and regularly contributes to more than twenty postgraduate tourism courses around the world. He is a registered European Commission IST evaluator and reviewer and Vice Chairman of the International Federation of Information Technology and Tourism (IFITT). Dimitrios was the immediate past Chairman of the Association of Tourism Teachers and Trainers (ATTT).

Anne Graham is a Senior Lecturer in Air Transport and Tourism at the University of Westminster. Before joining the university she worked in air transport consultancy. Anne has a first class BSc degree in Mathematics, a MSc degree in Tourism and a PhD in air transport and tourism management. Anne specialises in the teaching and research of tourism and air transport and has two key research interests. First the research of airport economics and regulation and in 2003 the second edition of her key book entitled *Managing Airports: An International Perspective* was published by Elsevier. Anne's other research interest is the modelling and forecasting of tourism and air transport demand.

Dimitri Ioannides received his PhD in Urban Planning and Policy Development from Rutgers University, New Jersey. For the last 12 years he has taught at Missouri State University and since 2003 he has also been a Senior Research Fellow at the Center for Regional and Tourism Research in Bornholm, Denmark where he spends approximately two months a year. His research interests include the tourist industry, tourism and sustainability, and tourism planning in transboundary areas. His publications include two edited books, including *The Economic Geography of the Tourist Industry* (Routledge).

Dimitris Koutoulas with a degree in Business Administration and a PhD in Tourism Marketing, works as a tourism and marketing consultant. He presently teaches at the Greek Open University. His consultation appointments include, among others, research projects as well as business and marketing planning on behalf of the Greek National Tourism Organisation, the European Union, the authorities of Athens, the Cyprus Tourism Organisation, the Organising Committee of the Athens Olympic Games, the Greek Organisation for Tourism Education and Training and the Athens Convention and Visitors Bureau. Dr Koutoulas also has extensive hands-on experience in applied marketing.

Zheng Lei is a Senior Lecturer in Tourism Management in the Ashcroft International Business School, Anglia Ruskin University, United Kingdom. He started his career in a tour operating business in China where he worked for six years. Having secured a three-year scholarship from the University of Surrey, Mr Lei is currently completing research at a doctoral level on low-cost carriers and their impact on regional tourism development. Zheng has co-authored papers in *Tourism and Hospitality Research* and the *Journal of Air Transport Management* and has presented his work at various international conferences including the German Aviation Research Society Workshop, the Hamburg Aviation Conference and the Air Transport Research Society Conference. His research interests include industrial organisation and air transport economics.

Gang Li is a Lecturer in Economics in the School of Management, University of Surrey, United Kingdom. His research interests include applied econometric modelling and forecasting, with an emphasis on international tourism demand analysis. He also researches in Chinese economic issues such as income inequity using econometric methods.

Gunnar Niels is Head of Oxera Competition, and has ten years' experience in the field of competition policy. Before joining OXERA in May 1999, Gunnar was Deputy Head of the Economics Directorate at Mexico's Federal Competition Commission. Gunnar is on the Advisory Board of the *Competition Law Journal* and has been guest editor for the *Antitrust Bulletin*. He has published several papers in these and other journals, such as the *European Competition Law Review, World Economy, European Journal of Political Economy* and *European Journal of Law and Economics*. Gunnar holds a PhD and MSc in Economics from the Erasmus University Rotterdam.

John F. O'Connell has a Masters degree in Air Transport Management from Cranfield and an MBA (Aviation) from Embry-Riddle. He began his career as a marketing analyst with Boeing by examining ways to optimise an airline's schedule network. John then joined Embry-Riddle Aeronautical University extended campus in San Francisco where he lectured in airline management, marketing and operations. While in the USA, he also lectured extensively at NASA at Moffett Federal Airfield, California on technical aeronautical issues. John then moved to Europe where he currently gives short courses for IATA and AACO to airlines globally and he also lectures in airline strategy in numerous universities. He also acts as independent consultant to airlines who wish to set up low-cost operations and has advised carriers in Malaysia, Singapore, India, Egypt and Morocco. Mr O'Connell has published articles in *Airline Business, Aircraft Economics* and in the *Journal of Air Transport Management*. John is also a member of the editorial board of the journal *World Review of International Transportation Research*. He is currently doing a PhD at Cranfield University on airline strategy.

Andreas Papatheodorou is an Assistant Professor in Industrial Economics with emphasis on Tourism at the School of Business Administration, University of the Aegean, Greece. He is also an Honorary Research Fellow of the Tourism and Travel Research Institute at the University of Nottingham and a Visiting Senior Fellow at the University of Surrey. Andreas holds a MPhil in Economics from the University of Oxford and a DPhil in Geography from the same university. He started his academic career as a Lecturer in Tourism at the University of Surrey. Dr Papatheodorou is actively engaged in tourism research, focusing on issues related to competition, pricing and corporate strategy in air transport and travel distribution. Most of his work is related to the Mediterranean region and has been published in international academic journals. Andreas has also offered his services as an Advisor to the Greek Government on tourism policymaking and development and conducts air transport and tourism education courses organised by AACO in the Middle East.

Evangelia Petridou Daughtrey teaches Greek at Drury University, Springfield Missouri. She is also a Political Science student at Missouri State University and a certified travel agent.

Haiyan Song is Chair Professor of Tourism in the School of Hotel and Tourism Management, The Hong Kong Polytechnic University, Hong Kong. He also holds a Visiting Professorship in the School of Management, University of Surrey, United Kingdom. Professor Song has a background in Economics. His main research area is tourism economics with a particular focus on tourism demand modelling and forecasting. He has extensive research and consultancy experience in such areas as foreign direct investment in China and economic issues related to China's tourism sector.

Reinder van Dijk is managing consultant at OXERA and specialises in competition policy and financial regulation. He has appeared as an expert witness on competition issues, and has worked with a range of clients on competition cases in the UK, Europe, Latin America and the Middle East. His experience in financial and economic policy includes working at the Netherlands Central Bank as an economist in the monetary and economic policy department. Reinder has an MSc in Economics from the Erasmus University Rotterdam in The Netherlands, and a postgraduate diploma in International Economic Law from the University of Warwick, UK.

Stephen Wanhill is Emeritus Professor of Tourism Research, School of Services Management, Bournemouth University and a Visiting Professor at the Universities of Limerick, Nottingham and Swansea, as well as for the Center for Regional and Tourism Research, Bornholm, Denmark. His principal research interests are in the field of tourism destination development and to this extent he has undertaken a wide range of tourism development strategies, tourism impact assessments, lecture programmes and project studies from airports to attractions, both in the UK and worldwide, covering some 50 countries. He has acted as tourism policy advisor to the Select Committee on Welsh Affairs, House of Commons and has been a Board Member of the Wales Tourist Board with responsibilities for the development and research divisions. He is the editor of the journal *Tourism Economics.*

Preface

I still remember that rainy morning in June 1995 when I visited Mr Andrea Boltho, my personal tutor, in his imposing office at Magdalen College in Oxford. It was time to decide on the topic of my MPhil dissertation and I had proudly announced him that I was interested in focusing on strategic trade theory and infant industries. In his usual polite manner, he convinced me that this was not the right topic for me; it would be better to choose something related to my home country, Greece. Tourism then came as a straightforward option to my mind and eventually I produced a thesis on the demand for international tourism in the Mediterranean Region. The tourism industry raised my interest so much that I subsequently decided to pursue a DPhil in the area focusing on the relatively unexplored supply-side of the sector from an economic geography perspective. Upon completion of my DPhil in 2000, I commenced my academic career as Lecturer in Tourism at the University of Surrey, an institution with a long tradition in tourism studies. My aim was to capitalise on my graduate studies and become an expert in the field of industrial economics and geography of tourism. In this context, I introduced a new MSc module entitled Competition Issues in Tourism in 2002; I also co-designed and led a new MSc Programme in Tourism and Air Transport Management in 2003.

By that time, I had reached the conclusion that there was a gap in the academic book market regarding the integrated treatment of industrial organisation matters in tourism. This was in sharp contrast with the rising market concentration observed in many related sectors. Dimitri Ioannides, whose work among others has inspired the topic of my DPhil, was very supportive when I discussed with him my ambition to edit a book in the area. He has kindly put me in contact with David Stonestreet from IB Tauris, who is the publisher of this book. Moving then to the University of the Aegean in Greece as an Assistant Professor in Industrial Economics with emphasis on Tourism was an ideal timing to bring the whole idea forwards.

Admittedly, the topic of the book is specialised; its importance, however, is crucial from a policymaking perspective, hence the need for a thorough treatment with contributions from a panel of experts. I would like to thank all of them, as without their help this book would not have materialised. On a personal note, I would like to express my gratitude to my family for their support.

Andreas Papatheodorou
Athens 2006

1

Corporate rivalry, market power and competition issues in tourism

An introduction

Andreas Papatheodorou

Oligopoly as the playground of corporate rivalry and market power

Economics are traditionally preoccupied with the achievement of market efficiency. The term 'market' has been heuristically used but essentially refers to
'a group of products that are reasonable substitutes for at least one good in the
group and have limited interaction with the rest of the economy' (Yarrow, 2001).
A realistic market definition should step beyond the physical characteristics of
the products involved and consider both demand and supply-side substitution,
i.e. whether consumers are able to find suitable product or supplier alternatives
(NERA, 2001). The term 'efficiency' is three-faceted. Productive efficiency involves
market equilibrium at the lowest average total cost and allocative efficiency exists
when price is equal to marginal cost and the allocation of resources cannot
improve consumer welfare (Pareto optimality). Both dimensions of efficiency may
be achieved under perfect competition. This is an idealistic market structure where
infinitesimal firms produce a homogeneous product and compete freely against
each other for the custom of infinitesimal rational, perfectly informed and mobile
consumers. In reality, the closest to perfect competition is monopolistic competition where part of productive and allocative inefficiency is traded for variety and
product differentiation.

Still, neither perfect nor monopolistic competition is compatible with the third
facet of efficiency, namely the dynamic one, which refers to product and process
improvements, development and innovation (OXERA, 2002). This is because both
market structures result in zero profits in the long run; hence they cannot support
research and development, which requires heavy and in most cases unprofitable
and non-recoupable (sunk) investment. On the other hand, a monopolist may
enjoy super-normal profits, which can be partly used to increase productivity and
achieve dynamic efficiency. These profits, however, are associated with productive
and allocative inefficiency; moreover, the monopolist has no incentive to invest in
technology or other improvements unless contested. In this context and from a
rather Schumpeterian point of view, the market structure of oligopoly where few

firms compete against each other in a strategic environment is a realistic alternative which under certain conditions may produce an acceptable balance among the three facets of efficiency and the subsequent generation of socio-economic welfare.

Dominance and mergers

Corporate rivalry and market power are, therefore, structurally intertwined in oligopolistic markets. In principle, everything may happen in an oligopoly as the competitive conduct ranges from market cartelisation and the replication of the monopoly outcome to destructive price wars. In fact, perfect competition and monopolistic competition do not give rise to strategic behaviour, while the uncontested monopoly produces rather predictable and explicit outcomes, which are best controlled by a suitable regulatory framework rather than any Competition Acts. On these grounds, the study of competition issues is of primary interest and importance in oligopolies to inspect business practices that may result in dominance and abuse of market power. More specifically, the term 'dominance' refers to a concentrated structure, where the leading firm possesses a very high market share. When a small number of companies form an effective oligopoly, collective dominance may also be present (Court of First Instance, 2002). Individual or collective dominance is not problematic per se; nonetheless, it may raise issues of market power abuse. Therefore, what matters is the restrictive conduct of dominant firms; if the latter are powerful enough to devise a strategy independently of their competitors, this may have a negative impact on market competitiveness. Modern competition policies should be designed to safeguard efficiency but also to cater for public interest by emphasising distribution objectives to raise consumer welfare (Morris, 2000). Therefore, dominance enquiries should pay more attention to market conduct that damages competition and the consumers rather than the other competitors per se. For example, a tour operator may succeed in becoming a market leader because of good service quality delivered to its clientele. If this service is good value for money and raises no complaints by potential or actual customers then the tour operator should not be penalised for its dominance: this could lead to market distortion by discouraging efforts to innovate and succeed. Nonetheless, corporations should play by the rules and avoid raising unnecessary market entry (or exit) barriers or signing non-transparent contracts with suppliers and distributors which restrict competition. Corporate conduct should be analysed in a dynamic context as short-run positive effects may be reversed in the longer term. For example, a predatory pricing strategy followed by a leading firm is harmful for competitors but beneficial for consumers in the short term. Nonetheless, if this strategy succeeds in inducing the exit of the other competitors in the longer run, the leading company may decide to abuse its market dominance without reservation causing a reduction in consumer welfare.

2

Similarly, the study of competition issues is topical in appraising mergers between companies within the same supply chain (vertical mergers) and especially in directly competing operations (horizontal mergers) (NERA, 1999). Production advantages and efficiency gains may emerge by avoiding duplication of fixed/sunk costs. Such cost savings may then finance research on product development – the merged firms take advantage of scale and scope economies by using resources previously spent in pointless revenue diluting rivalry (Schumpeter, 1996). In addition, a merger may save a weak firm from declaring bankruptcy; hence, unnecessary scraping of capital and labour redundancies are avoided. Therefore, a thorough merger investigation should perform a cost-benefit analysis to evaluate the importance of any potential production advantages against the emergence of a dominant position and the potential abuse of market power. Public interest should be prioritised and the customer must enjoy any savings in production costs either directly through price discounts and better quality products and/or indirectly through innovation. To this end, the merging firms should be prevented from restricting the market conduct.

Competition issues in tourism

Having established the validity of studying competition issues in general, the natural step forward is to explain their relevance and importance in the context of tourism. To do so, we first evaluate the complexity of the tourism sector from a supply-side perspective and then present those characteristics of the product which may be subject to market power abuse given the oligopolistic features of the related industries. The latter may be understood in the context of a notable dualism in market and spatial structures.

Tourism – a supply-side conundrum

Tourism does not have a unique base as an industry, because its related commodities are viewed as heterogeneous both in terms of consumption and production practices. In fact, the tourism industry may be regarded as an amalgamation of businesses and other organisations that serve customers with diverse incomes, tastes and objectives (Eadington and Redman, 1991). For example, the air transport sector may be classified together with rail under a transportation industry tag, because they both move people using engine power; similarly, hotels and rooms-to-let constitute part of the accommodation industry. But, according to Smith (1998: 36) 'there is no apparent commonality between moving people from place to place (transportation) and helping them stay still (accommodation)'. This situation induced Leiper (1990) to argue that tourism is like a red-hair industry, whose commodities have nothing in common apart from the colour of their consumers' hair. On the other hand, transport, accommodation and other services are functionally linked. They exhibit demand complementarities, since they all support the production of a tourism experience. Therefore, they are also subject to pecuniary externalities (Scitovsky, 1954) and cost complementarities, since a sharp increase in the price of one segment may have serious implications for the unit cost of the others. These linkages are strong enough to re-establish the tourism industry as a valid supply-side concept. More generally, however, the definitional obscurity of the tourism sector is largely dissolved by considering the Tourism Satellite Accounts. This is an accounting information system that assembles, classifies and interrelates statistics from the National Accounts, which describe all important and measurable aspects of tourism found in the various sectors of the economy (WTO, 1999). It is closely related to the tourism ratio, which measures the size of tourism demand as a percentage of the total industrial supply. For example, TSA analysis reveals that tourism is the major component of the air transportation market. Indeed, its tourism ratio is over 90%; similar results hold for hotels. On the other hand, the respective figure for groceries is less than 3%. As a useful though arbitrary rule-of-thumb, all industries with a ratio exceeding 15% are regarded as tourism ones (Smith, 1998). In terms of transport, air and cruising are of predominant importance for tourism. Similarly, hotels, holiday parks and related accommodation facilities are part of the tourism sector. The travel distribution circuit owes its existence to tourism almost entirely, while certain attractions such as cultural heritage and theme parks are elements of a system that comprises outdoor recreation and tourism.

In addition to the above industrial organisation connotations, it is important to encapsulate the spatial dimension of tourism. In fact, tourism is a geographical phenomenon par excellence and the explicit treatment of space is essential in a supply side analysis. According to the *Dictionary of Travel, Tourism and Hospitality* (Medlik, 1993), every area visited by tourists may be regarded as a tourist desti-nation. Commoditisation is independent of spatial scale and refers both to large entities such as countries and regions and to smaller areas like towns or even neighbourhoods. This raises, however, the issue of cognitive distance and the relationship between an origin and a potential tourist area (Vukonič, 1997). For example, in long-haul journeys, entire countries or regions are shrunk into single focal points of attraction. However, as soon as a tourist visits the destination, perception changes and the spatial scale becomes narrower; for example, tourists who come to Greece change their notion of tourist area to the Cyclades islands, Santorini or even Little Venice in Mykonos.

The importance of a geographical unit as a tourist destination is mainly determined by the level and content of its characteristics subject to the existing constraints. In particular, local attractions are associated with the natural/cultural tourist potential of a resort and the available accommodation, catering and entertainment infrastructure. Moreover, in contrast to the natural resources, which usually exist ex nihilo and have a free public good character, the provision of tourist services is conditional upon the sufficiency of tourist demand. If the latter exceeds a specific level, however, it may create congestion in the short term and destroy natural resources in the long run. In other words, local characteristics are subject to a dynamic spatial trade-off. In addition to this mutual exchangeability, the attractiveness of a destination is constrained by a number of transport and information impediments. The former are associated with financial and time costs, whereas the latter are a function of cognitive distance. Both constraints, however, are conditional upon the availability and quality of transport and information networks. As the nature of these features changes in space and time, the various barriers in tourism development become endogenously determined in the circuit.

Having the above discussion in mind, tourist commodities may be defined as all goods and services for which visitors constitute a large part of their aggregate demand. Space is an inherent characteristic of these products both in terms of mobility (i.e. transportation) and fixity (i.e. accommodation). Primary inputs and factors of production (land, labour and capital) are transformed into intermediate ones (physical facilities) such as visitor attractions and conference centres. Further processing creates intermediate outputs such as folklore shows or restaurant meals. These are taken by the visitor and processed into final products or experiences. This active consumer involvement during the last stage of production is a unique feature of the tourism industry, since without their participation intermediate outputs remain idle. Unfortunately, the TSA lags behind in this sense, as it is not designed to encapsulate the subjective experience of tourism (Smith, 1998). However, we can still acknowledge in principle the existence of a generic product, namely a tourism experience. This view is further enhanced by the existence of a number of characteristics, which are holistically attributed to tourism rather than to its constituent industries. In particular, the uniqueness of tourism lies in the voluntary displacement of people from familiar environments to relatively unknown ones. Tourists visit the site of production – the tourist factory – in contrast to commodity trade patterns; in fact, production and enjoyment of the purchased services coincide in time and location. Furthermore, as stated by Urry (1990), tourist services have an element of spatial fixity, where part of what is consumed is the commodified site. In addition, although tourism is a non-durable product in the proper sense, the positive benefit gained from holiday-taking extends beyond the time spent away from home. Therefore, while from a static perspective the choice of the consumer to spend a relatively high percentage of their budget on tourism goods is a paradox, such a decision may be fully justified within an inter-temporal framework.

Tourism characteristics and strategic behaviour

It should be noted, however, that the tourist product involves a number of characteristics that may be strategically used in the context of corporate rivalry. First, tourism may be regarded as an experience good, because the consumer cannot tell its quality and characteristics before its purchase (Tirole, 1988). This information problem is accentuated by spatial factors and may have serious implications for travelling decisions, given the relatively high cost of holidays. As a result, the potential consumer may seek professional assistance from the travel distribution system. In this context, the tour operators act as wholesalers who bundle different tourism services together and sell them jointly as a package at a unique price; similarly, travel agents are the retailers of the system who offer consulting services and sell individual travel components or whole tourist packages to the consumer. The travel distribution system is subject to dynamic economies of scale associated with reputation and experience. It may abuse its intermediary role by effectively manipulating prices, information and service quality to exercise oligopolistic power on consumers and set oligopsonistic conditions on transport, accommodation and other principals. Still, recent advancements in information and communication technologies such as the Internet have reduced the cost of information acquisition and encouraged disintermediation and the direct contact between consumers and tourism producers (Buhalis, 1998).

Second, the tourist product requires the combination of tangible assets and intangible services in ways that are occasionally subject to market turbulence and instability (Papatheodorou, 2002). In particular, tourism is characterised by substantial fixed costs in transport, accommodation and in some cases technological infrastructure; airports, hotels and electronic reservation systems are good examples. These costs are largely sunk as they cannot be easily recovered due to their spatial fixity (e.g. a hotel cannot move) and asset specificity (e.g. the functionality of an airport is limited to air transport services). As a result, they may constitute significant barriers to market entry and exit and provide risky and wealthy entrepreneurs with satisfactory returns and rents on quasi-natural monopolies and oligopolies. To deter rivalry the incumbents may invest excessively in such capacity and therefore accentuate the utilisation problem. In fact, the pathology of many tourism firms stems from the perishable nature of their services and the inability to store the product and sell it at a later date: a hotel bed or an airline seat that is not sold today is lost forever. To face this difficulty, firms may decide to engage in horizontal (i.e. variety) and vertical product differentiation (i.e. quality) to increase their clientele; in many cases, however, the tourism producers may be tempted to undercut their rivals and engage into a bid war leading to pricing according to marginal costs. Since the latter may be significantly lower than average total costs (due to the existence of economies of scale), such price wars may shake up the industry and cause bankruptcies and market exit. Inductively, entry may not occur at all. Consequently and similarly to the case of predatory pricing, short-term consumer benefits may be outweighed by long-term losses associated with the abuse of market power by dominant principals and large tourism intermediaries, which can play one firm against the other. The seasonal character of tourism in many destinations makes the above description very relevant especially in off-peak periods (Baum and Lundtorp, 2001).

Tourism and the dual dualism

Having the above in mind, we may argue that tourism is a legitimate sector of the economy. It has a number of unique characteristics some of which are subject to the abuse of market power. To conclude this section and show the relevance of competition issues, we need to discuss the oligopolistic nature of certain tourism services. From a superficial point of view, the tourism sectors are characterised either by 'backyard capitalism' (Krugman, 1995) of numerous small firms or by contestability conditions of costless market entry and exit (Baumol, 1982). In fact, an airline can be established by just leasing a turbo-prop aircraft while most residential buildings can be easily converted to apart-hotels. As for tour operations, all that is required to set-up a business is an office, a telephone/fax and some knowledge of the destination area. Such a market structure could ensure very efficient conduct and performance – to use Bain's (1956) classical paradigm – either because of active competition among infinitesimal non-cooperating firms or due to potential rivalry from entrants threatening the incumbents with a hit-and-run strategy. Under such conditions, therefore, any active competition policy would be simply a waste of public resources.

In reality, however, concentration and market structure dualism prevail nowadays in the transport for tourism, accommodation and travel distribution sectors (Papatheodorou, 2004). In addition to the monopolistically competitive fringe, airline consolidation and the creation of mega-carriers (such as Air France–KLM and Lufthansa–Swiss) is marching fast in the context of the three global strategic alliances, i.e. Star Alliance, SkyTeam and oneworld. National markets are also heavily concentrated and in the USA, the ten-firm ratio exceeded 90% in 2000 (Goetz, 2002). Likewise, the recent merger between Carnival and POPC has led to the dominance of the world cruise industry by three major companies, i.e. the newly merged company, RCCL and the Star Group, which collectively control almost three-quarters of the market (Papatheodorou, 2006). As for the accommodation industry, the small traditional hotels coexist with giant global hotel chains: illustratively, the ten largest groups controlled 3.5 million rooms in 29.6 thousand hotels in 2003 (Hotels, 2004) while the joint turnover of the seven largest hotel corporations in Britain amounts to 60% of the market (Davies, 1999). Concentration is also apparent in the global travel distribution system, where companies like TUI have followed an aggressive acquisition strategy over the last few years, establishing transnational conglomerates: among other firms, the World of TUI controls tour operators (e.g. TUI, Thomson), airlines (e.g. Hapag-Lloyd, Britannia), hotels (e.g. Grecotel) and travel agents (e.g. Lunn Poly). In Britain, the four largest holiday groups and companies were licensed to fly 46% of passengers on a tour package in 2004 (CAA, 2005).

These emerging changes in the market structure are inherent features of the growth process in the sectors of tourism. Once a critical size of visitor flows is attained, scale and scope economies develop in a self-reinforcing manner raising barriers to entry and leading to effective market foreclosure. In particular, the various routines and processes of corporate operations may come under severe pressure across the stages of the business cycle (Nelson and Winter, 1982). During periods of recovery and demand booming, new investment and expansionary strategies may be required to take advantage of the new business opportunities. On the other hand, periods of recession and demand stagnation may necessitate rational restructuring and radical downscaling to survive in a fiercely competitive environment. Whether firms are sufficiently flexible to adapt successfully to any exogenous macro changes depends on the ability of their entrepreneurs to act as rational forward-looking persons. Since the end of the Second World War and until the mid 1970s, the tourism industries have enjoyed a long period of uninterrupted stable growth, which allowed new market entry and corporate expansion of the incumbents. From the mid 1970s onwards, corporate rivalry gradually intensified, raising the need for effective price manipulation and product differentiation in a global, maturing market: company bankruptcies (e.g. Clarkson's in Britain) and a shake-up of the industry set the foundations for the subsequent observed rise in concentration. The emerging oligopolists serve mainly the mass leisure and business tourist markets: this is not coincidental, as capacity and price competition are objectively understood, while special features are often only subjectively assessed. Due to their lower risk, mainstream activities may have lower profit margins; nevertheless, entrepreneurs are compensated by the size of the business turnover, which is usually large enough to ensure a sustainable level of absolute profitability. On the other hand, the monopolistically competitive fringe specialises in high margin–low volume services in the context of product differentiation.

This market structure dualism has also its spatial equivalent in terms of an emerging Core–Periphery pattern in tourism destinations (Papatheodorou, 2004). Core resorts are usually popular sunlust and wanderlust destinations characterised by heavy tourist infrastructure and a variety of facilities within a densely purpose-built urban environment. These areas enjoy enhanced accessibility from tourism origins of major market potential due to good road networks and frequent public transport services offered e.g. by large charter carriers, which are parts of leisure conglomerates. In addition to traditional small hotels, core destinations host large tourism accommodation complexes managed or even owned by global hotel corporations. The promotion of these areas by vertically integrated tour operators complements the exhibited pattern. Moreover, corporate transnationalisation has effectively linked the origin markets through mergers, acquisitions and alliances; as a result, their service providers and intermediaries increase their bargaining power over the core tourism areas with potentially detrimental effects on the latter.

On the other hand, peripheral resorts are associated with areas promoting the idiosyncratic elements of their natural and built environment. Accessibility is limited as transport connections are less frequent and more expensive than in the Core – in some cases, services may be performed by small carriers or ship companies operating as local monopolies under a regime of public service obligations (PSO). Small-scale accommodation establishments prevail, usually owned by local families with basic hospitality training and know-how. Most tourists travel there independently as tour packages may not exist or be offered by small specialised operators with limited exposure to the market. The low level of overall tourism demand denies the seizure of scale and scope economies and sustains a pre-Fordist, artisanal corporate culture, which amalgamates economic rationality with personal relations among producers and consumers. The local monopolies or oligopolies in transport and other services can only abuse their market power ex post, i.e. once the tourist is there. Nonetheless, the multitude of peripheral destinations in the global tourism market makes the ex ante (before the decision) industrial configuration converge towards monopolistic competition. Inductively, the local tourist producers may behave competitively to achieve customer satisfaction and secure repeat visitors in the longer term.

A concise analytical framework

The above discussion may be constructively set in a concise analytical framework which combines the microeconomic theory of characteristics (Gorman, 1980; Lancaster, 1966, 1971) with evolutionary patterns in tourism (Papatheodorou, 2004). The characteristics theory argues that consumers derive utility from the consumption not of goods as such (as assumed by the classical microeconomic setting) but of characteristics intrinsically related to those goods. In tourism, such features may be collectively grouped into facilities and attractions at the macro-destination level or into core and ancillary (facilitating, supporting and augmenting) product characteristics when referring to specific sectors such as transport or accommodation. Tourists aim at maximising their utility subject to the structure of their preferences, the consumption technology which converts different tourist services into characteristics and the various constraints, namely disposable expenditure and time (Papatheodorou, 2001):

$$
\begin{aligned}
\max \quad & U = f(\mathbf{c}_{\text{tour}}) \\
\text{s.t.} \quad & \mathbf{c}_{\text{tour}} = \mathbf{J}\mathbf{d}_{\text{tour}} \\
& Y \geq \mathbf{p}_{\text{tour}}\mathbf{d}_{\text{tour}} + \mathbf{p}_{\text{trans}}\mathbf{v} \\
& T \geq \mathbf{v}'\mathbf{d}_{\text{tour}} + \mathbf{t}_{\text{trans}}\mathbf{v} \\
& \mathbf{c},\mathbf{d},\mathbf{p},\mathbf{t} \geq \mathbf{0} \quad Y, T \geq 0
\end{aligned}
\tag{1.1}
$$

U is the consumer's well-defined utility function and c_{tour} is the column vector of macro or sectoral tourism characteristics. J is the matrix of consumption technology coefficients, which converts the number of days spent in each destination d_{tour} into characteristics. The disposable expenditure constraint Y is subject to the daily price of the tourist product p_{tour} and the transport cost p_{trans}; v is a unit column vector and v' its transpose. Similarly, the time constraint T refers to the days spent in each destination plus the total transfer time t_{trans} from the origin to each of the available destinations. Equation system (1.1) is best understood in the context of continuous products that may be broken down on a daily basis. Good examples are composite tourist products (such as those offered by a tour operator's package or a cruise), hotel accommodation, museum visits and restaurant patronage. A reductionist approach is followed here regarding the transport element – the focus is solely on prices and time involved. A detailed analysis of this component requires an explicit reference to its characteristics (e.g. entertainment, convenience) and the consideration of its binary nature: we either travel to a destination or we don't. Moreover, the tourist is most likely to travel to a single destination during any one trip; hence discrete choice is an inherent feature of the consumption process (Papatheodorou, 2003). Having the above in mind, the equation system (1.1) may be treated effectively with the aid of appropriately adjusted non-linear programming techniques.

Figure 1.1 represents graphically the above model. For simplicity, three destinations (or tourism service providers) only are considered here, namely D_1, D_2 and D_3 associated with characteristics rays *OGA*, *OHB* and *OKC* respectively. These are based on the consumption technology and show the relative strength of each destination: D_1 focuses on facilities (or ancillary products), D_3 on attractions (or core products) while D_2 is in-between. Points *A, B,* and *K* show the quantities of characteristics enjoyed by the consumer as a result of consuming the maximum number of days afforded by the time constraint. Similarly, *G, H* and *C* refer to the expenditure constraint. As a result, the effective boundary is given by points *G, H*

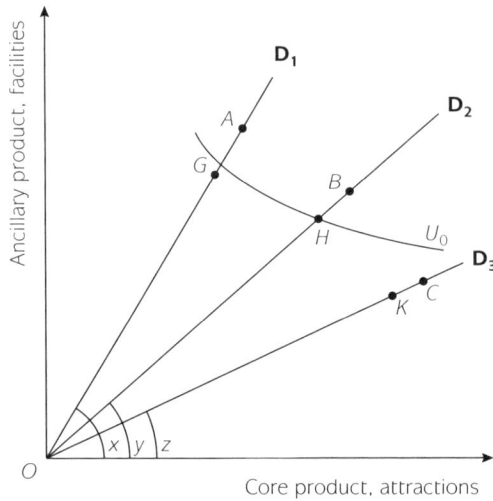

Figure 1.1 The characteristics model in tourism

and K: consumers are relatively more money-constrained in D_1 and D_2 and limited by time in D_3. Since none of G, H or K strictly dominates the other two points (i.e. none offers higher quantities of both characteristics), choice will be ultimately determined by consumer preferences: these are given by the indifference curve U_0; here, its curvature is such that the tourist finally selects D_2.

Corporate rivalry and market power may significantly influence the choice outcome in the above characteristics model. First, in the context of an oligopolistic setting, prices are subject to the competitive conduct prevailing in the specific tourism industry. A local price war among hotel chains or airlines may be destructive for market participants in the short run but will most probably result in increased tourism flows in the specific destination (as points G, H or C move to the right). Similarly, the formation of a cartel may allow supernormal profits leading, however, to the reduction of tourists (as points G, H or C move to the left). Rivalry in the tour operations industry is particularly important here due to the intermediary role of the sector and the emergence of an oligopsonistic (versus the producers) oligopoly (versus the consumers). In fact, the tour operators may manage to play the various destinations against each other and secure good deals and substantial cost savings. The latter may be subsequently passed to the consumers as lower prices if the market is competitive or kept by the tour operators as profits in case of restricted conduct. Nonetheless, prices are usually sticky in an oligopoly; hence non-price competition is also very critical in manipulating destination choice. Market participants may provide a greater variety or improve the quality of their tourist services by offering more characteristics for the same price and time spent in a destination: in this case, points A–K would move to the right. Aggressive advertising and information campaigns could have a similar effect: what matters then is not *actual* but *perceived* characteristics. Transport companies may also decide to compete in faster travelling, resulting in an outward shift of points A, B and K; for example, the recent enhancement of competition in the sea passenger market in Greece has also led to the introduction of modern and faster ships in the lines between Piraeus and certain Aegean islands. Finally, tour operators may introduce new destinations in the context of product differentiation leading to the emergence of another set of characteristics and a new ray in Figure 1.1.

The above relationships may also be expressed spatially as now shown in Figures 1.2 and 1.3. In the short run, interaction among the origin areas (depicted by F_1 between O_1 and O_2) can emerge as a result of corporate transationalisation and globalisation. For example, the TUI group may co-ordinate the time schedule and other flight operations of Britannia and Hapag-Lloyd to serve the British and German markets in a joint and more efficient manner. Certain tourism flows (F_3) are directed to the tourist Periphery, where the prevalence of monopolistic competition does not raise issues of corporate rivalry and abuse of market power. Nonetheless, the majority of tourists visit one of the destinations in the tourist Core (flow F_2), where strategic interdependence (shown by the two-directional arrows)

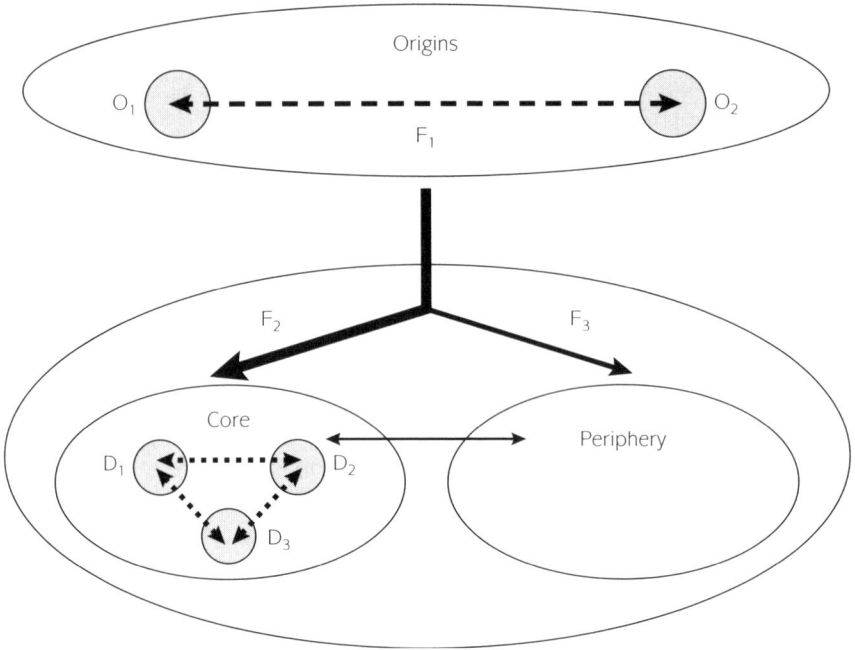

Figure 1.2 Short-run tourism flows

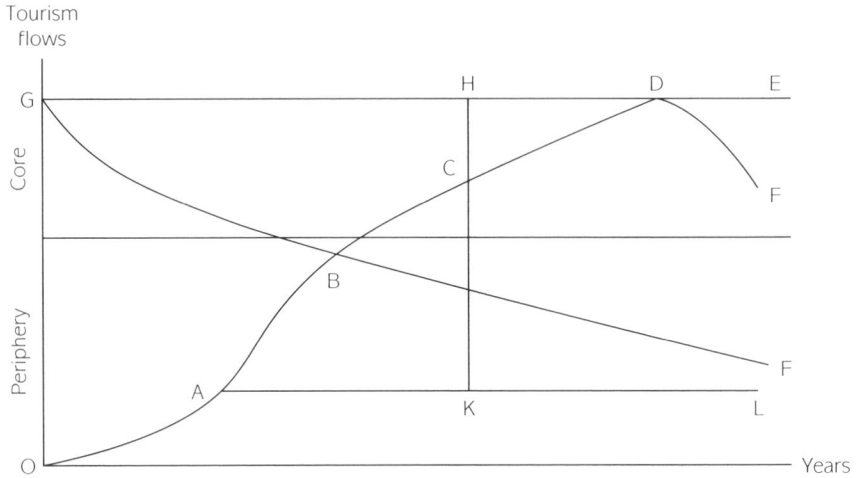

Figure 1.3 Long-run tourism flows

Source: Both figures are adapted from Papatheodorou (2004).

12

is apparent in the form of actions described in the previous figure. Interaction between Core and Periphery is limited; product characteristics and consumer preferences are very dissimilar, hence the impact of corporate rivalry and competition issues is small.

In the longer term, Core and Peripheries are endogenously determined in the context of an evolutionary process. Figure 1.3 shows alternative scenarios of development over time. In his seminal article on the resort life cycle theory, Butler (1980) identified a sinusoidal pattern depicted by OABCDF: resorts may manage to thrive but eventually become victims of their own success: tourism flows may exceed the carrying capacity of the area leading to unsustainable development and degradation of the physical and built environment.

This trend is likely to be fortified by corporate rivalry and the existence of a very competitive conduct which results in price wars: for example, tour operators may compete fiercely in core destinations once a critical threshold of tourists is secured (shown by the dotted line) allowing the reaping of scale and scope economies. Eventually, however, the tour operators may move to other destinations either because of service quality problems in the existing ones or in the context of their product differentiation and spatial portfolio strategy. As a result, abrupt patterns are also possible. Cancun in Mexico is an interesting example of successful co-ordination among the various tourism stakeholders leading to the creation of an 'instant resort' from point *O* to *G*. Nonetheless, sudden downscaling is also possible (e.g. from point *C* to *K*) not only because of natural (e.g. tsunami) or other disasters (e.g. war) but also due to corporate decisions. For example, overdependence of a destination on a single origin market or service provider (e.g. hotel, airline or tour operator) may have serious negative connotations if the latter enters into financial difficulties (Debbage, 1990). As a result and where the pursuance of a strategy to reduce overdependence is difficult, destinations may accept an abuse of market power from the provider's side to ensure its profitability and hence their own survival.

Structure of the book

It seems, therefore, that in addition to any impact on the welfare of consumers, corporate rivalry and the abuse of market power in tourism may have important implications for destination development. Although it was deemed necessary to raise this point in this introductory chapter, the book does not follow the standard political economy perspective that examines the impact of transnational conglomerates on destinations; this topic is covered elsewhere in a comprehensive manner (Britton, 1991; Shaw and Williams, 1994). Similarly, active or passive competition among tourist countries or regions (e.g. in the form of subsidies to tourist producers) is not discussed, to avoid divergence on issues of protectionism, strategic trade practices and jurisdiction. Moreover, the number of competition issues in tourism is potentially very large; to make a useful contribution, therefore, the book focuses on few of them. In particular, the book does not study general rivalry processes among different tourist products (e.g. sport tourism, health tourism) or customer segments (e.g. gay tourism or older tourism): it examines solely issues arising from corporate power and rivalry in the sector. For this reason, research areas where environmental or other non-economic regulation is of major importance (e.g. nature parks) are also beyond the scope of the analysis.

In essence, the book follows an industrial organisation approach to study and evaluate competition issues that have emerged in the tourism industry. Although much valued research on competition has been undertaken for individual tourism sectors, the treatment of competition issues in an integrated manner is still under-represented academically. Moreover, anecdotal discussions of the editor with competition policymakers, lawyers and economists show that for the prevailing conventional wisdom, competition issues are only marginally related to tourism: hence, the need for a useful benchmark study to challenge this belief. The book is written in a management rather than a hard-core technical economic style. An explicitly mathematical perspective would be appealing perhaps to theoreticians in academic economic departments but it would most probably discourage readers in business school communities (academics and students) and policymaking (at national and local scales) who are the primary target audience of this book. Under no condition, however, does this mean that the quality and insightfulness of the book have been compromised: inter alia, the decision to produce an edited rather than a single-authored book is justified on the grounds of bringing together a group of people who are recognised as experts in their own field.

Chapters 2 and 3 set the theoretical foundations of the book. Zheng Lei studies the pillars of industrial organisation and their application to tourism. He first focuses on the structure-conduct-performance (SCP) paradigm, which has dominated industrial economic analysis until recently. He then explores the implications of modern game theory as a useful study tool for oligopolistic markets and eventually integrates the two theoretical frameworks by providing appropriate examples from the airline, the hotel accommodation and the tour operations industries. Building on the above, Gang Li and Haiyan Song discuss the various quantitative techniques to treat competition issues in tourism. In fact, Chapter 3 is the only one in the book with explicitly mathematical contents albeit from an applied perspective. The authors focus first on market structure analysis and discuss concentration indices, such as the m-firm concentration ratio and the Herfindahl-Hirschman Index (HHI). They subsequently study price analysis in the context of cross-sectional tests, correlation coefficients and econometric modelling (price-concentration studies and hedonic pricing). The following section of the chapter discusses demand and substitution issues referring to single-equation demand models and the Almost Ideal Demand System (AIDS), while the final section presents a complementary view based on discrete choice modelling. Some of the techniques discussed in the chapter are complex and require detailed data, which are not always available. Still, they may produce insightful results which can either validate or reject the theoretical analysis of Chapter 2.

The following chapters analyse corporate rivalry and competition issues in specific tourism industries. Chapters 4 focuses on the airline industry. Following a detailed introduction on the performance of the sector, John F O' Connell studies the evolution of competitive airline markets mainly in the post-deregulation era. The first wave of impacts is related to hub-and-spoke operations and how hubs can effectively restrict competition. The second wave refers to the emergence of strategic alliances and their business conduct, while the third discusses the evolution and importance of frequent flyer programmes. Moreover, Chapter 4 explores the emergence of low-cost carriers as a credible competition threat to the market dominance enjoyed by traditional airlines; it also deals with the sensitive topic of corporate rivalry in equity partnerships and the competition issues behind open skies agreements.

Anne Graham discusses airport competition in Chapter 5. Following an analysis regarding airport commercialisation and the impact of airline deregulation, the chapter focuses on the nature of airport competition, which exists both between and within airports; provision of airport services and competing terminals are of major importance here. Moreover, the gradual emergence of airport systems may raise significant competition issues especially in the context of the current wave of privatisation. Given the natural monopoly character of airports, regulation is still deemed necessary in certain cases; the chapter explores its main principles and practice and deals also with the potentially anti-competitive issue of state aid. Finally, Anne Graham stresses the role of slot allocation as a major playground of corporate rivalry in airports; she discusses alternative mechanisms of allocation and associated restrictions and concludes by suggesting a closer relationship between airlines and airports and the need for an active slot reform.

Moving away from the air transport sector, Chapter 6 provides a fruitful synthesis of competition issues in the hospitality and the tour operations industries. In particular, Dimitris Koutoulas explores the market influence of the latter on the former using the Greek resort hotels as a case study. The chapter discusses the role of corporate rivalry in the distribution of resort hotel capacity through the inclusive tour market and evaluates the impact of recent sectoral developments in the alternative forms of competition. The chapter uses TUI as a vivid example of horizontal and vertical corporate expansion in tourism and then reports the findings from a very interesting hotel survey based on an electronic questionnaire in Greece. The results in tabular form reveal the intense corporate environment of hotel operations in Greece and the love-and-hate relationship that has developed between hoteliers and tour operators. The chapter concludes by suggesting effective competition strategies for resort hotels and suitable governmental policies in destination areas to alleviate the emerging problems.

Chapter 7 digs further into the travel distribution system by exploring the travel agent retail sector using the USA as a case study. In this way, Dimitri Ioannides and Evangelia Petridou Daughtrey aim at filling the existing gap in the distribution literature which has traditionally focused primarily on the impact of tour operators. The profile of the US travel agency sector is characterised by an impressive growth of the largest companies following a recent wave of mergers and acquisitions; to survive, the smaller companies are changing their business model. The chapter assesses explicitly the influence of the Internet as an effective distribution technology with a major impact on corporate rivalry and competition: the erosion of commissions, the development of dynamic packaging and the growth of online agencies are some of the challenges faced by brick-and-mortar companies. Innovation within a world of rapid changes and market consolidation is necessary; the deregulation of Global Distribution Systems (GDS) is an evolutionary move in this direction as it provides further agility but also intensifies competitive pressures on US travel agents.

It seems, therefore, that the information and communication technologies (ICT) have a very significant impact on tourism competition. Dimitrios Buhalis capitalises on these issues in Chapter 8 focusing primarily on the role of Internet and e-commerce in raising challenges but also providing solutions for the various tourism sectors. ICT can influence the market structure and the competitive conduct of the industry by reducing barriers to entry, facilitating the acquisition of travel information and enhancing the transparency of commercial transactions. As a result, they affect the performance and profitability of the tourism sector by allowing substantial cost savings but also setting requirements for investment on new infrastructure. The chapter deals with the role of ICT on tourism in a holistic manner but also examines the impacts on specific sectors such as the airlines, hospitality and intermediaries – horizontal and vertical integration are of primary importance here as they allow the reaping of scale and scope economies through the appropriate use of technology. The chapter concludes by raising the need for a paradigm shift in the tourism industry and the use of ICT to rationalise operations in an increasingly competitive environment.

Chapters 4–8 explore corporate rivalry, market power and competition issues in the context of specific tourism industries. The next two chapters have a somewhat different orientation in terms of focusing on competition related to a tourism characteristic par excellence, namely space. Both chapters provide an interesting amalgamation of theory with empirical evidence leading back to the foundations explored in Chapters 2 and 3. In particular, Stephen Wanhill discusses competition issues in attractions in Chapter 9. The nature and consisting characteristics of visitor attractions are analysed and a useful classification of the product into core and augmented imagescape, tangible features and support services is provided. The chapter presents various policies on admission charges based on alternative market structure regimes – emphasis is given on monopolistic competition and oligopoly. In fact, a dualism seems to have emerged (a theme explored earlier in this introductory chapter) where an 'aristopoly' of few, large attractions coexists with a competitive fringe of smaller and perhaps less publicised ones. Issues of ownership are of major importance here in terms of market exposure and charging policies. Not surprisingly, the majority of large built attractions such as Disneyland are controlled by transnational conglomerates who act as price-setters in a strategically interdependent market – given the sunk nature of the investment, uncertainty is an inherent characteristic of corporate rivalry. Likewise, governments should be careful when pouring money into public attractions to avoid a waste of resources.

Gunnar Niels and Reinder van Dijk focus on holiday parks in Chapter 10. While all previous contributors are academics, Dr Niels and Mr Dijk are both applied economists working for Oxera, a leading economics consulting company in Britain. In this context, they bring into the foreground the practitioners approach in dealing with competition issues. The chapter is based on a real project undertaken by Oxera to assess the impact of a merger in the European holiday parks sector; as mergers result in an increased market concentration, an appropriate definition of the market may act as a very useful structural benchmark for the competitive conduct and the actual performance of the sector. On these grounds, Chapter 10 studies the economic principles behind market definition and discusses relevant quantitative techniques such as the SSNIP test and critical loss analysis. In this way, it complements the framework provided in Chapter 3. The actual merger case study is based on a survey among holidaymakers in the Netherlands; inter alia, the results show that the relevant product market should be defined more broadly than holiday parks with a specific range of facilities; similarly, the relevant geographical market covers not only the Netherlands but the neighbouring countries too. Such studies are useful not only for authorities investigating the impact of mergers, but also for the companies under consideration which can acquire a better understanding of their business environment.

Having all the above in mind, Chapter 11 of the book summarises and provides some concluding remarks by Papatheodorou. Explicit reference is also made to the cruise sector which essentially combines elements of transport and accommodation in the context of an all-inclusive package. The chapter stresses the need for constructive policymaking and makes suggestions for the tourism policy agenda in the areas of corporate rivalry and competition.

References

Bain, J. (1956) *Barriers to New Competition*. Cambridge, Mass.: Harvard University Press.

Baum, T. and Lundtorp, S. (2001) *Seasonality in Tourism*. Oxford: Elsevier Science.

Baumol, W. J. (1982) Contestable Markets: An Uprising in the Theory of Industry Structure. *American Economic Review* 72: 1–15.

Britton, S. (1991) Towards a Critical Geography of Tourism. *Environment and Planning D. Society and Space* 9: 451–478.

Buhalis, D. (1998) Strategic Use of Information Technologies in the Tourism Industry. *Tourism Management* 19(5): 409–421.

Butler, R. (1980) The Concept of a Tourist Area Cycle of Evolution: Implications for Management of Resources. *Canadian Geographer* 14: 5–12.

Civil Aviation Authority (2005) *ATOL Business* 25 (January), London: Civil Aviation Authority.

Court of First Instance (2002) *Annulment of Commission's Decision C* (1999) 3022. Luxembourg: European Communities.

Davies, B. (1999) Industrial Organization: The UK Hotel Sector. *Annals of Tourism Research* 26(2): 294–311.

Debbage, K. (1990) Oligopoly and the Resort Cycle in the Bahamas. *Annals of Tourism Research* 17: 512–527.

Eadington, W. R. and Redman, M. (1991) Economics and Tourism. *Annals of Tourism Research* 18(1): 41–56.

Goetz, A. (2002) Deregulation, Competition and Antitrust Implications in the US Airline Industry. *Journal of Transport Geography* 10: 1–19.

Gorman, W. M. (1980) A Possible Procedure for Analysing Quality Differentials in the Egg Market. *Review of Economic Studies* 47: 843–856.

Hotels (2004) Hotels Corporate 300. *Hotels*, July.

Krugman, P. (1995) *Development, Geography and Economic Theory.* Cambridge, Mass.: MIT Press.

Lancaster, K. J. (1966) A New Approach to Consumer Theory. *Journal of Political Economy* 74: 132–157.

Lancaster, K. J. (1971) *Consumer Demand: A New Approach.* New York: Columbia University Press.

Leiper, N. (1990) Partial Industrialization of Tourism Systems. *Annals of Tourism Research* 17(4): 600–605.

Medlik, S. (1993) *Dictionary of Travel, Tourism and Hospitality.* Oxford: Heinemann.

Morris, D. (2000) Competition Policy and Regulation in the UK: A New Era. Lecture given in Lancaster University on 29 November 2000.

National Economic Research Associates (1999) *Merger Appraisal in Oligopolistic Markets.* Research Paper 19. London: Office of Fair Trading.

National Economic Research Associates (2001) *The Role of Market Definition in Monopoly and Dominance Inquiries.* Economic Discussion Paper 2. London: Office of Fair Trading.

Nelson, R. R. and Winter, S. G. (1982) *An Evolutionary Theory of Economic Change.* Cambridge, Mass.: Harvard University Press.

Oxford Economic Research Associates (2002) The Benefits of Competition. *Competing Ideas*, September: 1–3.

Papatheodorou, A. (2001) Why People Travel to Different Places? *Annals of Tourism Research* 28(1): 164–179.

Papatheodorou, A. (2002) Civil Aviation Regimes and Leisure Tourism in Europe. *Journal of Air Transport Management* 8(6): 381–388.

Papatheodorou, A. (2003) Modelling Tourism Development – A Synthetic Approach. *Tourism Economics* 9(4): 407–430.

Papatheodorou, A. (2004) Exploring the Evolution of Tourist Resorts. *Annals of Tourism Research* 31(1): 219–237.

Papatheodorou, A. (2006) The Cruise Industry – An Industrial Organisation Perspective, in *Cruise Tourism: Issues, Impacts, Cases* edited by R. Dowling. Wallingford: CABI Publishing.

Schumpeter, J. A. (1996) *Capitalism, Socialism and Democracy*. London: Routledge.

Scitovsky, T. (1954) Two Concepts of External Economies. *Journal of Political Economy* 62: 143–151.

Shaw, G. and Williams, A. M. (1994) *Critical Issues in Tourism – A Geographical Perspective*. Oxford: Blackwell Publishers.

Smith, S. (1998) Tourism as an Industry – Debate and Concepts, pp. 31–52 in *The Economic Geography of the Tourism Industry – A Supply Side Analysis*, edited by D. Ioannides and K. G. Debbage. London: Routledge.

Tirole, J. (1988) *The Theory of Industrial Organization*. Cambridge, Mass.: MIT Press.

Urry, J. (1990) *The Tourist Gaze*. London: Sage Publications.

Vukonič, B. (1997) Selective Tourism Growth: Targeted Tourism Destinations, pp. 95–108 in *Tourism, Development and Growth: The Challenge of Sustainability*, edited by J. J. Pigram and S. Wahab. London: Routledge.

World Tourism Organization (1999) *Tourism Satellite Account (TSA): The Conceptual Framework*. Madrid: WTO.

Yarrow, G. (2001) Economics of Market Definition. Presentation in the Regulatory Policy Institute, Oxford.

2

The theoretical pillars of industrial organisation in tourism

Zheng Lei

Industrial Organisation is a branch of Applied Microeconomics. It is concerned with the workings of markets and industries and in particular the way firms compete with each other (Cabral, 2000). It differs from microeconomics by empha-sising firm strategies characterised by market interaction and applying predictions and explanations to the real-world cases. The standard approach to the study of Industrial Organisation is based on the seminal works of Robinson (1933), Mason (1939), Bain (1956) and Chamberlin (1965), decomposing a market into structure, conduct and performance, commonly known as SCP paradigm. The fast development of game theory in the 1970s gave a push to the strategic approach to Industrial Organisation by providing analytical tools to study the strategic moves by firms. The aim of this chapter is to analyse the main theories in Industrial Economics focusing on the SCP paradigm, the recent developments in Game Theory and their application in the context of tourism.

Essence of the structure–conduct–performance paradigm

In the framework of the SCP paradigm, market structure is affected by basic supply and demand-side conditions. Structure means barriers to entry, how sellers interact with other sellers, with buyers and with potential entrants. It affects market performance through the conduct or behaviour of firms (pricing, advertising, entry deterrence, etc.). Market performance, which implies how competitive, efficient and profitable the industry is, depends upon the conduct. The government may have a profound effect on the market structure and conduct by employing a variety of public policy instruments such as taxes and subsidies, regulations and price control.

The SCP paradigm is based on the premise that the firms' performance can be inferred relatively easily from a few readily measured indicators of market structure. The SCP paradigm implies that good economic performance should flow automatically from proper market structure and the conduct to which it gives rise (Scherer and Ross, 1990). In the event of market failure and outcomes below acceptable norms, government agencies may choose to intervene and attempt to improve performance by applying policy measures that affect either market structure or conduct (ibid.).

While the SCP paradigm dominated the research in Industrial Organisation for over four decades, its drawbacks have also become apparent. By the 1970s there was growing dissatisfaction with the premise inherent in the SCP model that market structure was exogenously determined. Research indicated that market structure could also be endogenous; the conduct and performance of firms in the industry was also an important influence on structure. For example, mergers affect directly the size and distribution of firms, advertising and innovation could raise entry barriers and predatory pricing could force competitors out of the market – in essence behaviour that directly or indirectly raised the costs of entry into a market also influenced structure (Rickard, 2002).

Baumol et al.'s (1982) concept of contestable markets was further casting doubt on the idea that structure could shed much light on competitive rivalry. The theory argues that what is crucial in determining price and output is not whether an industry is actually a monopoly or not, but whether there is a real threat of competition. Baumol et al. argue that markets are contestable if a potential entrant has access to the same technology and resources as incumbents; the costs of entry and exit by potential rivals are low; and entry can be made very rapidly. In such cases, when the incumbent is making supernormal profits, new firms can employ hit-and-run tactics. The constant threat of entry forces existing firms to minimise their production costs and resist the temptation to raise prices to achieve supernormal profits. Thus conduct in contestable markets is not determined by market structure: the need to deter entry is the main influence on performance.

The traditional SCP paradigm is founded upon the neoclassical approach and 'static' analysis. However, most business environments are not in a state of equilibrium. Rather, they are characterised by some degree of change (McWilliams and Smart, 1993). Schumpeter (1942) points out that in changing environments, dynamic analysis is required to understand and predict the relative ability of firms to sustain competitive advantages.

Schumpeter's ideas were further developed by Austrian School economists and advocates of evolutionary economics. The Austrian approach to competition concentrates on the dynamic progress rather than structural issues, while evolutionary economics emphasise the inevitability of mistaken decisions in an uncertain world. Further work by researchers in the area of behaviour economics attempted to integrate concepts such as organisational knowledge and routines to Schumpeter's concept of dynamic competition (Nelson and Winter, 1982). Apart from all these significant developments in the area of Industrial Organisation over the past few decades, the most important breakthrough can be attributed to Game Theory, which will be addressed later on.

Despite the various criticisms, the SCP paradigm has a number of advantages. First, it gives us an overall picture to describe markets and to highlight key features as a necessary first step towards the analysis of market structures, behaviour and performance (Sinclair and Stabler, 1997). Moreover, since the approach is not industry-specific, it may be applied to many industries so making inter-industry comparison possible (Britton et al., 1992). Therefore, it is better not to view the SCP approach as a 'model' but a useful device for capturing the essential relationships between variables. Figure 2.1 below shows the SCP paradigm applied to a service industry modified from Sinclair and Stabler (1997). Here, all variables

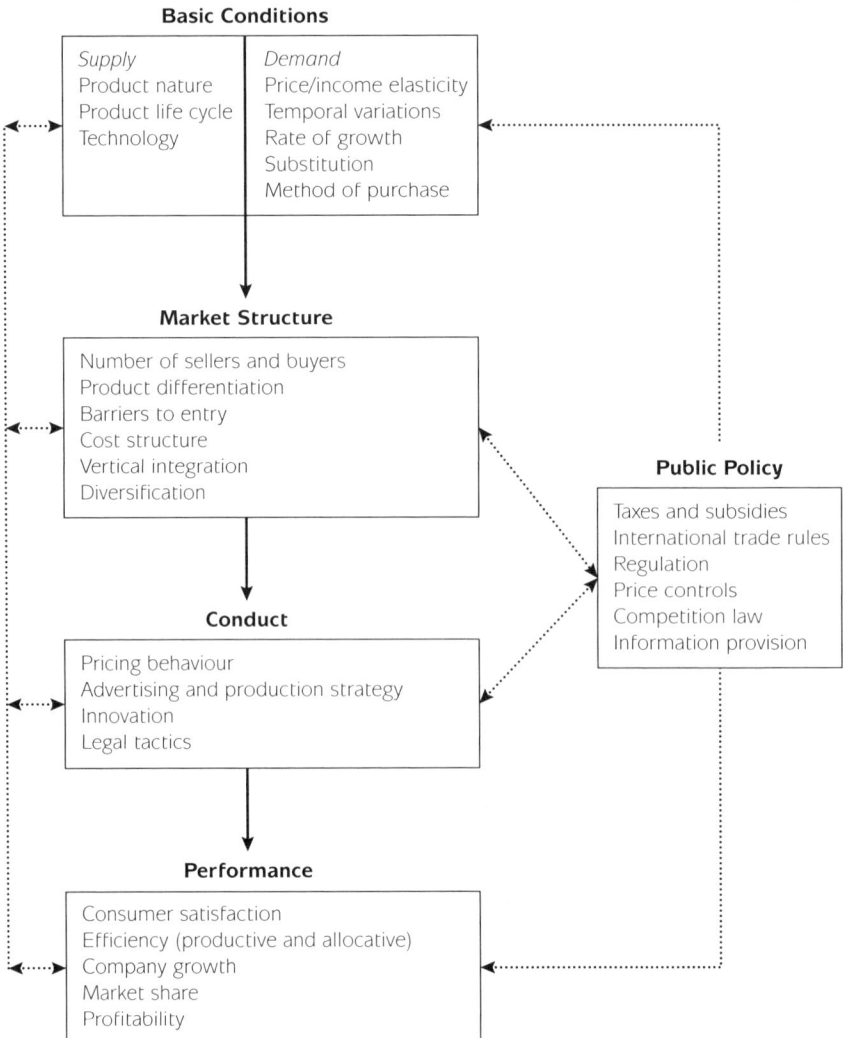

Basic Conditions

Supply	*Demand*
Product nature	Price/income elasticity
Product life cycle	Temporal variations
Technology	Rate of growth
	Substitution
	Method of purchase

Market Structure

Number of sellers and buyers
Product differentiation
Barriers to entry
Cost structure
Vertical integration
Diversification

Public Policy

Taxes and subsidies
International trade rules
Regulation
Price controls
Competition law
Information provision

Conduct

Pricing behaviour
Advertising and production strategy
Innovation
Legal tactics

Performance

Consumer satisfaction
Efficiency (productive and allocative)
Company growth
Market share
Profitability

Figure 2.1 The structure–conduct–performance paradigm

are endogenously determined because of interdependencies between variables of market structure, conduct and performance and feedback effects on basic condition and public policy. The remaining of this chapter, thus, endeavours to use this paradigm to analyse the tourism sector.

Basic conditions

The SCP paradigm is founded on the analysis of manufacturing industries. Use of the SCP approach in the service sector is not readily applicable because of the nature of services and their way of production. In a study of executive search and selection industry, Britton et al. (1992) demonstrate that the characteristics of intangibility, irreversibility, inseparability of production and consumption, heterogeneity and perishability have profound impact on the market structure, conduct and performance. In the tourism sector, intangibility means that services cannot be demonstrated or sampled before purchase, so consumers have to base decisions to purchase on other criteria while irreversibility means once tourism service is purchased, it cannot be refunded. As international tourism is usually expensive for most consumers, reputation and image of tourism companies plays a crucial role in the determination of consumer purchasing decisions.

Inseparability indicates that service products are consumed and produced simultaneously. The simultaneous process of production and consumption can lead to situations where it is difficult to ensure the overall satisfaction of consumers (Cooper et al., 2005). Heterogeneity implies that units of the service are not standardised. Hence, assurance of quality and standardisation of service outputs are important for service industries (Britton et al., 1992). The characteristic of perishability means that service products such as tourism, unlike goods, cannot be stored for sale on a future occasion (Cooper et al., 2005). For example, an unsold hotel bed or an airline seat is revenue that can never be recouped.

Apart from these generic characteristics common to all services, there are two further features that are particularly relevant to the tourism sector: seasonality and the interdependence of tourism products (Middleton, 2001). Seasonality means demand fluctuates greatly between seasons of the year. Summer is usually the peak season for many holiday destinations such as those in the Mediterranean, while winter is the busiest period for ski resorts in the Alps. At a micro level, hotels in a holiday destination usually have higher occupancy rate in the weekends than during weekdays; airlines often face stronger demand for early morning than for afternoon flights.

Interdependence means that visitor facilities in a destination are functionally related to other infrastructure (ibid.). For example, the required restaurant facilities in a holiday resort might be determined by the capacity of hotels, while the number of visitors is largely dependent on the transport links between the destination and the tourism-generating regions. The concept of Tourist Area Life Cycle (TALC) developed by Butler (1980) further shows that tourist facilities in a destination are subject to the influence of the stage where the destination lies on the cycle. This is particularly true in the hotel industry. Once a hotel is established, location of operations becomes fixed for the lifetime of the asset. Location, thus, is a major determinant of the profitability of an operation (Middleton, 2001). For example, seaside resort hotels in Britain have been in persistent difficulty since the 1970s as those destinations went to decline.

Like most other industries, technology is crucial for the tourism sector. Airlines led the way in the development and application of new technologies. Computerised reservation systems (CRS) emerged in the 1960s and, subsequently, developed into global distribution systems (GDS). To facilitate distribution of airfares, airlines then installed terminals of CRS, and later GDS, in travel agencies (Buhalis, 2003). Transnational hotel chains also developed their own reservation systems and made them available to travel agents through GDS connection.

As the initial capital investment on CRS and GDS is enormous, only major airlines and transnational hotel chains are able to afford the required investment. However, the Internet revolution changed the balance of the game as it significantly reduced the capital and operational requirements. This is particularly the case for low-cost carriers which bypass GDSs and sell their seats directly to the public at competitive prices. Nowadays, even small accommodation establishments and tour operators can take advantage of the Internet and promote themselves globally (ibid.).

In terms of demand, international tourism is generally considered a luxury commodity with high income elasticity rather than a necessity. Price and income elasticities are frequently calculated in international tourism demand studies. By using meta-analysis to examine 777 income elasticity estimates, Crouch finds that the mean income elasticity is +1.76, and the mean price elasticity is –0.39; both are significantly different from zero at the 1% level (Crouch, 1992). Although price elasticity is not as large as income elasticity, the empirical studies by Martin and Witt (1988) demonstrate that substitute prices play an important role in determining the demand for international tourism.

Structure

Absolute cost barriers are rather low, which encourages entry into the tourism sector (Papatheodorou, 2004). Similarly, product differentiation barriers are not too high either as tourism services can be easily benchmarked and copied by other firms due to their visibility and lack of patent protection (Cooper et al., 2005). On the other hand, the regulatory regime can become a barrier for new entrants in the airline industry. This is still the case in most part of the world. In the United States (USA) and European Union (EU), before their domestic aviation markets were liberalised, entry and exit were strictly restricted. However, since the USA and EU adopted policies towards deregulating their respective domestic airline market, this barrier has become virtually non-existent; any airline can apply for a licence and operate at market-determined prices. Currently, the regulation barrier tends to be lower as the trend of deregulation is spreading to other countries. For the accommodation sector, although star rating and quality control are common practices in many countries, regulation as an entry barrier is usually trivial. Tour operating business is often regulated by the bonding system, under which consumers are guaranteed to be compensated in the event of insolvency of tour operators. The bonding requirement can raise the entry cost barriers, but not very significantly.

Due to the intangibility, irreversibility and heterogeneity nature of the tourism service, the purchase of tourism products contains an element of risk. Companies in the tourism sector have to invest in physical facilities, to access distribution channels and to develop and maintain reputation. For a new entrant, establishing recognition and reputation among a significant number of customers could require significant amounts of time and monetary resources. These can become a considerable sunk cost if the companies exit the market. Therefore, entry into the mainstream market has become difficult for new entrants.

Evidence regarding the existence of economies of scale in the tourism sector is mixed. For airlines there are strong indications that an increase in the number of places and routes in an airline's network will not reduce unit costs. In a study, Caves et al. (1984) try to identify the cost advantage of trunk airlines over smaller regional airlines. Based on data from 1970 through 1981 in the USA, they find that any differences in scale have no role in explaining higher cost for smaller airlines. The primary factors explaining cost differences are lower density of traffic flows and shorter stage lengths for the regional airlines. Both earlier and later studies confirm that there are no significant economies of scale at the firm level (Caves, 1962; Strazheim, 1969; White, 1979; Gillen et al., 1990).

In the accommodation sector, transnational hotel chains can take advantage of economies of scale by mass purchases, marketing and reduction of overheads. These chains are more able to fund staff training and enjoy efficient production methods (Dunning and McQueen, 1982). Also, construction costs decrease with increasing plant size (Debbage and Daniels, 1998). For the tour operating business, economies of scale exist in terms of ongoing operational costs as well as in purchasing and marketing economies (Evans and Stabler, 1995). Major tour operators rely on volume bookings by mass tourists because of significant cost advantages in bundling the various travel components into single products.

Seeking economies of scale through horizontal integration and increased market concentration is a trait observed in the tour operating and hotel industries over the past few decades (Debbage and Daniels, 1998). A few transnational hotel companies now dominate the hotel industry (Go and Pine, 1995). The top four US-based consortia (HFS, Holiday Inn, Best Western and Choice Hotels international) control more than 11,500 properties (approximately 1.25 million rooms) world-wide (Debbage and Daniels, 1998). In the UK, the four largest tour operators control almost 75 per cent of the market (Global Market Information Database, 2004). Apart from horizontal integration, vertical integration has also been pervasive in the tour operating business. The four largest UK tour operators have all become vertically integrated in recent years, as shown in Table 2.1 below.

The rationale behind this wave is well summarised by Cooper et al. (2005). First, vertical integration can allow tour operators to pursue economies of scale through the linking of complementary activities, investing in new technologies and joint marketing activities. Moreover, it can also set costs and quality standards under the umbrella of one organisation. Third, it can secure suppliers and increase buying power. Finally, it can protect market position by guaranteeing access to retail outlets on prime high street sites and effectively deter entry of competitors. Compared to the successful vertical integration strategy in the tour operating industry, only limited success has been observed in the airline and hotel industries. Although it is common for scheduled airlines to form alliances with transnational hotel chains and hotels becoming involved with the business of travel agencies, there is no strong evidence that hotels and airlines can gain significant benefit from vertical integration (Debbage and Daniels, 1998).

In summary, the initial barrier arising from capital requirement to enter the tourism sector is low and product differences and regulation do not constitute significant barriers to entry either. However, the intangibility, irreversibility and heterogeneity nature of the tourism services force tourism companies to invest heavily in marketing promotion and distribution. These irreversible sunk costs constitute a serious barrier to potential new market entrants and lead to the emergence of a dual dualism as argued by Papatheodorou in Chapter 1 of this book.

Table 2.1 Vertical integration and consolidation in the UK charter industry, 2000

Airline	Tour operators	Market share 03	Travel agencies	Market share 03
Britannia	**Thomson**	21.8	Lunn Poly	21.4
MyTravel	**MyTravel**	23.2	MyTravel	
			Going Places	
			Travelworld	20.5
Air 2000	**First Choice**	14.0	Travel Choice	14.0
JMC Airlines	**Thomas Cook**	17.7	Thomas Cook	17.3

Source: Cooper et al. (2005) Global Information Database (2004).

Conduct

Market conduct involves pricing behaviour, advertising and production strategy, innovation and legal tactics. The nature of intangibility, inseparability and heterogeneity of the tourism product render recognition and reputation very important. Advertising, which differentiates the product, tends to boost market power and raise entry barriers, thereby increasing the price of products to consumers (Scherer and Ross, 1990). Innovation can be reflected in the application of information communication technology and the adoption of new business strategies, while legal tactics have always been employed by incumbent companies to deter entrants. The nature of the tourism product also has profound effect on the pricing behaviour of tourism companies. Middleton (2001) asserts that perishability makes tactical price-cutting by major competitors almost certain whenever supply exceeds demand; similarly, seasonality makes price adjustments necessary to manage demand for a given capacity in the short run.

In tourism sector oligopolies, a company's conduct is largely determined by its rivals' competitive behaviour. This interdependence is encapsulated by Game Theory which deals with the strategic interaction of rational individuals or economic agents. The goal of a game-theoretical model is to predict the outcomes of a list of actions adopted by each participant. It is especially useful when the number of interactive agents is small, in which case the action of each agent may have a significant effect on the payoff of other players (Shy, 1995). For this reason, Game Theory is extremely helpful in analysing industries consisting of a small number of competing firms, since any action of each firm, whether price choice, quantity produced, research and development, or marketing techniques, has strong effects on the profit levels of the competing firms (ibid.).

Probably, the most famous example in Game Theory is the Prisoners' Dilemma, which may be used to illustrate the static games of complete information. Assume the existence of two tour operators, A and B that compete on the same market. Each must decide to set its price for the upcoming year and each has two options: maintain the same price or cut it. When one tour operator cuts its price, it will achieve a larger market share and increase its profit at the other's expense. If both tour operators cut prices, both profits will be reduced. The consequences of each tour operator's choices are given in Table 2.2 below. The first entry is A's annual profit and the second is B's. Each tour operator will make its price decision simultaneously and independently of the other firm. A and B would be collectively better off by maintaining the price if they could reach an agreement. However,

Table 2.2 Price war game

		Tour operator B	
		Maintain price	Cut price
Tour operator A	Maintain price	8,8	1,10
	Cut price	10,1	4,4

cartel outcomes are not self-enforcing. Although collusion can raise tour operator A's profits, these may rise further if tour operator B maintains price while A cuts its own. Because this incentive structure is the same for tour operator B, each company will have an incentive to secretly cut price, thereby bringing about the collapse of the cartel. Thus, the equilibrium, which is called Nash Equilibrium, to this game is (4,4). In other words, both tour operators A and B choose to cut prices.

In the real world, Evans and Stabler (1995) observe that from the end of the 1960s there have been recurrent price wars in the UK tour operating industry, particularly in the early 1970s and 1980s, when the big tour operators were fighting for market share. As a result of the price war, certain companies were induced to exit the market and the industry became ever more concentrated. The rising concentration attracted investigation by the Monopolies and Merger Commission (MMC) (now renamed as the Competition Commission) to examine whether this constituted an abuse of market power and restriction of competition. The MMC concluded that the market was competitive due to the existence of strong price competition; a poor profitability record; a relative ease of entry into the market; and the ready expansion of smaller operators.

Oligopolists are pulled in two different directions. The interdependence of firms may make them wish to collude with each other. If they can act together and replicate a monopoly, they can jointly maximise industry profits. However, in most industrialised countries, the formal collusion between oligopolists is illegal despite the popularity of tacit agreements which can take various forms such as dominant-firm price leadership. On the other hand, aiming at larger market shares or industry profits provides individual firms with incentives to cheat. Cheating is difficult to spot when there are many firms in the market with a different cost structure and heterogeneous products (Scherer and Ross, 1990).

To complement the previous price war game, we may now consider a capacity expansion setting. Suppose that hotels A and B are the only two in a resort catering for the same holiday market. Each must decide whether to expand capacity by increasing hotel rooms in the upcoming year. Each has two options: no expansion and expansion. When one hotel expands its capacity (rooms), it will achieve a larger market share and increase its profit at the other's expense. If both hotels expand, this will put downward pressure on the market price and both profits will be reduced. Suppose A's cost is slightly higher than B's. The consequences of each hotel's choices are described in Table 2.3.

Assuming a static game of complete information, the Nash equilibrium is (2,4). In other words, A chooses not to expand its capacity with payoff of 2 while B expands with payoff 4. Let's consider the same two hotels in another scenario. Rather than moving simultaneously, A seeks to pre-empt B by making its capacity decision ahead. Thus, by the time B makes its decision, it will have observed A's choice and must adjust its decision-making accordingly. We can represent the dynamics of this decision-making process by the game tree in Figure 2.2.

Table 2.3 Capacity expansion game

		Hotel B	
		No expansion	Expansion
Hotel A	No expansion	4,3	2,4
	Expansion	3,2	1,1

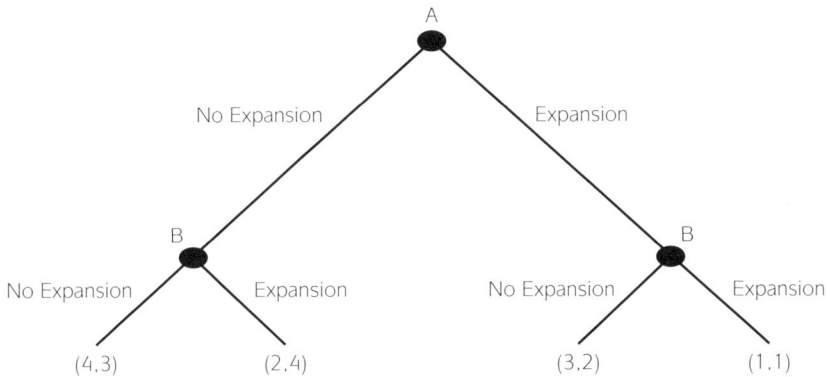

Figure 2.2 Decision tree for sequential capacity expansion game

By reasoning back the tree, we assume that A anticipates B to choose a profit-maximising response to any strategic move A might make. Given these expectations, we can then determine A's optimal strategy: if A chooses not to expand, B would react with Expansion and A's profit would be 2; if A chooses Expansion, then B's best response would be not to expand and A's profit would be 3. The Sub game–Perfect Nash Equilibrium is thus for A to choose Expansion and B to respond with no Expansion, yielding a payoff of (3,2). Note that the outcome of the sequential-move game differs significantly from the outcome of the simultaneous-move game. This is what we call a first mover's advantage: by making decisions first, A forces B into a disadvantageous position.

However, to make this strategy a success, Hotel A must convince Hotel B that it will deliver the promise it made. To give strategic move credibility, hotel A then has to take some other supporting actions that make a move reversal too costly or even impossible. This might be done by signing a contract with a construction company and paying a deposit to guarantee the contract. Breaking the contract is subject to severe penalisation: in this way, the commitment appears credible and hotel A can then achieve more profit than when both hotels act simultaneously.

The above example assumes symmetric and perfect information among all players. This restriction can be awkward for modelling situations where players have long-standing differences in information. In this context, entry deterrence is now used as an example to illustrate games of incomplete information. Let us assume that an airline monopolises the route between London and Athens. A potential entrant seeks to enter the market and competes with the incumbent airline. However, it is not certain about the incumbent's payoff from *Fight*. The payoff matrix is shown below in Table 2.4. X is the payoff of the incumbent airline from fighting with entrant; it is known to the incumbent but unobservable by the entrant.

We assume there are two types of incumbent airlines: strong and weak. A strong incumbent airline enjoys advantages such as better reputation, lower cost structure, more attractive frequent flyer programme and larger market power (control of slots, gates at airports) than a weak incumbent. In this context, fighting with a new entrant could generate more profit than accommodating it. This is very likely in the airline industry as consumers usually face greater uncertainty flying with a new entrant given the advantages that the strong incumbent enjoys. Therefore, by lowering fares through price discrimination based on a sophisticated yield management, a strong incumbent could stimulate demand for air travel, and generate more profits compared to the case of entrant accommodation. In contrast, if the incumbent is weak, fighting with a new entrant would make it less profitable than accommodating.

In choosing whether to enter, the entrant must predict the incumbent's type. If it is a strong incumbent, entrant's best strategy is to stay out; otherwise, to enter. If the game is dynamic and played either over time or in different markets (e.g. city-pairs), then the entrant would be able to observe the moves of the incumbent and modify its beliefs on the type of latter accordingly. In a seminal paper, Kreps and Wilson (1982) present some game-theoretical models to illustrate the impact of a firm's reputation on its payoffs. To apply the ideas of Kreps and Wilson's model to our case, an incumbent airline may seek to acquire a reputation for being tough early in the game to convince the potential entrants that it is strong. Later entrants, observing earlier moves, will revise their assessment of the types of the incumbent. Under such circumstances, a weak incumbent may be willing to fight

Table 2.4 Entry deterrence game

		Incumbent	
		Accommodate	Fight
Entrant	Enter	30,40	−10,X
	Not enter	0,100	0,100

entry early on to 'convince' subsequent entrants that it is 'strong', thus, deterring new entrants from challenging its monopoly position.

Another famous game-theoretical model, limit pricing, developed by Milgrom and Roberts (1982) can be also applied to our airline example. Here, an entrant is likely to know less about the incumbent's type than the incumbent itself does. The incumbent can, thus, send signals to the potential entrant. A strong incumbent has a lower cost structure than a weak one. Fare can be a strong signal as it is a function of costs. Because a weak incumbent could lower its price to disguise its costs, a strong incumbent would try to make sure that the entrant would recognise its cost advantage. To do so, a strong incumbent would lower its fares by a suffi- ciently large amount, so that the potential entrant is convinced that only a strong incumbent would price that low. In effect, a low fare becomes a credible signal that the incumbent's cost is low. Here a player has private information about their own cost type, but makes this information available to the other players by the signals they make. The model of limit pricing has been widely tested in the context of airline business. Strassmann (1990) investigates the role of potential competition using a structural model of interactions between prices, entry and concentration based on quarterly data from the USA after domestic air market liberalisation. He produces evidence that future entry is directly influenced by current prices. The latter thus appear to provide an important signal to potential entrants about the probability of profitable entry.

Performance

In the simple SCP approach, performance is the outcome of structure and conduct. This is usually measured as efficiency, company growth, market share and profitability. As it is relatively easy to measure, profitability is the most used indicator for performance. However, there are mixed results regarding profitability measurement in the context of the tourism sector.

In a study of structure, conduct and performance in the deregulated US airline industry, Evans and Kessides (1993) demonstrate that the substantial pricing power of a carrier is derived from the control of sunk and scarce airport facilities rather than the structure of the airline industry itself. Similarly, Davies (1999) finds that in spite of the fact that the leading UK hotel companies have a significant market share, no firm seems capable of exhibiting monopolistic behaviour. Market share is more easily explained than profitability and appears to be a key strategic variable in firm behaviour. However, the results are highly sensitive to both the choice of model and the definition of the industry. In another paper, Davies and Downward (2001) examine the British tour operator/travel agency business from 1989 to 1993. The results show that there is an even inverse relationship between concentration and profitability, suggesting that market structure cannot explain performance in the large company segment.

Apart from the mixed results arising from the measurement of profitability in the tourism sector, a fundamental problem is how to measure customer satisfaction, which is closely related to product quality. In the manufacturing industries, this is usually assumed to be constant, but this is often not the case in services (Britton et al., 1992). Therefore, customer satisfaction or quality must be taken into account when measuring performance of the tourism sector.

Conclusions

This chapter examined the SCP paradigm and attempted to analyse the basic conditions, the market structure, the conduct and the performance of the tourism industries. Service characteristics are crucial in understanding the SCP linkages in the tourism sector. Intangibility, irreversibility, inseparability, heterogeneity, perishability, seasonality and interdependence all have important implications for the application of the SCP paradigm in tourism. The basic forms of game theoretical models have been illustrated with examples from tourism to study the competitive behaviour of large firms. However, the topic of Game Theory is vast and some of the mathematics and statistics involved are cumbersome. We only hoped to touch on some of the essentials of Game Theory here, leaving the details for the interested readers to explore.

Although it appears fruitful to apply the SCP paradigm to study the market structure and conduct of tourism industries, the approach encounters difficulties in the analysis of performance. The empirical studies examined in this chapter also show unsatisfactory links between market structure, conduct and performance. Moreover, most of the usual performance indicators do not readily apply to tourism services as the quality factor is difficult to measure. Still, the SCP is a major theoretical pillar in industrial organisation and can provide a useful analytical benchmark for the applied chapters of this book.

References

Bain, J.S., 1956, *Barriers to New Competition* (Cambridge, MA: Harvard University Press).

Baumol, W., Panzar, J. and Willig, R., 1982, *Contestable Markets and the Theory of Industrial Structure* (New York: Harcourt Brace Jovanovich).

Britton, L.C., Clark, T.A.R. and Ball, D.F., 1992, 'Modify or extend? The application of the structure conduct performance approach to service industries', *The Service Industries Journal*, 12(1), 34–43.

Buhalis, D., 2003, *eTourism: Information Technology for Strategic Tourism Management* (London: FT Prentice Hall).

Butler, R., 1980, 'The concept of a tourist area cycle of evolution: implications for management of resources', *Canadian Geographer*, 14, 5–12.

Cabral, L.M.B., 2000, *Introduction to Industrial Organisation* (Cambridge, MA: MIT Press).

Caves, D.W., Christensen, L.R. and Tretheway, M.W., 1984, 'Economies of density versus economies of scale: why trunk and local service airline costs differ', *Rand Journal of Economics*, 15(4), 471–489.

Caves, R., 1962, *Air Transport and Its Regulation* (Knoxville, TN: University of Tennessee Press).

Chamberlin, E., 1965, *The Theory of Monopolistic Competition* (Cambridge, MA: Harvard University Press).

Cooper, C., Fletcher, J., Fyall, A., Gilbert, D., Wanhill, S., 2005, *Tourism Principles and Practice*, 3rd ed. (London: Pearson).

Crouch, G.I., 1992, 'Effect of income and price on international tourism', *Annals of Tourism Research*, 19, 643–664.

Davies, B., 1999, 'Industrial organization in the UK hotel sector', *Annals of Tourism Research*, 26(2), 294–311.

Davies, B. and Downward, P., 2001, 'Industrial organization and competition in the UK tour operator/travel agency business, 1989–1993: an econometric investigation', *Journal of Travel Research*, 39, 411–425.

Debbage, K. and Daniels, P., 1998, 'The tourist industry and economic geography: missed opportunities', in D. Ioannides and K. Debbage (eds), *The Economic Geography of the Tourist Industry: A Supply-Side Analysis* (London: Routledge).

Dunning, J.H. and McQueen, M., 1982, 'Multinational corporations in the international hotel industry', *Annals of Tourism Research*, 9, 69–90.

Evans, N.G. and Stabler, M.J., 1995, 'A future for the package tour operator in the 21st century', *Tourism Economics*, 1(3), 245–264.

Evans, W., and Kessides, I., 1993, 'Structure, conduct, performance in the deregulated airline industry', *Southern Economic Journal*, 59(3), 450–467.

Gillen, D.W., Oum, T.H., Tretheway, M., 1990, *Airline Costs and Performance: Implications for Public and Industry Policies* (Vancouver, Canada: Centre for Transport Studies, University of British Columbia).

Global Market Information Database, 2004, 'Travel and Tourism in the United Kingdom', Global Market Information Database (www.euromonitor.com/GMID/default.asp), accessed on 19 March 2005 (London: Euromonitor International).

Go, F.G. and Pine, R., 1995, *Globalization Strategy in the Hotel Industry* (London: Routledge).

Kreps, D.M. and Wilson, R., 1982, 'Reputation and imperfect information', *Journal of Economic Theory*, 27, 253–279.

Martin, C.A. and Witt, S.F., 1988, 'Substitute prices in models of tourism demand', *Annals of Tourism Research*, 15, 255–268.

Mason, E.S., 1939, 'Price and production policies of large scale enterprizes', *American Economic Review*, 29, March, 1939.

McWilliams, A. and Smart, D., 1993, 'Efficiency v. Structure–Conduct–Performance: implications for strategy research and practice', *Journal of Management*, 19(1), 63–78.

Middleton, V.T.C., 2001, *Marketing in Travel and Tourism*, 3rd ed. (Oxford: Butterworth Heinemann).

Milgrom, P. and Roberts, J. 1982, 'Limit pricing and entry under incomplete information', *Econometrica*, 50, 443–460.

Nelson, R. and Winter, S., 1982, *An Evolutionary Theory of Economic Change* (Cambridge, MA: Ballinger).

Papatheodorou, A., 2004, 'Exploring the evolution of tourism resorts', *Annals of Tourism Research*, 31(1), 219–237.

Rickard, S., 2002, 'Industrial Organisation Economics', in M. Jenkins and V. Ambrosini (eds), *Strategic Management: a Multi-Perspective Approach* (New York: Palgrave).

Robinson, J., 1933, *The Economics of Imperfect Competition* (London: Macmillan).

Scherer, F.M. and Ross, D., 1990, *Industrial Market Structure and Economic Performance*, 3rd ed. (Boston: Houghton Mifflin Company).

Schumpeter, J., 1942, *Capitalism, Socialism and Democracy* (New York: Harper and Row).

Shy, O., 1995, *Industrial Organization: Theory and Applications* (Cambridge, MA: MIT Press).

Sinclair, M.T. and Stabler, M., 1997, *The Economics of Tourism* (London: Routledge).

Strassmann, D.L., 1990, 'Potential competition in the deregulated airlines', *The Review of Economics and Statistics*, 72(4), 696–702.

Strazheim, M., 1969, *The International Airline Industry* (Washington, DC: The Brookings Institution).

White, L.J., 1979, 'Economies of scale and the question of natural monopoly in the airline industry', *Journal of Air Law and Commerce*, 44, 545–573.

3

Quantitative techniques for tourism competition analysis

Gang Li and Haiyan Song

This chapter introduces various quantitative techniques for competition analysis and draws on the applications of these methods in the tourism context. The utilization of quantitative techniques has arisen from the need to answer such questions as market structure, pricing and demand for consumer goods. The aim of this chapter is to illustrate how some of these key techniques can assist tourism competition analysis.

Market structure analysis

The structural characteristics of an industry, to a great extent, determine the nature and intensity of competition within it (Grant 1995). The larger the number of businesses in the market is, the higher the competition intensity. Meanwhile, the level of market concentration also affects the nature of competition. A lower concentration level may indicate more competition within an industry. Market concentration is usually assessed by two measures: m-firm concentration ratio (CR_m) and the Herfindahl-Hirschman Index (HHI).

The *m-firm concentration ratio*

The m-firm concentration ratio is the market share of the m largest firms in an industry. It can be expressed as:

$$CR_m = s_1 + s_2 + s_3 + \ldots + s_m \tag{3.1}$$

where s_i ($i = 1, 2, \ldots, $ m) is the market share of the ith largest firm.

The most commonly used measures are the four- and five-firm concentration ratios (CR_4 and CR_5). A value of CR_m close to zero indicates an extremely competitive industry. If CR_1 is greater than 90 per cent, this suggests that the market is effectively a monopoly. The lower the concentration ratio is, the lower the barriers to entry of this industry are. As a result, new firms can enter the market

Table 3.1 The top tour operators in Germany and Italy

German market	Market share ('99)	Italian market	Market share ('98)
TUI Group Deutschland	21.1	Gruppo Alpitour	23.5
C&N	17.8	Costa Crociere	5.9
LTU	8.3	HIT	5.9
Dertour	5.0	Viaggi del Ventaglio	5.2
FTI	5.0	Valtur	4.3
CR_5	**57.2**	CR_5	**44.8**

Source: Adapted from Buhalis and Laws (2001: 143, 147).

with relative ease, and this can increase the competition pressure in the industry concerned. For example, Table 3.1 shows the market shares of the top five tour operators in Germany and Italy in 1999 and 1998, respectively. The calculated CR_5 values indicate that both markets are highly concentrated, and the Italian market is more competitive than the German one, as CR_5 in Italy is lower than that in Germany. Over the last few years, mergers and acquisitions have been evident in the European tour operations markets. The increasing market concentration has led to economies of scale. Those large regional or international operators have strengthened their dominant positions, while the small or independent firms have become increasingly less competitive.

The calculation of the concentration ratio is simple and straightforward. However, it only presents an incomplete picture of concentration in an industry, because it does not use the market shares of all the firms in the industry. It also does not take into account the distribution of firm size. For example, even if there is a significant change in the market shares among the top five firms, the value of CR_5 will not be affected.

Herfindahl-Hirschman Index (HHI)

The HHI provides a more complete picture of industry concentration than CR_m. The HHI uses the market shares of all firms in the industry, and these market shares are squared in the calculation to place more weight on the larger firms. Given an industry with n firms, the HHI is calculated from:

$$HHI = \sum_{i=1}^{n} s_i^2 \tag{3.2}$$

Unlike the concentration ratio, the HHI will change if there is a shift in market share among the larger firms. The value of the HHI varies between 0 and 10,000.

The lower the index is, the more competitive the market. If there is only one firm in the industry, that firm would have 100 per cent market share and the HHI will be equal to 10,000. In the other extreme, if there are a very large number of firms, each of which has almost zero market share, then the HHI will be close to zero, indicating nearly perfect competition.

An HHI of less than 1000 implies a relatively non-concentrated market; an HHI between 1000 and 1800 represents a moderately concentrated market; while markets having HHIs greater than 1800 are considered highly concentrated. The HHI is often used by regulatory authorities including the USA and UK especially for evaluating mergers. A merger that creates a market with over 1800 points of HHI will raise concerns (Fishwick 1993). According to Brooks *et al.* (2004), the value of the post-merger HHI has to be less than 1000 for a merger not to be considered having a significant adverse impact on the market competition.

The HHI has been applied to tourism competition analysis in various sectors such as hospitality and airlines (see, for example, Pan 2005 and Janić 1997, respectively). Table 3.2 shows the HHIs of Taiwanese international tourist accommodation market in the three metropolitan areas (Pan 2005). These values indicate that the accommodation market in Taipei is highly competitive while the markets in the other two areas are less so. With regard to the variation of competition over time, the accommodation market in Taipei is rather stable, while the other two have become increasingly more competitive.

It should be noted that concentration measures of a market only reflect one aspect of competition and they should be applied in conjunction with other measures when assessing market competition (Brooks *et al.* 2004).

Table 3.2 HHIs of Taiwanese international tourist accommodation markets

Year	Taipei	Taichung	Kaohsiung
1989	660	5460	3220
1990	590	4300	3110
1991	610	4630	3350
1992	660	4070	3540
1993	710	3690	3880
1994	660	3830	3740
1995	650	3900	1940
1996	650	3040	2130
1997	660	2880	1870
1998	660	2880	1990
1999	650	2300	1930
2000	640	2300	1620
Mean	650	3610	2690

Source: Adapted from Pan (2005: 3).

Price analysis

The analysis of prices, price trends and the relationships between prices is an important aspect of competition investigation. Once the prices of products are analysed along with their quality features, implications of products' competitiveness can be generated. Among the various quantitative methods for price analyses, two statistical tests of prices and price trends and two regression techniques are introduced in this section.

Cross-sectional price tests

Cross-sectional price tests are used to examine uniformity between two sets of prices which may be associated with different geographic areas, two different time periods or two related products. These tests are based on statistical grounds without economic or behavioural underpinnings. They are useful in analysing the market power or the effect of cartelization (Hoehn *et al.* 1999).

The cross-sectional price tests require that the two sets of prices being compared should be randomly sampled from two populations. The null hypothesis is that the two populations have identical distributions. The two samples of prices can be either independent or paired. For example, to examine if the bus fares in London are higher than those in Paris, the samples in two areas can be regarded as independent. If it is assumed that the two samples depend on each other to some extent, for instance, the bus fares in London and south England, or the prices before and after a new pricing strategy is adopted, these samples in related areas or periods should not be considered independent but paired. Different assumptions of the relationship between the two sets of prices lead to two different statistical tests.

The independent-samples *t* test

Given two sets of prices P_1 and P_2 in relation to two independent samples, both drawn from normally distributed populations with means μ_1 and μ_2 and identical variance σ^2, the average prices in the two samples ($\bar{P}_1$ and $\bar{P}_2$) are unbiased estimates of μ_1 and μ_2, and the pooled sample variance S_p^2 is an unbiased estimate of σ^2. S_p^2 can be expressed as a weighted average of the two sample variances S_1^2 and S_2^2, i.e.

$$S_p^2 = \frac{S_1^2(n_1 - 1) + S_2^2(n_2 - 1)}{n_1 + n_2 - 2} \tag{3.3}$$

where n_1 and n_2 are the sample sizes. The hypothesis $\mu_1 = \mu_2$ can be tested using the following statistic:

$$t = \frac{\bar{P}_1 - \bar{P}_2}{S_p\sqrt{\dfrac{1}{n_1} + \dfrac{1}{n_2}}} \; or \; \frac{\bar{P}_1 - \bar{P}_2}{\sqrt{\dfrac{S_1^2(n_1-1)+S_2^2(n_2-1)}{n_1+n_2-2}\left(\dfrac{1}{n_1}+\dfrac{1}{n_2}\right)}} \tag{3.4}$$

which is distributed as a student's *t*-statistic with degrees of freedom equal to ($n_1 + n_2 -2$). To accept the null hypothesis, the estimated *t* must be lower than the tabulated critical values at a significance level of 10 per cent or less.

The conditions for using the independent-samples *t* test are random sampling, normally distributed populations, independent observations and identical population variance (Grimm 1993). It is difficult to meet all of these conditions in practice, especially the last two. Therefore, unless there is very strong justification for the validation of these assumptions, the paired-sample test should be used for the cross-sectional prices examination.

The paired-samples *t* test

Assume each score in sample P_1 is related to another score in sample P_2. Both P_1 and P_2 are drawn from two normally distributed populations with means μ_1 and μ_2 and variances σ_1^2 and σ_2^2. The hypothesis $\mu_1 = \mu_2$, equivalent to $\mu_1 - \mu_2 = 0$ can be tested using the following statistic:

$$t = \frac{\bar{P}_1 - \bar{P}_2}{S_D\sqrt{1/n_p}} \tag{3.5}$$

where

$$S_D = \sqrt{S_1^2 + S_2^2 - 2S_{12}}$$

and S_{12} is the covariance of the two samples; n_p is the number of pairs of observations. Formula (3.5) follows Student's *t*-distribution with degrees of freedom equal to ($n_p - 1$). The testing procedure is the same as that of the independent-samples test. The paired-sample test is more powerful than the independent-samples alternative as $S_D < S_p$ and there is a greater likelihood of rejecting a false null hypothesis when using the paired-samples test.

The paired-samples test can be illustrated using the data of London public transport fares. Docklands Light Rail (DLR) and bus services are both available in some areas in London (see Table 3.3). The change of the DLR fares is likely to influence bus fares. Therefore, the paired-samples test is more appropriate to analyse the difference of the fares between the two competing transport services. This analysis can be done by SPSS. Table 3.4 presents the result, which suggests that travel by DLR is significantly (at 1 per cent level) more expensive than by bus, i.e. bus services are sold at a relative price discount.

Table 3.3 The average fares per passenger kilometre in London

Period	Fares of DLR (P$_1$)	Fares of buses (P$_2$)
1987/88	16.00	12.40
1988/89	13.00	12.80
1989/90	13.50	13.30
1990/91	13.20	13.30
1991/92	12.50	13.80
1992/93	14.80	14.00
1993/94	15.00	15.10
1994/95	15.40	15.40
1995/96	16.20	15.40
1996/97	16.70	15.50
1997/98	15.70	15.20
1998/99	16.00	15.50
1999/00	15.90	15.50
2000/01	16.00	14.70
2001/02	17.20	13.70
2002/03	16.50	12.50
2003/04	16.40	11.90
Mean	15.30	14.12
Standard deviation	1.42	1.26

(Unit: Pence, at 2003/04 prices)
Data source: London Travel Report 2004, Transport for London.

Table 3.4 Paired-samples test for fare differences

Mean of (P$_1$–P$_2$)	Standard deviation	*t* statistic	Degrees of freedom	Significance
1.180	1.673	2.899	16	0.010

Price correlation

Correlation analysis is used to investigate the degree of association between two price variables and to determine if the two products or one product in two geographically different areas belong to the same market. To some extent, this technique can bring to light evidence of collusive agreements. It can also be employed to examine the interdependence between prices and other related factors such as market shares and the degree of market concentration.

Given two variables x and y, let σ_x and σ_y represent their square roots of the variances, respectively, and σ_{xy} is the covariance between x and y. The correlation coefficient r_{xy} is calculated as:

$$r_{xy} = \sigma_{xy} / \sigma_x \sigma_y \tag{3.6}$$

The value of the correlation coefficient ranges between -1 and 1; $r_{xy} = -1$ and $r_{xy} = 1$ indicate perfect negative and positive correlations respectively. A coefficient of zero implies no correlation detected, but it does not necessarily mean that the two variables are independent. In practice, the significance of a value of r largely depends on the sample size. It is customary to calculate r using the natural logarithm of the price series, due to both efficiency reasons and the economic meaning of the first log differences, which can be interpreted as the growth rate (Hoehn *et al.* 1999). To investigate price uniformity in terms of the trend and speed of price change, correlation coefficients should be computed based on both price levels and differences in logarithm.

The correlation analysis is illustrated using the data related to local bus fares in the UK. Table 3.5 shows the national fare index and the area breakdown indices. Using SPSS the Pearson correlation coefficients can be calculated using

Table 3.5 UK local bus fare indices (1995 = 100)

Period	National bus fare index	Area breakdown of local bus fare index				
		London	England	Scotland	Wales[1]	Outside London
1985/86	81.2	73.8	79.1	93.8	–	82.9
1986/87	87.0	76.1	85.6	94.3	–	89.4
1987/88	88.4	76.8	87.4	94.5	–	91.0
1988/89	88.4	80.4	87.7	92.7	–	90.2
1989/90	88.6	82.2	88.3	90.4	–	90.0
1990/91	88.9	82.7	88.8	88.7	–	90.3
1991/92	92.4	86.4	92.4	91.2	–	93.7
1992/93	94.7	90.2	94.6	94.5	96.9	95.8
1993/94	97.3	95.8	97.5	96.2	98.8	97.8
1994/95	99.2	98.7	99.2	99.4	99.9	99.3
1995/96	100.5	100.4	100.5	100.1	100.0	100.5
1996/97	103.1	102.2	102.9	104.7	101.2	103.4
1997/98	105.1	102.6	104.6	109.3	103.3	105.9
1998/99	106.6	103.5	106.0	110.9	105.9	107.6
1999/00	109.3	105.0	108.9	112.3	109.5	110.6
2000/01	109.9	101.9	109.5	113.0	110.9	112.3
2001/02	112.0	99.1	111.7	113.0	114.5	116.0
2002/03	112.9	96.4	112.7	112.9	117.1	118.2
2003/04	113.6	95.5	113.6	111.8	118.9	119.5

[1] Note: Bus fare indices for Wales prior to 1992/93 are omitted because insufficient data are available.
Data source: DfT surveys of operators, Department for Transport, UK.

Table 3.6 Correlations between UK local bus fare levels in different regions

	National	**London**	**England**	**Scotland**	**Wales**	**Outside London**
National	1					
London	0.890**	1				
England	0.999**	0.898**	1			
Scotland	0.927**	0.784**	0.907**	1		
Wales	0.963**	0.121	0.969**	0.868**	1	
Outside London	0.992**	0.824**	0.988**	0.930**	0.990**	1

** Correlation is significant at the 1 per cent level (2-tailed).

both the levels and differences of the bus fares in logarithm to examine the associations between the trends of fares and their variations in different areas. The correlation coefficients of the price levels (see Table 3.6) suggest that the general trends of fare movements over time in different areas are highly correlated with the national trends, with only one exception between London and Wales. The highest correlation appears between the national average fares and those of England, which implies that, to a great extent, the variations of bus fares in England can represent the national trends. This implies that there are common factors that simultaneously influence the bus fare movements in different areas and in the same direction. The computation of correlations between bus fare changes in different areas provides a clearer picture of the associations between fare variations and suggests closeness of regional markets. The degree of correlation between the fare changes, however, is much lower and less significant than those between the fare levels. This suggests that although some factors have common effects on bus fares across regions, the degree of the influence is different. Although the fare changes are in the same directions among regions, the speed of changes varies across regions. The bus fare fluctuations in England and outside London are good indicators for the national bus fare variations. As we know, public transport in London is always more expensive than other areas, which may be associated with the larger number of tourists and different pricing strategies. These explain why the correlations between bus fares in London and those of other areas are relatively low and none is significant where the growth rates are concerned.

Correlation analysis, together with cross-sectional price analysis, can be used to investigate competition in many other sectors of the tourism industry in addition to the above case. For example, high correlation and insignificant difference between the air fares of different airlines on the same route indicates that some sort of collusive agreement may exist in this market, which is likely to reduce the degree of competition and raise market entry barriers.

Table 3.7 Correlations between UK local bus fare changes in different regions

	National	London	England	Scotland	Wales	Outside London
National	1					
London	0.380	1				
England	0.987**	0.385	1			
Scotland	0.451	0.239	0.312	1		
Wales	0.275	−0.223	0.347	−0.176	1	
Outside London	0.943**	0.054	0.925**	0.413	0.637**	1

** Correlation is significant at the 1 per cent level (2-tailed).

Correlation analysis is straightforward and can provide useful indications for the relationships between products and their prices. However, as with cross-sectional price analysis, correlation analysis is purely a statistical tool and does not have any theoretical underpinnings and takes no account of causal effect between variables. Therefore, spurious correlations are likely to occur. For example, two price series could be correlated simply because they share a common component. In order to draw a robust conclusion, correlation analysis should be complemented with more sophisticated techniques such as Granger causality tests and counteraction tests. The explanation of these techniques is available from a number of econometric texts (see, for example, Greene 2003), and is beyond the scope of this chapter.

Price-concentration studies

Price-concentration studies are based on the structure-conduct-performance paradigm developed by Bain (1951). According to this theory, market structure, usually measured by market concentration in empirical analysis, affects market performance measured by profit margin via its effect on pricing. If there is a strong positive correlation between prices/profits and market concentration, a merger in this market which has a significant impact on concentration should raise anti-competitive concerns.

The theoretical underpinning of Bain's paradigm can be represented using the Lerner index of monopoly power (Lerner 1943), which is written as:

$$\frac{P - MC_j}{P} = \frac{\theta_j + \left(1 - \theta_j\right)S_j}{\varepsilon_p} = \frac{\theta_j}{\varepsilon_p} + \frac{\left(1 - \theta_j\right)}{\varepsilon_p}S_j \qquad (3.7)$$

where P is the market price, MC is the marginal cost, $(P - MC_j) / P$ indicates the degree of profitability and can be measured by various accounting profit variables;

S_j is the share of firm j in total industry output; ε_p is the industry price elasticity of demand; θ_j is the conjectural variation term, measuring the percentage change in output that firm j expects other firms in the industry to undertake in response to a 1 per cent change in its own output. The value of θ indicates the relationship between firms and the market structure. For example, a value of θ equal to zero means no reaction on behalf of other firms to an increase in its own output. It indicates that this firm operates in a Cournot oligopoly. In practice, regression analysis in relation to the above equation is used to test the relationship between prices/profits and concentration, assuming that θ_j/ε_p and $(1 - \theta_j)/\varepsilon_p$ are the parameters to be estimated. The analysis can be carried out with data at both firm and industry levels. At the industry level, profitability is regressed against market concentration measures (with the CR_m or HHI being used as proxy). At the firm level, both industry concentration and the firm's market share affect its performance and therefore should be included in the regression. With regard to the data requirements, time-series, cross-sectional or preferably panel data (pooling both time-series and cross-sectional data) can be used in regression analysis.

In the context of tourism, the application of the price-concentration analysis can be seen in Pan (2005). In this study, the aggregated before tax ratio of accounting profits to sales for international tourist hotels is regressed against the HHIs for both the accommodation market and the food-beverage market. The pooled data of three geographic areas in Taiwan in a 20-year period are utilized in a panel regression model. The results show that market concentration in accommodation market significantly improves the international tourist hotels' profitability, while concentration of the food and beverage markets has a positive but insignificant effect. These results imply that the collusive relationship may be strong in this particular industry, which may raise concerns from the competition authority.

The price-concentration analysis is based on the assumption that firms' performance (prices/profits) is affected by the degree of concentration but no feedback effect exists. However, this is not always true in practice, as high prices may lead to new entries or more imports and consequently result in lower concentration. This methodology is also criticized for not taking the efficiency gains and the existence of differentiated products into account (Baker and Bresnahan 1992). For instance, in the study by Pan (2005), another possible explanation of the results is that greater efficiency (rather than the collusive behaviour) of large firms could lead to higher profitability in a more concentrated industry. The price-concentration analysis is not able to identify the true explanation and therefore should be complemented by other techniques in order to draw a robust conclusion.

Hedonic price analysis

Hedonic price analysis is based on Lancaster's (1966) characteristics theory, which postulates that goods can be regarded as 'bundles' of characteristics and therefore the price of a particular product is associated with the attributes or characteristics of the goods concerned. Hedonic price analysis is developed to purge prices of the effect of a set of characteristics such as quality differences, so that the pure price difference between 'standardized' products can be isolated and examined (Hoehn *et al.* 1999). Therefore, hedonic price analysis can provide more accurate information for competition analysis, with regard to the relationships between the prices of two differentiated products or of one product in two periods, during which product differentiation or quality change has occurred. For example, if the non-adjusted price increases dramatically over a certain period, while hedonic price analysis identifies that the quality-adjusted price decreases significantly, the indication would be that the price change may not lie in the anti-competitive behaviour of the supplier or monopolistic abuse but, more likely, in the improve-ment of product quality. If the quality-adjusted price of product A is similar to that of product B, while the non-adjusted price of B is much higher than that of A, this implies that product A has gained more competitive advantages over B and therefore is more likely to win the competition with B.

The hedonic price analysis is a regression analysis developed by Rosen (1974). Given a good Z consisting of characteristics $z_1, z_2, \ldots, z_n$, the price of Z can be expressed as:

$$\ln P(Z) = \alpha + \sum_{i=1}^{n} \beta_i z_i + u \tag{3.8}$$

or

$$\ln P(Z) = \alpha + \sum_{i=1}^{n} \beta_i \ln z_i + u, \tag{3.9}$$

where α and β are parameters to be estimated and u is the disturbance term.

In the tourism context, the hedonic price analysis has been used to investigate the price competitiveness of specific tour operators, tourism resorts, and holiday packages. For example, Papatheodorou (2002) examines competitiveness in Mediterranean resorts using the hedonic analysis in which the prices of holiday packages are regressed against a number of package characteristics and operator and location scaling factors. A double-log regression model is utilized, in which the estimated coefficients represent the relative price differentials (in logarithm). In order to measure the percentage price differences, the following transformation has to be made: $100 \cdot (e^{\ln X} - 1)$. For example, the estimated coefficient of '2-star official accommodation classification' in this study is -0.07, the indication of which is that the 2-star establishments are sold at a 6.75 [$= 100 \times (e^{-0.07} - 1)$] per cent discount in relation to the base, i.e. the 3-star classification (Papatheodorou 2002).

As the residuals of the regression have removed the characteristics that differentiate the products, competitiveness of individual products can then be measured in terms of the sign and how far the residuals deviate from zero. If the prices (the dependent variables) are transactions prices, negative residuals indicate 'bargains,' as the product costs less than one would expect from the quantities of characteristics they possess. On the contrary, positive residuals suggest that the product costs 'too much' for what it provides in terms of characteristics. The larger the positive residuals are, the less competitive a product is. Therefore, the residual analysis of a hedonic price model can provide indication of relative market positions of competing products. However, little empirical research focusing on this method has been conducted in tourism completion analysis.

Although the hedonic analysis is useful in price analysis, especially in dealing with differentiated products, the reliability of the results largely depends upon the proper model specification and the quality of the empirical data. The strong interrelationship among independent variables (multi-collinearity) makes the regression coefficients unstable with large variance which results in non-significant parameter estimation. Omission of important variables (representing character-istics) may also lead to biased estimates and misleading interpretation of the results.

Demand and substitution analysis

Demand and substitution analysis here refers to the econometric analysis of demand for substitute products based on the classical consumer theory. Analysis of demand-side substitution helps to understand to what extent consumers are willing to switch to substitutes in an event of a price increase. If the number of the consumers who are likely to switch is large enough, it may prevent a hypothetical monopolist from maintaining prices above the competitive levels (Hoehn *et al.* 1999). In other words, a weaker substitution effect implies a greater market power that the producer has gained in competition.

In an econometric model, the demand for a product is regressed against the price of the product concerned, prices of hypothetical substitutes as well as complementary products, consumers' income and other influencing factors. Such a demand model can be expressed as:

$$Q_i = f\left(P_i, P_s, Y, X\right) \tag{3.10}$$

where Q_i is the quantity demanded for product i, P_i is the price of product i, P_s is the price of the hypothetical substitute product, Y is the income of consumers and X represents other influencing factors. When the model is expressed in logarithms, the estimated coefficients provide indicators for demand elasticities, which is useful for analysing the degree of substitution between alternative products and their price competitiveness. For example, coaches and trains are two competing transport modes especially for domestic travel. Modelling the demand for both transport means can help to examine the degree of competition between them to find out which has more competitive advantages.

The empirical demand analysis in the context of tourism predominantly focuses on the demand for international tourist destinations in order to investigate the interrelationships between alternative destinations and their relative market positions in competition, though the methodology is also applicable at disaggregated levels as long as the data required are available. Two broad categories of econometric models are used most often in tourism demand studies: single-equation models and system-of-equations models.

Single-equation demand models

Demand analysis especially for tourism often use time-series data. Each single-equation model is associated with the demand for one product only. If a group of products are concerned, their demand needs to be modelled and estimated separately. A number of different functional forms of single-equation models have been applied to tourism demand studies. The overviews of the methodologies and their applications to tourism studies can be seen in Song and Witt (2000) and Li *et al.* (2005). The double-log regression model is the most often used function form, in which both dependent and independent variables are transformed into logarithms. By doing so, the estimated coefficients have direct relations with demand elasticities.

For example, Song *et al.* (2003) examined demand for Thai tourism by seven key international source markets with the competition among Thailand and its neighbours including Malaysia, Indonesia, Singapore and the Philippines being investigated. The estimated reduced autoregressive lag distribution model for the UK is:

$$LTOU_t = -12.064 + 0.410LTOU_{t-1} + 2.904LGDP_{t-1} - 0.244LRRCP_t$$
$$(2.232) (0.109)\phantom{LTOU_{t-1}} (0.514)\phantom{LGDP_{t-1}} (0.138)$$
$$+ 0.330LRSUB_{t-1} - 0.184DUM97$$
$$(0.145)\phantom{LRSUB_{t-1}} (0.097) \tag{3.11}$$

where the letter *L* in front of the variable names stands for logarithm, *TOU* is tourist arrivals from the UK, *GDP* is the income of UK tourists, *RRCP* is the tourism price level in Thailand relative to that of the UK, *RSUB* represents the relative substitute price level of tourism in competing destinations, and *DUM* is a dummy variable capturing the effect of the 1997 Asian financial crisis. The subscripts *t* and *t*–1 refer to the current and previous periods, respectively. The values in parentheses are standard errors. The coefficient of LRSUB suggests significant substitution effects between Thailand and its neighbouring countries in terms of competing for UK tourists.

Single-equation models are easier to estimate due to the smaller number of variables incorporated into the model. However, the limitation is that this approach is incapable of analysing the interdependence of budget allocations to different tourist products/destinations. Lacking a strong underpinning of economic theory, the single-equation approach is specified and estimated on an *ad hoc* basis. As a result, it is difficult to attach a strong degree of confidence to the empirical results (in particular with regard to demand elasticities).

Almost Ideal Demand System (AIDS)

The system-of-equations approach embodies the principles of demand theory, and is more appropriate for demand analysis. Amongst a number of system approaches available, the AIDS introduced by Deaton and Muellbauer (1980) has been the most commonly used method because of its considerable advantages over others. The AIDS model is specified in the form:

$$w_i = \alpha_i + \sum_j \gamma_{ij} \log p_j + b_i \log(x/P) + u_i \tag{3.12}$$

where w_i is the budget share of the ith good, p_i is the price of the ith good, x is total expenditure on all goods in the system, P is the aggregate price index for the system, and u_i is the disturbance term. The aggregate price index P is defined as:

$$\log P = a_0 + \sum_i \alpha_i \log p_i + \frac{1}{2} \sum_i \sum_j \gamma_{ij} \log p_i \log p_j \tag{3.13}$$

where a_0, α_i and γ_{ij} are parameters to be estimated. Replacing P with the Stone price index (P^*) as in equation (3.14), the linearly approximated AIDS is derived and termed 'LAIDS':

$$\log P^* = \sum_i w_i \log p_i \tag{3.14}$$

Within the LAIDS framework, the expenditure elasticity (ε_{ix}), the compensated own-price elasticity (ε_{ii}^*) and cross-price elasticity (ε_{ij}^*) can be calculated as: $\varepsilon_{ix} = 1 + \beta_i/w_i$, and $\varepsilon_{ii}^* = \gamma_{ii}/w_i + w_i - 1$ and $\varepsilon_{ij}^* = \gamma_{ij}/w_i + w_j$, respectively. These elasticities have more solid theoretical grounds than those of single-equation models, and therefore provide more precise and reliable information for substitution analysis.

The LAIDS model and its recently developed dynamic version (error correction LAIDS) have been applied to tourism destination competitiveness analysis (for example, Durbarry and Sinclair 2003; Li *et al.* 2004; Papatheodorou 1999).

Table 3.8 Long-run compensated price elasticities of UK tourism demand in key European destinations

	France	Greece	Italy	Portugal	Spain
France	**−1.17**	0.19	−0.16	0.08	**1.15**
Greece	0.48	**−2.75**	−0.03	−0.43	0.23
Italy	−0.35	-0.03	−0.93	**0.33**	−0.11
Portugal	0.35	−0.80	**0.69**	**−1.16**	−0.05
Spain	**0.77**	0.06	−0.03	−0.01	**−1.52**

Note: the values in bold type are significant at the 5 per cent significance level.
Source: Abstracted from Li *et al*. (2004).

Li *et al*. (2004) applied the dynamic LAIDS to modelling UK tourist expenditure allocation in the main European destinations: France, Greece, Italy, Portugal and Spain, and investigating the price effects between them. The calculated own-price elasticities suggest that UK tourists are the most sensitive to price variations in Greece, and least to the changes of prices in Italy. The positive values of the cross-price elasticities (in bold type) imply the significant substitution effects between France and Spain, and between Italy and Portugal. Therefore, if tourism prices in one destination (e.g. France) increase, UK tourists are likely to choose to visit the competing destination (e.g. Spain). However, the degrees of substitution between the two destinations are different. For example, if the prices in Spain increase by 1 per cent, the demand for France will increase by 1.15 per cent. On the other hand, if the prices in France increase by 1 per cent, the demand for Spain will increase by only 0.77 per cent. This indicates that France has stronger market power over Spain in the competition for attracting UK tourists' expenditure.

Although the AIDS/LAIDS models have advantages over single-equation models, applications to tourism competition analysis are still limited due to their technical complexity (such as simultaneous estimation) especially in the dynamic version of the model.

Discrete choice analysis

Discrete choice analysis can be used to model consumers' individual choices among mutually exclusive and collectively exhaustive sets of alternatives such as a set of tourist destinations. This technique helps to investigate the influencing factors of consumers' choice amongst the competing alternatives. In a demand-driven market, these factors are driving forces for suppliers to adjust their production arrangement and marketing strategies in order to achieve favourable positions in the competition. Therefore, these key factors identified from discrete choice analysis are the focus of competition investigation. Meanwhile, the results of discrete choice analysis provide indications for product differentiation and market segmentation in a competitive market.

Different from the above demand analysis which is derived from the classical consumer theory, discrete choice analysis is based on Lancaster's characteristics theory, as with the hedonic price analysis. The difference between the discrete choice model (DCM) and the hedonic price model is that the DCM attempts to recover a full demand function (as opposed to just a pricing function). The consumer j's utility (U_{ij}) from the purchase of alternative i is:

$$U_{ij} = f(X_i) + \varepsilon_{ij} \tag{3.15}$$

where $f(X_i)$ is the function of the attribute vector (X) related to i, and ε_{ij} is a random disturbance term. In a binary choice context, the probability that an alternative is chosen or not chosen is written as:

$$\text{Prob}(Y = 1|X) = F(X, \beta) \tag{3.16}$$

$$\text{Prob}(Y = 0|X) = 1 - F(X, \beta) \tag{3.17}$$

where β is a set of parameters reflecting the impacts of changes in X on the probability. Based on different assumptions of the distribution of disturbance ε_{ij}, two commonly used models – *probit* and *logit* models are identified, written in and (3.18) and (3.19), respectively (see Greene 2003):

$$\text{Prob}(Y = 1|X) = \int_{-\sigma}^{x'\beta} \phi(t)dt = \Phi(X'\beta) \tag{3.18}$$

$$\text{Prob}(Y = 1|X) = \frac{e^{X'\beta}}{1 + e^{X'\beta}} = \Lambda(X'\beta) \tag{3.19}$$

where $\Phi(\cdot)$ and $\Lambda(\cdot)$ are notation for the standard normal distribution and logistic cumulative distribution, respectively.

More often a consumer faces multiple choices, therefore multinomial DCMs should be applied. Given a hierarchical decision-making process among several aspects of a heterogeneous indivisible good, the nested multinomial model, the extension of the multinomial model, should be employed. The data used for DCMs are usually collected from consumer (or potential consumer) surveys. The demographic structure of households is an important influencing factor in determining a consumer's choice, and the DCM can easily accommodate this factor as an attribute in the model. In the tourism context, the DCMs have not been applied widely. Eymann and Ronning (1997) utilized the nested multinomial logit models to analyse the determinants of German tourists' choice among eight aggregated destination regions. The results suggest that the impact of the price index of one-day vacations is not significant. It implies that tourists adjust the level of consumption to the regional price level rather than choosing 'inexpensive' vacation resorts. In other words, price competition is unlikely to be a key issue dominating the investigated market. Other non-price factors have greater effects on tourists' choice and determine the market power of the alternative destinations concerned. For example, this study shows that the sunnier the climate of a destination, the higher the frequency of visitors who choose the destination because of its sunny climate. Moreover, the frequency of first-time visitors is higher at newly developed vacation areas. This is to say, the newly developed areas have gained more competitive advantages over their older counterparts in attracting first-time visitors. These results provide some useful marketing implications regarding how to differentiate the tourist resorts in different destinations and how to segment the tourism market.

Discrete choice analysis is useful for investigating the influencing factors of individual choices and the determinants of market competition, the results of which provide useful information for suppliers to project effective marketing strategies. However, the technical complexity restricts its utilization only to econometric experts. Moreover, the model specification may seriously affect the reliability of the results, especially in the cases where multiple choices and hierarchical decision-making processes are presented. The appropriate specification is subject to complicated statistical tests, which may not be powerful enough to draw a robust conclusion.

Summary

This chapter introduces a number of useful quantitative techniques for tourism competition analysis. The complexity of these techniques increases from simple measures like the CR_m and the HHI, to statistical tests, such as the independent- and paired-samples t tests and correlations, and to the econometric models, such as the hedonic price model, the single-equation model, the AIDS and the DCM. The applications of these techniques to tourism competition analysis are illustrated with examples. The limitations of each method are discussed and suggestions for combining different techniques in analysing the competition issues in tourism are presented. Due to the space constraints, only those quantitative approaches that have been successfully applied to tourism competition analysis are introduced with many of the available techniques in the general economic literature being omitted. The quantitative techniques presented in this chapter complement the practitioner's perspective explored in Chapter 10 and provide a good reference point for those interested in competition measures related to tourism.

References

Bain, Joe S. (1951). 'Relation of Profit Rates to Industry Concentration: American Manufacturing, 1936–1940', *Quarterly Journal of Economics* 65: pp. 293–324.

Baker, Jonathan B. and Timothy F. Bresnahan (1992). 'Empirical Methods of Identifying and Measuring Market Power', *Antitrust Law Journal* 61: pp. 3–16.

Brooks, Ian, Jamie Weatherston and Graham Wilkinson (2004). *The International Business Environment* (Harlow, Pearson Education).

Buhalis, Dimitrios and Eric Laws (2001). *Tourism Distribution Channels: Practices, Issues and Transformations* (eds) (London, Continuum).

Deaton, Angus and John Muellbauer (1980). 'An Almost Ideal Demand System', *American Economic Review* 70: pp. 312–326.

Durbarry, Ramesh and M. Thea Sinclair (2003). 'Market Shares Analysis: The Case of French Tourism Demand', *Annals of Tourism Research* 30: pp. 927–941.

Eymann, Angelika and Gred Ronning (1997). 'Microeconometric Models of Tourists' Destination Choice', *Regional Science and Urban Economics* 27: pp. 735–761.

Fishwick, Francis (1993). *Making Sense of Competition Policy* (London, Kogan Page).

Grant, Robert M. (1995). *Contemporary Strategy Analysis: Concepts, Techniques, Applications* (Oxford, Blackwell).

Greene, William H. (2003). *Econometric Analysis*, 5th edition (Upper Saddle River, New Jersey, Prentice Hall).

Grimm, Laurence G. (1993). *Statistical Applications for the Behavioral Sciences* (New York, John Wiley & Sons).

Hoehn, Thomas, James Langenfeld, Meloria Meschi and Leonard Waverman (1999). 'Quantitative Techniques in Competition Analysis', Research paper provided for the Office of Fair Trading by LECG Ltd.

Janić, Milan (1997). 'Liberalisation of European Aviation: Analysis and Modelling of the Airline Behaviour', *Journal of Air Transport Management* 3(4): pp. 167–180.

Lancaster, Kelvin J. (1966). 'A New Approach to Consumer Theory', *Journal of Political Economy* 74: pp. 132–157.

Lerner, Abba (1934). 'The Concept of Monopoly and the Measurement of Monopoly Power', *Review of Economic Studies* 1: pp. 157–175.

Li, Gang, Haiyan Song and Stephen F. Witt (2004). 'Modelling Tourism Demand: A Dynamic Linear AIDS Approach', *Journal of Travel Research* 43(2): pp. 141–150.

Li, Gang, Haiyan Song and Stephen F. Witt (2005). 'Recent Development in Econometric Modeling and Forecasting', *Journal of Travel Research* 44(1): pp. 82–99.

Pan, Chih-Min (2005). 'Market Structure and Profitability in the International Tourist Hotel Industry', *Tourism Management* 26(6): pp. 845–850.

Papatheodorou, Andreas (1999). 'The Demand for International Tourism in the Mediterranean Region', *Applied Economics* 31: pp. 619–630.

Papatheodorou, Andreas (2002). 'Exploring Competitiveness in Mediterranean Resorts', *Tourism Economics* 8: pp. 133–150.

Rosen, Sherwin (1974). 'Hedonic Prices and Implicit Markets: Product Differentiation in Pure Competition', *Journal of Political Economy* 82: pp. 34–55.

Song, Haiyan, Stephen F. Witt and Gang Li (2003). 'Modelling and Forecasting Demand for Thai Tourism', *Tourism Economics* 9(4): pp. 363–387.

Song, Haiyan and Stephen F. Witt (2000). *Tourism Demand Modelling and Forecasting: Modern Econometric Approaches* (Oxford, Pergamon).

4

Corporate rivalry and competition issues in the airline industry

John F. O'Connell

Competitive strategy and general trends in the airline industry

Porter (1996) defines competitive strategy as a combination of the ends (goals) for which the firm is striving and the means (policies) by which it is seeking to get there. Strategy itself is conceptualised as a firm's realised position in its competitive marketplace (Mintzberg, 1987; Porter, 1980). The competitive pressure within the airline industry to maintain and exceed the expectations of service, schedules, yields and the accompanying need of operations performance have become a global reality. Big influences in modern-day airline competition now stem from integrated cost leadership/differentiation strategy (Coulter, 2002; Hitt et al., 2003) or the best-cost provider strategy (Thompson and Strickland, 2001). In the hypercompetitive airline industry, successful companies integrate strategies based on fundamental economic advantages with complementary marketing initiatives so that they can present a consistent product to the marketplace. In many industrial sectors, competitive pressure now requires companies to compete on several dimensions simultaneously. Changes in the competitive landscape and the blurring of industry barriers are making it increasingly difficult for firms to sustain valuable market position over time. Porter's theory that rivalry among existing firms is the core force that drives industry competition certainly fits the profile of airline competition as there are multiple threats from new entrants and existing carriers that offer extended substitute products.

Competitive strategies that are available to airlines include a number of typologies such as core concentration, vertical or horizontal integration, and diversification through the impetus of differentiation. As the competitive interaction between carriers further evolves, constant competitive responses of rivals must be deciphered for sustainability since, as oligopoly and game theory suggest, a firm may use strategic deterrence and threats of retaliation to erode the market position of its rival (Tirole, 1990; Chen and Miller, 1994). The airline business experiences excessive competition, overcapacity, falling yields, high cost structures and a constantly changing strategic outlook, while governed by a regulatory platform, all of which are accountable for the industry's shortfall in profit generation. The industry has never earned a real rate of return on its investors' capital in its 60+ years of existence, and Taneja (2002) argues that airlines must stop going after profitless growth. Nonetheless, the airline industry is essential as it provides the access for tourism and the framework for business development (Papatheodorou, 2002).

IATA's traffic levels for 2004 were 6.5% above the 2001 levels, while cargo levels were 15.5% up over the same time period. According to the World Travel and Tourism Council (2004), world travel and tourism is estimated to generate $5,490 billion worth of economic activity (total demand) in 2004, growing (nominal terms) to $9,557 billion by 2014. Travel and tourism is expected to grow by 4.5% per annum in real terms between 2004 and 2014.

Figure 4.1 shows the historical growth of the global air travel market from 1970 to 2003 in terms of Revenue Passenger Kilometres (the output that the airline industry generates). It shows that there has been a compound annual growth rate of approximately 6% per annum and that traffic is resilient in that it recovers quickly, even after a major catastrophe like September 11, 2001. Consumers have continued to benefit overall from a deregulated industry, as fares have consistently decreased since the 1980s by a compounded reduction of around 2.5% per annum as shown in Figure 4.2, while the Consumer Price Index has increased by 3.5% over the same period, clearly benefiting the consumer.

The difficulty associated with the airline industry is that it is highly cyclical, as shown in Figure 4.3. In times of war, terrorism, recessions, low GDP, etc., airlines

RPKs Trillions

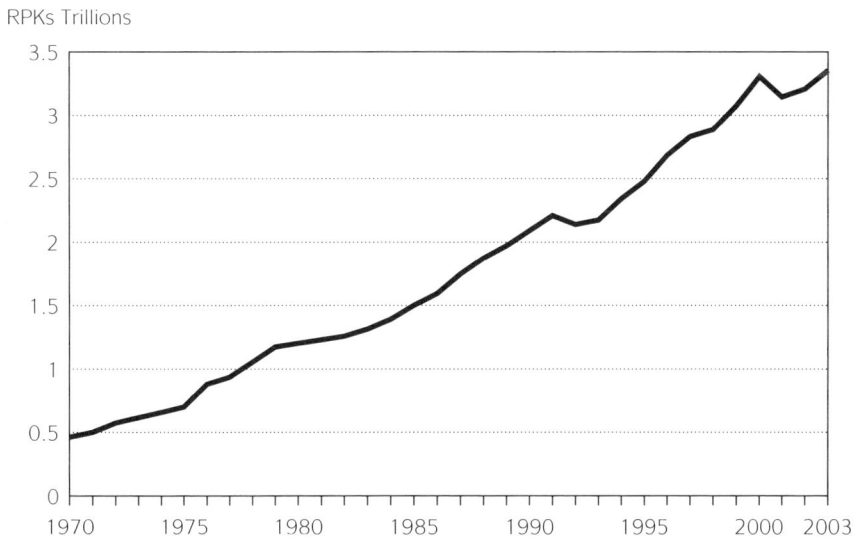

Figure 4.1 World air transport growth airlines (domestic and international)

Source: IATA, ATA.

Real
Yield*
(US Cents per RPK)

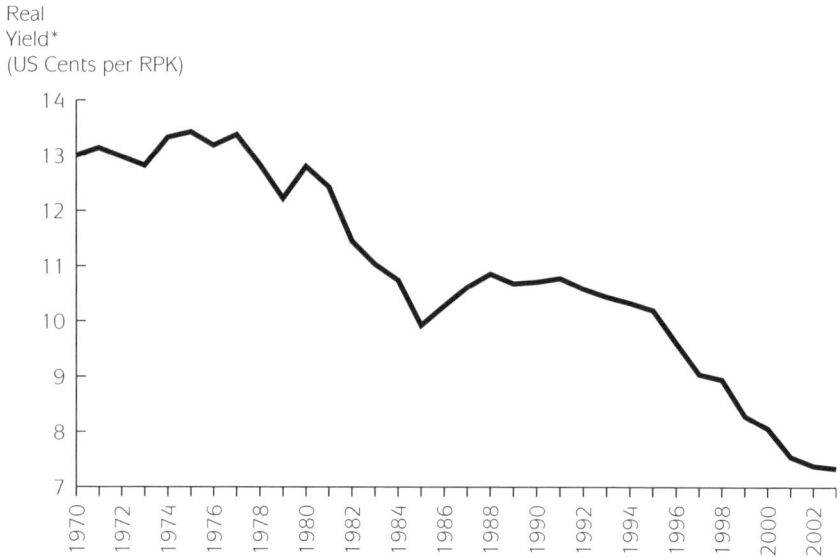

Figure 4.2 Yield decline of world airlines (scheduled)
*Including deflation by US CPI; 1990 = 100.

Source: ICAO.

are the first to experience the adverse effect and traffic levels generally fall in reciprocation. Historically, the airlines' respective governments have protected the industry; however, competitive practices under deregulation have virtually eliminated this umbrella effect. In deregulated markets, few industries can match airlines for their volatility. During economic upturns customers will be more service sensitive, and during economic downturns they will be more price sensitive. Air traffic as a product is basically a service that is offered to the customer and the industry suffers from the typical service industry's problem, namely the inability to store up the product offered to the customer. In addition the core product itself is hard to differentiate, especially for airlines that are in the same alliance. IATA surveys indicate that fare, frequent flyer programmes and schedules are the primary core drivers that influence the passenger's decision when selecting a specific airline.

However, the competitive landscape of global oscillatory cycles makes it very difficult for the airline industry to maintain linear growth. In the three years leading up to the end of 1992, the world's scheduled airlines made losses of $11.5 billion, which is greater than the accumulated net profit generated by the airline industry from its inception (Harkes, 1993). Then this was followed by a period (1995–2000) of profitability fuelled by strong economic growth, high employment, large disposable incomes, the dotcom boom and global stability through the absence of

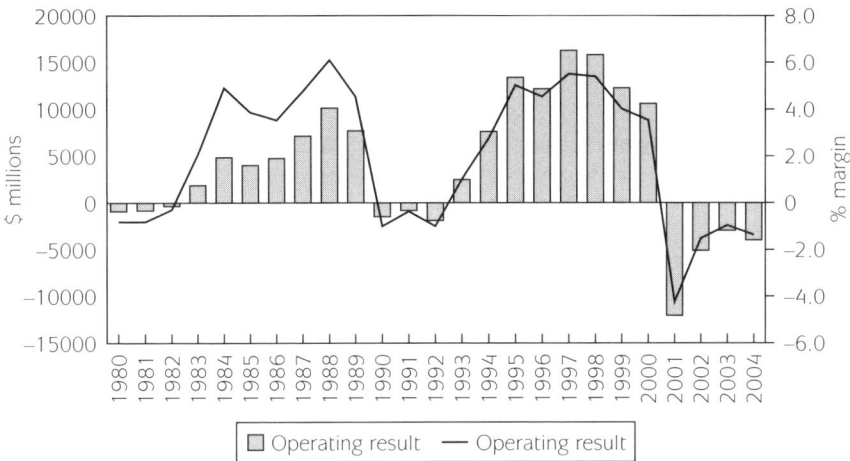

Figure 4.3 Industry operating profit and margin

Source: ICAO, IATA.

terrorism and wars. The global airline industry had a net profit in this period of $37.6 billion, however it was short lived, as 2001 was the catalyst for a severe economic downturn and a complete erosion of airline profitability. The industry had a net loss of $12.6 billion in 2001 alone, representing one-third of what the industry gained from 1995–2000. It lost another $11.5 billion and $6.5 billion for 2002 and 2003 respectively with another $5 billion loss estimated for 2004. Further exacerbating the profitability issue is the fact that the breakeven load factor for IATA international scheduled airlines has risen by 4.7% from 1998 to 2003. The revenues are primarily derived from selling the perishable aircraft seat and the belly-hold cargo capacity, of which 25% of the total aircraft capacity often goes unsold.

Competing airlines offer a range of products and services that is creating industry convergence, and thus differentiation is paramount for competitive advantage. In an attempt to differentiate itself, the airline industry has different types of models, each of which has a unique business plan and operates in different market conditions, while all are driven by the pursuit of profitability or by a good rate of return on the investment. Table 4.1 below outlines the different types of airline business models since 2002 that all compete for similar market share. It outlines the vast portfolio of options available to airline management and associated complexities of airline rivalries.

Table 4.1 Airline models formed since 2002

- Full-service airlines such as Etihad in the United Arab Emirates, established in 2003, which placed an order for 24 Airbus aircraft in July 2004 valued at $7 billion
- Low-cost carriers such as Air Asia in Malaysia and Air Arabia in Sharjah
- Traditional airlines rebranded as low-cost variants like Aer Lingus and America West
- Low-cost carriers within full-service carriers, such as Ted (UAL), Song (Delta), Atlas Blue (Royal Air Maroc), Snowflake (SAS)
- Regional airlines such as Lagun Air in Spain and Styrian Spirit in Austria
- Regional airlines which have been converted to low-cost carriers, such as Independence Air in the USA, and Norwegian Airlines
- Independent charter airlines such as Air Finland and Zoom in Canada
- Niche carriers such as Air Burbon linking Paris to the Island of Reunion

---

Evolution of competitive airline markets in pre-deregulation era

In the early days, governments finalised the approval on all aviation issues and airlines were highly constrained in what they could do. In the United States, Congress regulated the industry through the inauguration of the Civil Aeronautics Board (CAB) in 1938. It controlled the decision on important activities such as fares, route selection, capacity, flight products and mergers. CAB attempted to strengthen weaker carriers by giving them access to lucrative routes. Between 1950 and 1974 CAB received 79 airline applications but none was granted and CAB refused to award new routes to existing carriers. The board traditionally prohibited price reductions by requiring that carriers charge equal fares for equal distances. Thus it became difficult for carriers to lower fares in densely populated markets in order to stimulate demand and the board clearly failed to recognise price elasticity, leading to uncontrollable inefficiencies. In addition, airlines were not free to withdraw from certain routes regardless of the commercial implications. Meanwhile, carriers operating in the 'liberalised' states of California, Texas and Florida were offering very competitive services at fares below the prevailing rates in the rest of the United States. Carriers such as Pacific Southwest Airlines (PSA) and Southwest were more efficient and enlarged the markets they entered due to the low fares, as it attracted more passengers than the regulated high fare carriers (Oum et al., 1991). Regulators allowed airlines to purchase larger aircraft, predicting that the economies of scale resulting from the aircraft's lower seat mile cost would allow fare levels to fall in accordance. However this did not occur and load factors fell due to the increased capacity.

Economists such as Straszheim (1969) began to question the limitations of regulation and argued the benefits of freer competition in air transport. Leading reformists such as Levine (1965) and Jordan (1970) reported the efficiency achieved in the deregulated Californian market. Keeler (1972) concluded that regulation diluted any profits derived from CAB's fare system due to excess capacity, Douglas and Millar (1974) built a competition model that showed more efficiency in terms of capacity control if fares were not regulated. Devany (1975), however, reported that regulation was actually in the consumer interest as fares were set close to the output maximising level. Keeler (1978) in a later study reported that CAB's regulation was costing passengers $2.7 billion in excess charges per year. They all supported policy actions that would facilitate freer market competition by reforming outdated constraints. The early regulated government owned airlines lobbied constantly for subsidies that impeded economic development and above all, failed to boost economic growth. They were the symbol of overstaffed, inefficient, bureaucratic, high-priced monopolies that had a constant lifeline to government funding. The protectionist approach by CAB resulted in inefficient and uncompetitively run businesses.

CAB (1975) concluded that the consequences of the regulatory legislation included key anti-competitive issues such as the exclusion of new airlines from long-haul trunk markets, protection of inefficient carriers, high labour costs and little price competition. If these regulations were relaxed, a more competitive environment would emerge and provide enormous benefits to the consumer in the form of lower fares through innovative pricing and the generation of greater product differentiation between carriers. Economists such as Friedrich Hayek and Ludwig Von Mises emphasised 'laissez-faire', stating that competition can take the place of government regulation in a more efficient way. Thus, serving the consumer better in the long run by allowing firms to gain flexibility and explore ways to maximise profit, under the auspices of accepted ethics.

Deregulation would push airlines to re-examine their costs, thus forcing them to improve their efficiency, productivity and allow flexible yield management to capture segmented markets and thus overall grow market share. The US Deregulation Act was passed in 1978 and signified that market economics and subsequent competition came to the forefront of aviation policy making. It encompassed most of the requirements by allowing competitive pricing and eliminated restrictions on capacity and frequency, allowing airlines the freedom to operate on any route. In addition, it allowed multiple designation of carriers, liberalised the chartered airlines and made cargo more competitive. Meanwhile, the European scheduled carriers complained of the inroads which cheap and unregulated charter services were making into their potential traffic and profits. They campaigned for stricter controls. But the public and the tourist industry were pressing for deregulation as the charters offered lower fares. Three deregulation packages, agreed by the European Council of Ministers in 1987, 1990 and 1992, fully deregulated European air transport. It was the 'Third Package' under the constitution of the Council Regulation 2409/92 that effectively removed all remaining government-imposed restrictions regarding designation, market access and capacity. In effect it liberalised the licensing of carriers, the routes they fly and the prices they can impose. It also opened up cross-border and domestic markets (including cabotage) and removed national ownership restrictions. The European

Commission has also taken measures to ensure that the 'competition rules' that apply to other industries also applies to airlines. Restrictions were rigidly introduced, eliminating state aid.

The following events or waves represent the different strategies that emerged from deregulation and the competitive implications that resulted.

Deregulation's initial waves: hub-and-spoke operations

Viscusi et al. (1998) argue that one of the unanticipated developments after deregulation has been the widespread adoption of the hub-and-spoke system, which has drastically changed route structures. During the first ten years of deregulation, the major airlines shifted dramatically from point-to-point linear route systems to hub-and-spoke alternatives, which provided superior network connectivity, and so wider market coverage.

Many network carriers have tried to maximise the number of possible connections available in a reasonable period of time as effective alliance implementation demands a good linkage between partners' networks. The strategic advantage is that any given number of points can be linked over a hub with fewer departures than non-stop or direct services would require. Furthermore, once a hub has been established each additional spoke magnifies the linkage benefits and through services. Consequently, consumers clearly benefit from hub-and-spoke systems in that they can fly to many more points with higher frequencies and shorter connecting times. By combining point-to-point traffic with transfer traffic at a central hub, airlines are able to offer a wider variety of destinations to consumers with high daily frequencies at these airports. Concentration of traffic at the hub may lead to cost savings for airlines, especially for those airlines with high marginal costs per passenger (Brueckner and Spiller, 1994; Pels, 2000). Baltagi et al. (1995), for example, researched the domestic operations of 24 trunk and local US airlines from 1971 to 1986 and calculated that the associated airlines experienced 9.7% lower costs primarily saved by operating from a hub. To further support the advantages of hubs, Williams (1993) concluded that aircraft load factors increased by 5–10% because of centralising passengers at a hub. Load factors in commercial aviation are now approaching 70% up from a level in the low to mid-1950s before deregulation. Transferring passengers from small communities into the hub of the major carrier associates sparked the growth in recent times of regional affiliate airlines. These small communities were then served with frequent high-quality air links to major cities, growing rural economies.

Hubs can effectively limit competition

The increase in competition within airline markets does not mean that deregulated markets constitute a level playing field for everyone. In fact several barriers have reinforced the position of the incumbent airlines. Among the most relevant are infrastructural, network-related and marketing barriers such as lack of slots in the profitable trunk routes or scope of the network. Incumbent flag carriers enjoy a significant advantage as they control the large majority of the slots due to their dominant hub position. 'Grandfather rights' have effectively made these airports fortresses for the incumbents, limiting competition. Slots have become a highly competitive defence mechanism as British Airways, for example, paid United Airlines $20 million in 2003 for two favourable slot pairs in exchange for two unfavourable ones, boosting the home carrier's slot ownership to 41% at Heathrow (Pilling, 2003). This indicates the immeasurable commitment to hub development and domination by today's airline management.

European carriers operating hub-and-spoke systems have developed an extensive network of short-haul and long-haul routes that converge at the hub. Network carriers can cross-subsidise those less profitable routes with the traffic from other routes, which is a strategy that has been repeatedly used to push other competitors out of the market. Small airlines with limited networks and small hubs are disadvantaged when they operate independently of larger airlines. When there is concentration at the hub airport, one carrier tends to dominate operations by controlling the majority of the flights. The dominant carriers at hubs can boost frequencies on the connecting routes in order to offer more departures from the origin to destination than the competitor is able to mount. This often deters the level of competition at the fortress hub. Table 4.2 shows the impact of hubs and alliance partnerships. American Airlines had 100% of the market in 1994 but the competitive strength of the code-sharing partnership of United and Lufthansa, operating from their respective hubs, has forced American Airlines off the route, thus reducing the competition.

Another example of hub anti-competitiveness cites United Airlines in 2001 controlling 74% of the traffic at Denver Airport and 44 of its 91 gates. Regional airline Frontier, with just four gates, was the second largest airline at Denver. In 1999 American Airlines increased capacity and simultaneously cut fares by 30% below the flights variable cost in order to drive out smaller competitors and retain their 67% control of the Dallas Fort Worth hub.

Other carriers have abandoned the risk of positioning large numbers of aircraft at hub airports as the incumbent's territorial strength deters competitors. When

Table 4.2 Changes in hub-and-spoke market shares

Market	1994 (%)	1995 (%)	1996 (%)	1997 (%)	1998 (%)
Chicago–Dusseldorf					
American Airlines	100	100	0	0	0
United/Lufthansa	0	0	100	100	100

Source: Merrill Lynch, 1999.

a carrier has a strong presence at a hub its local distribution channels can also be dominated, as the domiciled carrier can influence local travel agents and corporations. The community is also very much aware of the airline brand that serves its local airport and passengers may book without further investigating alternative airlines. Challengers have to spend heavily to overcome this marketing disadvantage, particularly when it is reinforced by frequent flyer membership and corporate deals. Hub-and-spoke operations also deprive passengers of direct services, their journey times become longer and the fares may be higher if there is no alternative routing. Further evidence by Winston (1992) estimated that the time lost by passengers travelling through hubs accumulated in financial terms to over $1 billion. Studies by Borenstein (1989), Levine (1987) and Morison and Winston (1995) have found that fares on routes to and from hub cities have indeed risen above the industry average. In 1990, the US General Accounting Office examined trends and services at 15 concentrated airports and compared them with trends at 38 less concentrated airfields and concluded that the yields (average fare per mile) increased more at the concentrated airports and that fares charged by the dominant carriers tended to rise as their aggregate airport enplanement share increased (Belobaba and Van Acker, 1994). However studies on the whole industry have demonstrated that fares actually decreased overall as Winston (1992) calculated that consumers in the USA have saved in the region of $6.5 billion from lower fares (1990 dollar terms). Button and Taylor (2000) researched the impact of lower fares due to deregulation and concluded that US traffic grew from 93.4 million passengers in 1993 to 126.1 passengers in 1998 as a result of the continued degradation of air fares. This contrast of fare levels indicates that hubs are used as mediums for fare discrimination and uncompetitive practices.

One of the most competitive aspects arising from effective hub-and-spoke operations is the extent to which individual airline networks can become self-sufficient in meeting demand, enabling operators to keep passengers on their own rather than lose them to interline connections. Dennis (2001, cited in Doganis, 2002) illustrated that at London Heathrow Airport 27% of transfer passengers were British Airways to British Airways in 1984. By 1991 this had grown to 43%, and by 2000 it was approaching 60%.

Deregulation's second wave: alliances

In recent years, limited liberalisation in international civil aviation has allowed airlines to be more innovative and to develop new initiatives for serving new markets. Increasingly, these initiatives involve business arrangements that permit airlines from different countries to serve the global market together. Alliances have become the primary means for expanding and strengthening airline global service networks. Alliances have provided a way for carriers to mitigate the limitations of bilateral agreements, ownership restrictions, and licensing and control regulations. To accomplish this, they need to have foreign partners. Taneja (2004: 38) explains that alliances and code-sharing can overcome constraints due to regulatory barriers and thus expand operations more globally and develop a seamless product.

A vast amount of literature exists on airline alliances, covering areas such as the causes and effects of equity alliances (Youssef, 1992), selection criteria for alliance partners (Harvey and Lusch, 1995), motivations to enter alliance arrangements (Glaister and Buckley, 1996), the effect of code-sharing on international fare levels (Oum et al., 1998), the factors affecting the operational success of alliances (Bissessur, 1996; Bissessur and Alamdari, 1998), performance issues between alliances (Park and Cho, 1997), the price effects of international alliances (Brueckner and Whalen, 1998), key factors for alliance success and demise (Li, 2000), the regulatory issues concerning global alliances (Oum et al., 2001) and the impact of alliance airlines on partners' traffic (Iatrou, 2004).

By late 2004 there were three global alliance partnerships, namely Star, Oneworld and SkyTeam, and there has been greater ontogenesis between carriers. The Star Alliance (17 members, led by Lufthansa and United Airlines) serves 798 destinations in 140 countries, while Oneworld (8 members, led by British Airways and American Airlines) serves 591 destinations in 136 countries; SkyTeam (10 members, led by Air France and Delta Airlines) serves 512 destinations in 125 countries. Consequently the alliance groupings have a significant impact on the geographical passenger market share. The three alliances constitute a significant proportion of the world's passenger market share as the Star partnership accounted for 19.5%, while SkyTeam and Oneworld respectively constituted 18% and 11.9% in 2004. The remaining 49.4% of the world's passenger market belongs to all those carriers that are outside these three core alliances and include large carriers such as Japan Airlines, Emirates and Virgin Atlantic. In the same year, the three alliance partnerships had 72.5% of the European–American capacity, 60% of the European–Asia Pacific capacity and 45.2% of the American–Asia Pacific capacity (Field and Pilling, 2004). Airline alliances provide around 56% of the IATA freight volume. Global travel requirements today favour 'seamless' journeying via a number of points across the globe and alliances accommodate this facility, going beyond what a single airline could provide.

Initially, the alliances encompass easy-to-implement marketing agreements that help build a sound foundation for a more ambitious strategic integration. Partnerships can take many forms and range from minor tactical commercial agreements such as interlining, through-ticketing and ground handling contracts, to more strategic commitments such as code-sharing and antitrust immunity for joint fare-setting. The commercial alliance does not cement the relationship and allows a carrier to exit, though it does become increasingly difficult, the longer the alliance has been in existence, especially if cooperation in most of the cost-cutting areas has been implemented. The strategic alliance further integrates the relationship and it represents the interconnectedness or tightness of the coupling between partners. Doganis (2001: 65) elaborates that a strategic alliance is where the partners co-mingle their assets in order to pursue a single or joint set of business objectives. These alliances are a less than perfect substitute for mergers, which are prohibited by foreign ownership laws. The Chicago Convention makes international alliances with antitrust immunity a second-best solution to the challenge of global integration. Nevertheless, these cross-border arrangements are having a substantial impact on the structure of the airline industry.

The competitive behaviour of airline alliances

The majority of global airlines (with the exception of most low-cost carriers) participate in code-sharing. Code-sharing is by far the most widespread feature of airline alliances. It is a cheap marketing tool that helps airlines achieve a presence on routes that they do not serve or access to restricted markets and it can positively influence the traffic flow overall. Brueckner (2003) states that code-sharing among Star Alliance partners alone yielded annual incremental revenues of around $20 million. Code-share trips are usually priced with greater flexibility than under traditional arrangements. However, outright collaboration in pricing is not allowed in the absence of antitrust immunity.

The three global airline alliances today account for about half of the total world's Revenue Passenger Kilometres (RPKs) (Morley, 2003; Baker and Field, 2003). These global airline alliance consortia enjoy unmatched sustainable competitive advantage through their integrated synergies and it becomes anti-competitive for new carriers and for those not affiliated to an alliance. These synergies include enhanced resource utilisation, combined purchasing power, shared facilities, joint services, benefits and loyalty programmes that are all long-term sustainable competitive cost advantages. In more recent times the airlines are beginning to standardise the service across the alliance, thus making the service increasingly seamless for the customer. Some of the newer and more revolutionary synergies that have resulted from alliances include joint purchasing of fuel by Star partners. Star announced in late 2003 that it planned to form a joint company called Star Alliance FuelCo to manage the procurement of jet fuel at selected airports around the world (ATI, 2004). Smaller airlines within the alliance can benefit from the higher credit-rating quality of the group in obtaining fuel discounts. Those airlines not associated with the alliance will have to compete out of the same market with higher fuel costs.

Anti-competitive effects from airline alliances

Governments are increasingly becoming concerned about the potential anti-competitive aspects of alliances, which can result in less traffic for smaller, independent airlines, especially those operating in domestic or deregulated regions. Major carriers can advance their goals of predatory behaviour and eliminate small start-up airlines by excluding those new entrants from joint-fare or code-sharing practices. If effective, such exclusion could have a major impact on non-aligned competitors. An alliance creates the potential to capture market share, to fix prices with competitors in dominant markets, and to reduce competitive capacity in certain key markets. Anti-competitive effects are of greatest concern when the allied airlines' networks overlap but departure times are sequenced so as not to cause conflict. If only a handful of airlines serve a particular market, the coordination of two of those airlines could lead to a significant reduction in competition on overlapped routes. Alliances can also lead to higher prices in certain markets. These negative consumer effects would be felt most strongly in gateway cities, as shown in Table 4.2, as these two carriers basically operate as a single airline that dominates the route. Their alliance would eliminate some competition on this route and push prices upward, particularly for time-sensitive travellers. This effect has stymied attempts by American Airlines and British Airways to gain antitrust immunity. Brueckner and Whalen (1998) conducted a study of the impact of airline alliances on fares and concluded that an alliance between two competitive carriers would raise fares by about 5% in gateway-to-gateway markets.

Consumer protectionist groups insist that travellers are being directed towards a particular group of airlines and are often misled into thinking that the service is being provided with only one carrier. By advertising multiple designators for a single service, airlines can achieve significant marketing benefits as carriers can gain more favourable Computer Reservations Systems (CRSs) positioning. The anti-competitiveness of screen-padding within parallel code shared non-stop flights is very effective as the flight is listed twice on the CRS screens because both partners list the same flight as if it were their own flight. Code-shared connecting flights get listed ahead of interline flights on the CRS. Strongly branded airlines such as British Airways can position weaker brands such as Aer Lingus higher up the travel agent screen due to the code-share link, giving the Irish carrier a competitively better positioned flight from its linkup with BA.

Deregulation's third wave: frequent flyer programmes

Frequent flyer programmes (FFPs) are designed to be a competitive strategy to build customer loyalty and encourage repeat patronage from passengers. The need to attract, leverage and retain customers is still of primary concern to most businesses. Several studies have indicated that the average company loses around half its customers every five years and that it costs five to ten times more to gain a new customer than to keep an existing one (Kalakota and Robinson, 2001). A method cleverly adopted by airlines to attract customers is to incentify the travel agent by offering generous override commissions in exchange for steering passengers towards their carrier. The number of participants in a loyalty programme best represents its strength and by 2003 there were approximately

120 million frequent flyer members globally. The United States accounted for about 74 million, with Europe and Asia accounting for around 24 and 21 million respectively (Ferguson, 2003).

Airlines look for ways to increase the range of their product differentiation and obtain market advantage, and one strategy is to offer generous mileage points in exchange for continued passenger loyalty. The frequent flyer programmes separate passengers into different tiers, and customers with elite status get extra privileges such as upgrades, extra baggage allowances, etc., providing an increased incentive for regular travellers to achieve such a status. Palmer et al. (2000) state that two-thirds of airlines that have loyalty programmes have declared the scheme to be particularly effective in targeting high-value, frequent customers. Airlines are also increasingly using customer relationship management (CRM) as a cost-cutting tool to track their high-value passengers.

Empirical evidence demonstrates that frequent flyer programmes are a competitive weapon, as Reichheld and Teal (1996) emphasised that customer loyalty is a key determinant in predicting market share. Reinartz and Kumar (2000) and Yi and Jeon (2003) argue strongly that customer loyalty cannot be over-emphasised in the severely competitive business world of today. There are numerous examples that highlight the strength of the frequent flyer programme, such as authors like Nako (1992), who found that frequent flyer programmes significantly influenced business travellers' decisions regarding airline choice. Similarly, a survey conducted by the Official Airline Guide, cited in Hanlon (1999: 53) found that 90% of the world's business travellers participated in a FFP, and for those passengers making more than 20 trips per year, the figure is as high as 97%. The 2004 IATA survey also indicates that corporate passengers now rank it the second most important factor affecting airline selection for both the short-haul and long-haul markets.

Anti-competitive effects of frequent flyer programmes

In a study undertaken for the European Commission in June 1992 concerning new entrants in air transport, it was confirmed that FFPs can be an anti-competitive method employed by larger carriers which cannot be matched by smaller carriers, and can prevent them from competing profitably (Drabbe, 1996). The report also claimed that the pooling of FFPs by airlines within the same alliance constitutes a considerable entry barrier. Passengers travelling on airlines from the same alliance can amalgamate and redeem points on any of their partner carriers, who are thus effectively offering a joint programme. This endows these airlines with a superior competitive advantage as passengers become loyalty members to a group of specific carriers that reside within the alliance. Jurgen Weber, President of Lufthansa Airlines, explains that: 'frequent flyer programmes are the glue that holds an alliance together' (Gallacher, 1997). Further concerns of anti-competitive behaviour arose from studies conducted by Proussaloglou and Koppelman (1999), where research indicated that frequent business and leisure travellers were willing to pay a premium of $72 and $26 respectively to travel on a carrier that had a frequent flyer programme, further indicating that loyalty programmes are a powerful marketing weapon. In 2003 Sweden's competition authority requested the European Commission to undertake a study of the anti-competitive effects of frequent flyer programmes by SAS which commanded the dominant market position in Scandinavia. It stated that SAS' programme had, over the past ten years, led to the airline's business fares rising in comparison with those of other airlines. The increase amounted to 12% of the average ticket price. The study also found that the SAS programme affected the competition as it pushed up the cost of customers switching carriers (ATI, 2003).

Deregulation's fourth wave: low-cost airlines

Between 80 and 85% of new carriers launched in the USA after deregulation went bankrupt soon after while from 1993 to 1996, 60 out of 80 new European airlines failed. Developing robust new strategies or reinventing a new business model has become essential in order to compete against the branding and service of the conventional airline. One such alternative was a low-fare, point-to-point carrier called Southwest Airlines. Its origins predate deregulation, but deregulation enabled it to expand its unique short-haul, no-frills and low-priced service into the new liberated states. In Europe the low-cost carriers took on an exponential impetus as Europe's 'Third Package' of deregulation effectively removed all remaining government-imposed restrictions regarding designation, market access and capacity. It aimed to liberalise air travel within the European Union and challenge the dominance of flag carriers such as British Airways, Air France and Lufthansa. These three major airlines controlled 40% of the available passenger-kilometres on scheduled intra-European flights through bilateral agreements, regulated by the International Air Transport Association (IATA). Liberalisation slowly changed as new operators entered unrestricted markets and began to challenge the flag carriers, which had high cost bases and inefficient operating practices.

Deregulation has paved the way for low-cost carriers to enter markets where high fares had previously prevailed. Low-cost carriers have reshaped the competitive environment within liberalised markets. As was the case in the USA, no-frills carriers in Europe have used the freedoms of the deregulated market to capture market share, which had previously been controlled by the full-service network carriers. These new entrant airlines have pursued simplicity, efficiency, productivity and high utilisation of assets to offer low fares. The established low-cost carriers are profitable even in cyclical downturns, with for example, Southwest and Ryanair returning high annual operating margins and large annual increases in the numbers of passengers carried.

In the USA, low-cost carriers account for 25% of domestic traffic, and this is expected to grow to 40% or more by 2009. These new business models have quickly spread throughout the world. Low-cost carriers provided 14% of Europe's airline capacity in 2003 with Ryanair and easyJet accounting for 9% of the market. In the domestic markets of Canada and Australia, Westjet has almost a 20% share and Virgin Blue over 30%. Air Asia currently has a 30% share of the domestic Malaysian market. GOL, launched in 2001, has since become Brazil's third largest carrier, with 22% of the market. Consumers are the primary recipients reaping the benefits from the low-fare carriers. According to Tarry (2003), economy fares on routes between the UK and Western Europe fell by 30% during 2002. A study by the European Low Fares Airline Association (ELFAA) claims that low-cost carriers are saving passengers approximately €12 billion a year on intra-European travel. This enormous saving also comes from legacy carriers responding to the low-cost sector by reducing their respective fares in order to compete. The lobby group has also stated that its members have benefited Europe's regions with revenues of up to €3–4 billion through inbound tourism.

Competitive reaction by incumbents to the low-cost threat

The competition between the network airline and low-cost carrier is intense as the incumbent is quickly losing market share and the domestic yield has fallen dramatically. The incumbents have lower productivity coupled with higher operating costs. The unit cost gap between the low-cost carrier and the network carrier is typically between 1.5 and 3 eurocents per Available Seat Kilometre (Nuutinen, 2004). British Airways has had substantial losses on its European network, which are critical feeder routes to its long-haul network at Heathrow. However, it has reduced its losses from over £300 million ($560 million) to £60 million in four years. It has restructured its business model by lowering fares, de-hubbing Gatwick airport, basing fewer aircraft away from Heathrow and outsourcing activities extensively. It lowered its labour costs by £460 million, procurement expenses by £123 million and distribution costs by £212 million (Aviation Strategy, 2003).

Aer Lingus is another example of an airline that has extensively restructured itself in order to compete against Ryanair and won itself the 2004 Air Transport World Phoenix award for achievement. It coupled a 30% cost reduction with a 6.2% increase in passenger numbers fuelled by an aggressive average European fare of €85 that has helped to push its average load factor to 81%. It discontinued business class on short-haul flights and reconfigured the aircraft to have a higher seating density. It removed all ticket restrictions on all routes and on all fares. It launched 30 more routes between 2001 and 2004, with more emphasis on leisure travellers. More drastic measures included cutting one-third of the work force, including a 60% reduction in the management group, and introducing a pay freeze. Subsequently it ended 2003 with 9.7% operating margin and a profit of €83 million, causing Ryanair's profits on the Dublin–London routes to fall by 20% in 2003. Other airlines have set up low-cost airlines within the parent group as a separate brand. Some examples include Value Air (Singapore Airlines) and Jetstar (Qantas), which were set up as a counteractive measure to impede the growth of established low-cost carriers and deter others from entering the market. The infrastructure of today's aviation industry is also responding to low-cost carriers as Changi Airport in Singapore is setting up a dedicated low-cost terminal.

Deregulation's fifth wave: equity partnerships

Foreign ownership laws relaxed after deregulation. Equity partnerships represent cross-border acquisitions of other airlines; however, the ability to buy into foreign companies is still heavily constrained by governments. Equity stakes are sometimes a way to pre-empt competitors from teaming up with another airline. Most of the investments are motivated by an airline's interests in creating and operating strategic alliances. These airlines accept suboptimal returns on investment because they anticipate synergistic revenue from the passenger feed, and thus reconfigure competition into gain. In 1996 SAS had 18.4% equity in Continental, KLM had 25% in Northwest and British Airways had 24.6% in USAir. These European airlines were investing in the American-based carriers because of their strong US domestic network that moved passengers into the international gateways. Lufthansa's and SAS' interest in British Midland International primarily focused in the carriers' ownership of 14% of the slots at Heathrow.

This buy-in of equity represents a long-term interest in the new company, and thus fosters a genuine interest in developing the weaker carrier. However, equity investment also allows some control over its partner. Ownership laws and nationality clauses in bilateral air service agreements limit cross-border mergers and acquisitions. Airlines cannot assume full control of foreign carriers in the way that firms in the manufacturing or services sectors can acquire companies in other countries. Morrell and Gibson (2004) found that among the world's alliance members, the government is still the largest shareholder in 45% of the alliance members, which is limiting and has a damaging effect in the direction of the company. However, more airlines are now being privatised and substantial equity is being purchased by foreign carriers. At the end of 2001, over 60 airlines had shareholdings in foreign airlines while about 200 had equity owned by foreign investors (ICAO, 2000). In late October 2004, Icelandair purchased a 10.1% stake in easyJet.

The Oneworld Alliance members British Airways and American Airlines have some cross-equity participation in Iberia, which is the dominant carrier between Europe and South America. This carrier has carved itself a niche in the market and the other carriers also gain, due to their investment, as they are virtually absent from this market. Weaker airlines that lack the investment capital are competitively disadvantaged, as airlines that have equity partnerships have a foothold in foreign markets. Douma (2000) points out that less than 5% of all alliances ultimately lead to mergers. One recent merger was the amalgamation between Air France and KLM in mid-2004. The combination also brings together two of the top four airports in Europe, notably Schipol and Charles de Gaulle. According to Buyck (2004), the KLM Group controls around 70% of the flights at Schipol, while Air France controls 45% of the traffic at de Gaulle. The merger would have a combined optimised network of 226 destinations and the amalgamation will coordinate sales, revenue management, IT, fleet, cargo and maintenance. It will have combined aggregate revenue of $19.2 billion, making it the largest global airline revenue earner and any start-up carrier operating from the region will face insurmountable pressure from the reinforced incumbent.

The final waves of deregulation: Open Skies

The USA has been at the forefront in its drive to liberalise the air transport industry, after being the first country to deregulate its domestic market in 1978. The regulation of inter-country air transportation was governed by a maze of bilateral and multilateral agreements between governments and air carriers. Fares were controlled by the International Air Transport Association (IATA) system and it also regulated the inter-airline pooling agreements. By the late 1970s, the Netherlands wanted to push for a liberal agreement by allowing unlimited authority from any point in the USA. The latter wanted to eliminate the restrictions on capacity, frequency and route-operating rights and to create new and greater opportunities for innovative and competitive pricing, and the added flexibility to include multiple designators. On 31 March 1992, the US Open Skies agreement was initiated with the Netherlands. The final order defining Open Skies (DOT Order 92–8–13) consisted of eleven points outlined in Table 4.3 below. Although public comments solicited during the drafting period suggested that cabotage and ownership/control terms could be added to these eleven points, the Department of Transport (DOT) rejected both these terms.

The US Government also granted antitrust immunity (joint pricing and full collaboration on scheduling and marketing decisions) and access to additional US gateways to alliance partners in exchange for agreements to a more liberal ingress of international markets, frequencies and pricing freedoms. However, some differences have emerged between the EU and the USA on multinational air transport agreements, now referred to as the Open Aviation Area (OAA). This would essentially create a free trade area for air transport between the EU and the USA, and would give EU and US airlines complete freedom to serve any pair of airports in the EU and USA. Thus only the strongest carriers will survive, and there may be a further wave of airline consolidations into the future.

Table 4.3 Eleven major characteristics of Open Skies

- Open entry on all routes
- Unrestricted capacity and frequency on all routes
- Unrestricted routes and fifth-freedom traffic
- Double-disapproval pricing required in third- and fourth-freedom markets
- Liberal charter arrangements
- Liberal cargo regimes
- Conversion and remittance arrangements
- Open code-sharing opportunities
- Self-handling provisions
- Pro-competitive provisions on commercial opportunities, user charges, fair competition and intermodal rights
- Explicit commitment for non-discriminatory operation of, and access for, computer reservation systems

Some competitive issues associated with Open Skies

With Open Skies, airlines will be more flexible in developing new demand-oriented services, setting new fares and adjusting frequencies. It creates enormous opportunities for the consumer as the choice and quality of the operating airlines increases. However, it also puts pressure on those countries that have not signed up. Button and Taylor (2000) found that Open Skies between the USA and Canada increased transborder traffic to 14.3 million passengers in 1995 (up by 10% over the previous year). Consumers benefited from 102 new transborder routes that offered many cities their first non-stop service. Dresner and Tretheway (1992) conclude that Open Skies has had a serious impact on international fares as $325 million were saved in 1992 alone on the North Atlantic destinations.

However, Open Skies would seem to be the ideal free open aviation market where all competitive barriers are removed. This was witnessed in Europe as the 'Third Package' of liberalisation granted unlimited traffic rights including 'Seventh Freedom' rights (allowing an airline to carry revenue traffic between points in two countries on services lying entirely outside its own home country) and domestic cabotage (traffic rights on linking two points in a third country). At the same time ownership and nationality constraints on airlines registered in any member state were also removed, provided that the airline was European. However, there remain protectionist and anti-competitive effects that misdirect the openness of the emancipation act. In Chapter 5, Anne Graham examines such issues in terms of airport state subsidies and slot allocation. Oum (1998) argues that Open Skies is inherently flawed because increased competition usually means some players win while others lose.

If we consider the disparity of strength between airlines of different countries, there are indeed some inequalities that impede open internationalisation and competition. Examination of the United States Open Skies bilateral agreements reveals that they are protective of US carriers in several respects. For example, when the USA signs an Open Skies agreement with both Singapore and another ASEAN economy, US carriers would have unrestricted access to routes between Singapore and its ASEAN partner; however, airlines between the two ASEAN economies only have free access on their direct routes to the United States, but not necessary between themselves. Open Skies also prevents domestic operations by foreign carriers (cabotage) that operate to the United States, thus US carriers have the advantage of being able to draw on their extensive domestic networks to which foreign carriers do not have direct access. Also, because of US law, American citizens must own 75% of the voting stock of any US airline and the United States Government continues to insist that any international travel by its employees must be completed on US airlines. These restrictive issues will form the basis for the further evolution of international deregulation, by which all the remaining barriers will be removed and true Open Skies will completely liberate markets and remove barriers.

In conclusion, the airline industry is characterised by strong corporate rivalry. This has evolved over different institutional regimes and has become multidimensional as shown by the various competitive waves in the deregulation era. Restrictive practices and potential abuse of market power are apparent though. These may be the result of market liberalisation; alternatively, their cause may lie in the remnants of the old regulatory framework and the unresolved issues in the international marketplace. In any case, the airline industry is currently in a state of flux, which makes it a very interesting sector to study from an industrial organisation perspective.

References

Air Transport Intelligence (2003). Swedish competition body calls for European FFP analysis, Air Transport Intelligence news, 31st March.

Air Transport Intelligence (2004). Star sees benefits from joint fuel purchasing, Air Transport Intelligence news, 4th June.

Aviation Strategy (2003). British Airways: the devilish detail of FS&S, April 3–6.

Baker, C. and Field, D. (2003). Where are they now? Airline Business, July, 43.

Baltagi, B. H., Griffin, J. M., Rich, D. P. (1995). 'Airline Deregulation': The cost pieces of the puzzle, International Economic Review, 36(1), 245–260.

Belobaba, P. P. and Van Acker, J. V. (1994). Airline market concentration, Journal of Air Transport Management, 1(1), 5–14.

Bissessur, A. (1996). The identification and analysis of the critical success factors of strategic alliances. Unpublished PhD thesis, Air Transport Group, College of Aeronautics, Cranfield University, Bedford.

Bissessur, A. and Alamdari, F. (1998). Factors affecting the operational success of strategic airline alliances, Transportation Journal, 25, 331–355.

Borenstein, S. (1989). Hubs and high fares: dominance and market power in the US airline industry, Rand Journal of Economics 20, 344–368.

Brueckner, J. K. (2003). The benefits of codesharing and antitrust immunity for international passengers, with an application to the Star alliance, Journal of Air Transport Management, (9), 83–89.

Brueckner, J. K. and Spiller, P. T. (1994). Economies of traffic density in the deregulated airline industry, Journal of Law and Economics 37, 379–415.

Brueckner, J. K. and Whalen, W. T. (1998). The price effects of international airline alliances, unpublished paper, University of Illinois at Urbana-Champaign, November.

Button, K. and Taylor, S. (2000). International air transportation and economic development, Journal of Air Transport Management, 6, 209–222.

Buyck, C. (2004). Air Transport World, Marriage de Raison, January, 24–26.

Civil Aeronautics Board (1975). Report of the CAB special staff on regulatory reform, Washington, DC.

Chen, M. J. and Miller, D. (1994). Competitive attack, retaliation and performance: an expectancy-valence framework, Strategic Management Journal, 15(2), 85–102.

Coulter, M. K. (2002). Strategic Management in Action, 2nd edition, Prentice Hall, Upper Saddle River, NJ.

Dennis, N. (2001). The impact of airline industry changes on airports, Airport Economics and Finance Symposium, College of Aeronautics, Cranfield University, March.

Devany, A. S. (1975). The effect of price and entry regulation on airline output, capacity and efficiency, Bell Journal of Economics, 6, 327–345.

Doganis, R. (2001). The Airline Business in the 21st Century, Routledge, London.

Doganis, R. (2002). Flying off Course: The Economics of International Airlines, 3rd edition, HarperCollins, London.

Douglas, G. W. and Millar, J. C. (1974). Economic Regulation of Domestic Air Transport, Theory and Policy, Brookings Institution.

Douma, M. U. (2000). Strategic alliances: managing the dynamics of fit, Long Range Planning, 33, 579–598.

Drabbe, H. (1996). Frequent flyer programmes competition aspects, European Air Law Association Conference Paper, Copenhagen, 8th November, 1–8.

Dresner, M. and Tretheway, M. W. (1992). Modeling and testing the effect of market structure on price: the case of international air transport, Journal of Transport Economics and Policy 25, 171–183.

Ferguson, R. (2003). Nothin' but blue skies, Colloquy 11(2), 4–6 and 12–13.

Field, D. and Pilling, M. (2004). Team spirit, Airline Business, September, 46–48.

Gallacher, J. (1997). Power to the plans, Airline Business, 13(8), 34–47.

Glaister, K. W. and Buckley, P. J. (1996). Strategic motives for international alliance formation, Journal of Management Studies 33, 301–332.

Grant, T. D. (1994). Foreign takeovers of United States airlines: free trade process, problems and progress, Harvard Journal on Legislation, 31, Winter, 63–151.

Hanlon, P. (1999). Global Airlines: Competition in a Transnational Industry, 2nd edition, Butterworth-Heinemann, Oxford.

Harkes, J. (1993) Shooting for the moon, The Economist, 30 October.

Harvey, M. G. and Lusch, R. F. (1995). A systematic assessment of potential international strategic alliance partners, International Business Review 4 (2), 195–212.

Hitt, M. A., Ireland, R. D. and Hoskisson, R. E. (2003). Strategic Management, Competitiveness and Globalization, 5th edition, South-Western, Mason, OH.

Iatrou, K. (2004). Unpublished PhD thesis Cranfield University, Cranfield, UK.

International Civil Aviation Organisation (2000). Traffic by flight stage, digest of statistics, No. 495. International Civil Aviation Organization, Montreal.

Jordan W. A. (1970). Airline Regulation in America, Effects and Imperfections, Johns Hopkins University Press, Baltimore, MD.

Kalakota, R., Robinson, M. (2001). e-Business 2.0 Roadmap for Success, Addison-Wesley, Boston, MA.

Keeler, T. E. (1978). Domestic trunk airline regulation, an economic evaluation, studies on federal regulations, US Senate Committee on Government Affairs, Washington, DC.

Keeler, T. E. (1972). Airline regulation and market performance, Bell Journal of Economics, 3, 399–424.

Levine, M. (1987). Airline competition in deregulated markets: theory, firm strategy, and public policy, Yale Journal on Regulation, 4, 393–494.

Levine, M. (1965). Is regulation necessary? California Air Transportation and National Regulatory Policy, The Yale Law Journal, 74, 1416–1447.

Li, M. Z. F. (2000). Distinct features of lasting and non-lasting airline alliances, Journal of Air Transport Management, 6, 65–73.

Merril Lynch (1999). Global Airline Alliances Conference, New York, June.

Mintzberg, H. (1987). The Strategy Concept I, 5 Ps for strategy, California Management Review, 30(1), 11–24.

Morison, S. C. and Winston, C. (1995). The Evolution of the Airline Industry, The Brookings Institution, Washington, DC.

Morley, CL. (2003). Impacts of international airline alliances on tourism, Tourism Economics 9(1): 31–51.

Morrell, P. and Gibson, W. (2004). Theory and practice in aircraft financial evaluation, Journal of Air Transport Management, 10, 427–433.

Nako, S. (1992). Frequent flyer programs and business travellers: an empirical investigation, Logistics and Transportation Review, 28 (4), December, 295–414.

Nuutinen, H. (2004). US LCCs: reaching critical mass? Aviation Strategy, 80, June 6–9.

Oum, T. H. (1998). Overview of regulatory changes in international air transport and Asian strategies towards the US open skies initiatives, Journal of Air Transport Management 4, 127–134.

Oum, T. H., Stanbury, W. T. and Tretheway, J. (1991). Airline deregulation in Canada and its economic effects, Transportation Journal, Summer, 6.

Oum, T. H., Yu, C. and Zhang, A. (2001). Global airline alliances: international regulator issues, Journal of Air Transport Management, 7(1), 57–62.

Palmer, A., McMahon-Beattie, U. and Beggs, R. (2000). Influences on loyalty programme effectiveness: a conceptual framework and case study investigation, Journal of Strategic Marketing, 8, 47–66.

Papatheodorou, A. (2002) Civil aviation regimes and leisure tourism in Europe, Journal of Air Transport Management, 8(6), 381–388.

Park, N. K. and Cho, D. S. (1997). The effect of strategic alliance on performance, Journal of Air Transport Management, 3(3), 155–164.

Pels, E. (2000). Airport economics and policy. Efficiency, competition and interaction with airlines, PhD Thesis, Vrije Universiteit, Amsterdam.

Pilling, M. (2003). BA grabs yet more Heathrow slots, Airline Business, November, 19.

Porter, M. E. (1996). What is Strategy? Harvard Business Review, November–December.

Porter, M. E. (1980). Competitive Strategy, Free Press, New York.

Proussaloglou, K. and Koppelman, F. S. (1999). The choice of air carrier, flight and fare class, Journal of Air Transport Management, 5, 193–201.

Reichheld, F. F., and Teal, F. (1996). The loyalty effect – the hidden force behind growth, profits and lasting value, Harvard Business School Press, Boston, MA.

Reinartz, W. T. and Kumar, V. (2000). On the profitability of long-life customers in a noncontractual setting. An empirical investigation and implication for marketing, Journal of Marketing, 64, 17–35.

Straszheim, M. R. (1969). The International Airline Industry, The Brookings Institution, Washington, DC.

Taneja, N. K. (2004). Simpli-Flying Optimizing the Airline Business Model, Ashgate Publishing Limited, Aldershot, England.

Taneja, N. K. (2002). Driving Airline Business Strategies through Emerging Technologies, Ashgate Publishing, Aldershot, England.

Tarry, C. (2003). A step change in fares, Airline Business, June, 82–83.

Thompson, A. A. and Strickland, A. J. (2001). Strategic Management: Concepts and Cases, 12th edition, McGraw Hill, New York.

Tirole, J. (1990). The Theory of Industrial Organisation, MIT Press, Cambridge, MA.

Viscusi, W. K., Vernon, J. M. and Harrington Jr, J. E. (1998). Economics of Regulation and Antitrust, 3rd edition, MIT Press, Cambridge, MA.

Williams, G. (1993). The Airline Industry and the Impact of Deregulation, Ashgate Publishing, Aldershot, England.

Winston, C. (1992). Economic deregulation: days of reckoning for microeconomists, Journal of Economic Literature, 30.

World Travel and Tourism Council (2004). The fourth global travel and tourism summit, Doha, Qatar, 1–3, May 2004. www.wttc.org/2004tsa/PDF/Executive%20Summary.pdf.

Yi, Y. and Jeon, H. (2003). Effects of loyalty programs on volume perception, program loyalty and brand loyalty, Journal of the Academy of Marketing Science, 31, 229–240.

Youssef, W. (1992). Causes and effects of international airline equity alliances, PhD. dissertation, Institute of Transportation Studies, University of California, Berkeley.

5

Competition in airports

Anne Graham

Introduction

This chapter investigates the complex issue of airport competition. It begins by considering the driving forces which have been responsible for creating greater opportunities for airports to compete in recent years. This leads on to an assessment of the types of competition which exist and to a discussion of the significance of the new airport organizational structures which are evolving. Any consideration of competition would be incomplete without an examination of the need for economic regulation and so this is the next area to be covered. The chapter concludes by discussing one of the most significant obstacles to competition, namely slots constraints, and assesses the relative merits of different slot allocation processes.

Historically airports were very much run as public utilities. Many were simply seen as monopoly providers of infrastructure, and airport competition was not an issue of much relevance. Little attention was paid to the commercial and business aspects of airport operations. Moreover the airline regulatory environment meant that airline choice of airport was often severely limited because of the system of restrictive bilateral agreements between different countries. Slot congestion did not exist.

However, in the last three decades two major developments have gradually occurred which have significantly increased the scope for competition between airports. Firstly commercialization has taken place within much of the airport industry. This has meant that airports have become much more commercially oriented and more businesslike management philosophies have been adopted. Links with government owners have been loosened with the setting up of more independent airport authorities or by establishing airport companies. Greater emphasis has been placed on activities such as financial management, non-aeronautical revenue generation and airport marketing. In some cases there has been airport privatization which has meant that control and often ownership has been transferred, partially or totally, to the private sector. In addition a small number of airport companies have begun to expand beyond previously well-defined national barriers, which has produced a much more international or global airport business. All this has resulted in airport operators having a much more competitive outlook to seeking new or retaining existing customers.

The second major development has been the deregulation of the airline industry. This began in 1978 with the US domestic market and many more markets have been subsequently deregulated. In some cases this has been as the result of the adoption of more liberal bilateral air services agreements – as has occurred on a number of the North Atlantic and Pacific routes. In the European Union (EU), deregulation has been achieved with a multilateral policy that evolved over a number of years with the introduction of three deregulation packages. Since 1997 any carrier based in the EU can fly any route between two countries with virtually no controls on pricing or capacity. Deregulation has opened up markets to more potential or actual competition between airlines and, as a result, between airports as well. One of the major consequences has been the emergence of low cost carriers (LCCs) who often use airports as part of their competitive strategy.

The nature of airport competition

The nature of airport competition is complex partly because there are two types of competition which have to be considered. Firstly there is the competition between airports. Secondly there is the competition within airports, such as the competition for the provision of a certain service or competition between airport terminals. Moreover, airport competition is often confused by the examination of competition between airlines (Morrell, 2003). For example, two airports may be described as being in strong competition with each other but this may be because they are served by airlines which are themselves in fierce competition. The passengers' choice of airport will be largely determined by the nature of the airlines which serve the airport in terms of the fares, destinations and services on offer. Hence from a passenger viewpoint airport competition will be closely linked to the amount of airline competition which exists.

Competition between airports

The exact amount of competition which exists between airports is a fiercely debated subject, although there is some general consensus as to how competition can occur (ACI-Europe, 1999; Starkie, 2002; Cranfield University, 2002). If airports are located on small islands or remote regions, the scope for competition is very limited or non-existent. However, if airports are physically close, their catchment areas may overlap and airport competition can develop. The catchment area will not be fixed and can vary, for example, depending on whether short-haul or long-haul services are being considered.

In some major urban areas or cities there are a number of situations when more than one airport serves the population, such as in London, Paris, New York and Washington. When there are overlapping catchment areas, one airport often tends to become the dominant player with the other airports playing a more secondary role. In the London area, for example, Heathrow airport is considered by many passengers, particularly those travelling on business, to be the 'London airport' in spite of a range of services being offered at the other London airports. Secondary airports tend to fulfil more specialized roles such as overspill airports when the major airport has inadequate capacity. Alternatively centrally located secondary airports may be able to attract domestic or short-haul traffic, particularly business-related traffic, as with London City airport in the London area. Other airports may specialize in charter or freight operations. In recent years the reduced military requirement for airports has meant there are more sites available for the development of secondary airports.

The development of the European LCC industry has created opportunities for a number of secondary airports to market themselves as low-cost alternatives to the major airports (Barrett, 2000). These airports often offer faster turnarounds, short walking distances from the terminal to the aircraft and fewer delays. However, they may be situated substantially further from the town or city. Sometimes these airports may be owned by the same operator which has control of the competing airports, for example, BAA owns Stansted airport and Fraport owns Hahn airport. In these cases the airport operator may be able to exert some influence over the type of traffic which is attracted to each airport.

There is a particular issue when a new airport is built to serve the same traffic as an older airport which has become too congested. The newer airport may be perceived as less attractive if it is situated in a less convenient location and this may mean that the newer airport may never be able to compete effectively. This was the case with Montreal's Mirabel airport which was built in the 1970s to provide extra capacity in addition to Dorval airport or more recently with the new Milan Malpensa airport which competes with Milan Linate airport. The alternative is to avoid any competition and to close the old airport as has happened in locations such as Munich, Hong Kong, Oslo and Denver. Competition for the new Athens airport is even more limited as not only has the old airport closed down but also no new airport development within the same catchment area is allowed.

Finally, certain airports can compete for the role as a hub. This may be for passenger traffic or cargo operations, particularly express parcel services. A relatively central geographic position is required, along with appropriate infrastructure which will enable good flight connectivity and efficient passenger transfers. Ultimately, however, the development of a hub airport will be very much dependent on the operating strategies and network plans of airlines or airline alliances.

Many factors will affect an airport's overall competitiveness. Park (2003) classified these into five categories, namely spatial and locational factors, facility factors, demand factors, service factors and managerial factors. Their relative importance and controllability varies considerably (Meincke, 2002). Location, and the associated catchment area, is the most important aspect but the airport operator can have no influence over this. Airport operators also tend to have little control over other key factors such as the availability of slots or environmental restrictions. They do have much greater influence over the 'attractiveness' of the airport in terms of the quality and size of the aeronautical and commercial facilities but the impact of these on airport choice, once a certain minimum standard has been reached, may be fairly marginal.

As regards price, airport charges represent a relatively small part – on average around 4 per cent – of an airline's total operating costs. Thus it can be argued that any price difference will have a minimal impact on airlines and will significantly limit an airport's ability to compete. However, different types of airlines have varying degrees of sensitivity to price. Airport charges can be substantially more important for short-haul operations as they are levied more frequently. For low-cost and charter operations they can be even more significant because these airlines will have minimized many of the other airline costs. In these cases, airport price competition can be very real particularly if additional pricing incentives are offered.

Competition within airports – provision of airport services

Many airport services, such as air traffic control, security, ground handling and the provision of commercial facilities, can be provided either by the airport operator or by a third party. The way in which they are offered, and whether there are competing services, can have a major impact on an airport's competitive situation in both price and service quality terms. Competing services tend to be the most established in the commercial areas such as airport retail outlets, restaurants, hotels and car parks.

A key airport service for airlines is ground handling. These services can be provided by the airport operator, the airline itself (self-handling), another airline or an independent handling agent. In the United States, airport operators tend not to get directly involved but they do elsewhere, particular in Europe (De Neufville and Odoni, 2003). The issue of competition with the provision of handling services has always been controversial as traditionally it was quite common for the national airline or airport operator to have a monopoly or near monopoly in providing these services. Examples in Europe included Iberia and Olympic and the airport operators at Austrian, German and Italian airports. As a result airlines often complained of excessive costs or poor service levels. For this reason, some regulatory authorities insist that there is always at least a choice of two providers of handling services. However, whilst it is usually fairly easy to allow a number of airlines or agents to provide passenger handling in the terminal, capacity constraints of the equipment and space for ramp handling tends to make it much more difficult to provide competition in these areas. Also it is often argued that if there are too many handlers, economies of scale will be lost.

Within the European Union, a directive was passed in 1996 which provided for the phased liberalization of ground handling services. For third party handling (at airports with more than two million passengers) there has to be a minimum of two suppliers for certain types of service, with at least one of these being independent of the airport or dominant carrier. In addition at least two airlines should be allowed to self-handle. In reality the transition from a monopolistic to competitive situation at some airports has proved to be a difficult and slow process. There were delays in transposing the directive into the national legislation and also some airports, such as Frankfurt, Paris CDG and Düsseldorf, were granted temporary exemptions on the basis of shortage of capacity.

A major study for the European Commission on the impact of the directive concluded that handling prices had gone down in most cases and the number of third party handlers had increased (SH&E, 2002). So to some extent it appears that the directive has achieved its aims. However, it is not entirely clear what role the directive played in causing these developments. Cost cutting by many financially weak airlines has also put a downward pressure on handling prices. In addition, a number of airlines are opting to sell off their handling activities to concentrate on their core functions and hence third party handling has grown. Large global handling companies, such as Globeground, Worldwide Flight Services and Menzies, have emerged and are able to take advantage of their size to offer competitive price deals to the airlines.

Whilst prices have dropped, there is less evidence of improvements in the quality of service. The airport industry feels that this can be resolved by introducing service level agreements between handlers and airport operators whilst the handlers tend to take the view that quality is an issue to be tackled between themselves and their airline customer. This typifies a key problem faced by airport operators in trying to offer an attractive airport product. Sub-contracting and opening services up for competition may bring price benefits but loss of overall control may mean that service levels become more difficult to guarantee. The European Commission is expected to propose revisions to the handling directive in 2005 which will address some of these service quality issues.

Competition within airports – terminals

Potentially the greatest competition within airports could be achieved by having competing terminals under different ownership offering competition in terms of price and service quality. Varying quality standards and facilities could be offered to serve different services such as low cost, short haul, long haul or business – although the more specialized the terminal is the less scope exists for competition with other terminals. However, strategic planning could be much more difficult with the lack of single ownership and economies of scale could be lost.

In the UK there has been some discussion of the benefits of having competing terminals at Heathrow (Civil Aviation Authority, 2001a). Rather predictably, BAA, the airport owner, challenged the premise that separate ownership or management would create any benefits whilst BA was more in favour of the idea (BAA, 2001; BA, 2001). However, an important issue at Heathrow is that there are capacity constraints which are likely to minimize the basis for competition. Competition between terminals is much more likely to be effective when unused terminal capacity is available or new facilities are built. Within this context, in 2002 the Irish Government asked for expressions of interest from organizations which might wish to develop a competing terminal, possibly for LCCs, at Dublin airport. Thirteen companies responded including international airport groups and airlines. Such interest showed that at least these companies thought that it was a sound idea (Department of Transport, 2003). Elsewhere there is a growing number of airports, such as Singapore Changi, Geneva, Marseilles and Amsterdam, which are planning for separate 'low cost' terminals for their LCCs. However, these are not going to be operated under different ownership and the concept of competing terminals does not seem to have generated much widespread interest of support.

In practice there is only limited and insufficient industry evidence to conclude whether it is possible to have successfully competing airport terminals. In 1986, Terminal 3 at Toronto airport was handed over to a private consortium to provide new investment. However, in 1996 it was bought back under the responsibility of the Greater Toronto Airport Authority to allow for the development of the airport master plan. Elsewhere, at Birmingham airport, the Eurohub terminal was at one stage operated separately but has now been brought back under single management at the airport. In Brussels there were not competing terminals but the management of the airside and the terminal was split. However, in 1998 this division of management was reversed with the establishment of the Brussels International Airport Company. These cases suggest that the experience of competing terminals or split management was not too favourable. On the other hand, in the United States and particularly at JFK airport in New York, there are permanent examples of competing terminals being operated by airlines.

Airport organization and competition

There is another aspect of airport competition which relates to whether different airports should be operated as individual entities or as a group or system. To some extent the issues are similar to those raised when considering competing terminals. Arguments favouring group ownership and operations include economies of scale and enhanced career opportunities for employees, a stronger financial structure which can support the investment peaks and troughs at different airports and a more consistent strategic planning and investment policy. On the other hand, supporters of individual operations claim that separation would produce more competition, superior local management and prevent any cross-subsidization which occurs between airports.

This issue has been particularly contentious in the UK where BAA operates London Heathrow, Gatwick and Stansted as well as four other smaller UK airports. Since privatization in 1987, the arguments for and against splitting the group have been fiercely debated (Barrett, 2000). There have been various government reviews but these have generally concluded that the additional benefits of competition would be more that offset by the strategic and operational disadvantages (Toms, 2004). In the latest government review in 2000, it was concluded that capacity constraints in the London area together with the planning regime would severely limit the chances for greater competition if the group was split up (Civil Aviation Authority, 2000a). By contrast in Australia the government chose individual privatizations for the major international airports. In Ireland in 2003, the government decided to split up Aer Rianta, which operates Dublin, Shannon and Cork, with the objective of achieving more choice and competition – in spite of fierce opposition from the airport operator.

Privatization has enabled a number of airport companies to expand beyond previously well-defined national barriers and to operate groups of airports from different countries. This expansion has occurred not only with well-established airport companies such as BAA and Schipol, but also with a number of non-airport companies, whose previous experience in running airports was rather limited or non-existent, such as the property company TBI, the financial investor Macquarie or the construction company Hochtief (Graham, 2003). There clearly is some synergy between airport operations and the traditional activities of these non-airport companies and developing airport interests can, for example, enable construction firms to also secure lucrative construction contracts on their own terms.

For many industries, including travel-related businesses such as hotels, travel agents and tour operators, a key motive for such international expansion is to create market power and brand strength, and hence to reduce competition. This is not the case with the airport sector. Indeed the benefits of international expansion seem less clear but are likely to be more associated with risk-spreading, cost synergies and knowledge transfer. Unlike the airline industry there is only one significant airport alliance, called Pantares, which was set up between Schipol and Fraport in 1999. Again its aim was not to increase market accessibility but to reap benefits from shared knowledge, expertise and financial resources. To date, however, such benefits have proved rather limited.

Airport regulation

Regulation principles and practice

When an industry is considered to have considerable market power and not capable of sustaining competition, the usual practice is to use economic regulation to prohibit potential abuse of this monopolistic power. However, with the airport industry, the rationale for regulation is not so straightforward. It has been argued that no longer can all airports be viewed as natural monopolies because of the improved forces of competition which have occurred due to increased liberalization and commercialization. Therefore market power varies but tends to be the strongest at airports which have a high concentration of services, both short haul and long haul. These airports appeal most to the traditional scheduled carriers who have networked services. In these cases it would be difficult for other airports to act as substitutes and provide much competition, even if it was possible to overcome the problems for competing operators in getting access to suitably well-located sites. Starkie (2001) identified these economies of scope factors, as the result of established air service network services, together with the fixity of locational inputs, as the key determinants of market power. However, for the point-to-point services of charters and LCCs, there is much more scope for substituting different airports in overlapping catchment areas, and economies of scope factors are less important. For these airlines avoiding the congested major airport may often be seen as a benefit.

In addition regulation is often justified because most industries with monopolistic characteristics experience increasing returns to scale. However, within the airport industry, the evidence suggests that economies of scale tend to disappear once the annual output of an airport reaches around three million passengers and as airports grow much larger there may in fact be diseconomies of scale – primarily because the airport operation becomes that much more complex (Graham, 2003; Pels et al., 2000). This suggests that cost factors or economies of scale should not be a barrier to competitive entry (Starkie, 2002).

Even if market power exists, it is debatable whether airports are likely to exploit this power. Normally any company with profit-maximizing policies would be likely to set prices which lead to high returns. However with the airport industry, the arguments of demand complementarity also need to be taken into account. An increase in traffic at an airport will increase the demand for retailing and property facilities at airports. This will increase commercial revenues and will mean that the airport operator may be able to secure higher rents for retailing and property because of the attractiveness of the high traffic volumes. Hence the airport may have a strong incentive not to raise airport charges – even if not regulated – as any downward pressure on traffic demand could have a detrimental impact on the non-aeronautical side of the airport business. In other words, there are commercial incentives for airports to work with airlines to grow the total traffic.

This is particularly significant since many airports are increasingly relying on commercial activities to grow their businesses (Starkie, 2001; Starkie, 2002; Papatheodorou, 2003).

These unique characteristics of the airport industry have resulted in a considerable amount of debate as to whether airport regulation is necessary and if so, what type of regulation is the most appropriate. The most common form of regulation within the airport industry is price cap regulation, with a maximum price formula linked to inflation and an efficiency factor. A key decision has to be made concerning which airport facilities and services are to be considered under the pricing regime. There are two alternative approaches, namely the single till approach when all airport activities are included, and the dual till approach when just the aeronautical aspects of the operation are taken into account. With the single till concept growth in non-aeronautical revenue can be used to offset increases in aeronautical charges. Within the airport industry such single till practices are fairly widespread. The alternative dual till concept treats the aeronautical and non-aeronautical areas as separate financial entities and focuses on the monopoly aeronautical airport services. In this case the price cap is established by just considering the aeronautical revenues and costs rather than the total airport operation. This in itself is a difficult task because it involves allocating many common costs between the aeronautical and non-aeronautical areas (Civil Aviation Authority, 2000a).

The rationale for the single till is that without the aeronautical activities, there would be no market for the commercial operations and hence it is appropriate to offset the level of airport charges with profits earned from non-aeronautical facilities. This is the justification which the airlines use in favouring such a system which is clearly likely to bring the lowest level of actual charges for them. However, there is also a major logical argument in not including commercial activities within the regulatory framework since these cannot be considered as monopoly facilities. In addition, the single till leads to aeronautical charges being set below the true costs. This does not make economic sense at congested airports as this below-cost pricing mechanism cannot be used to make the best use of the scarce resources. London Heathrow is an example of an airport using the single till approach. Since being regulated in 1987 its charges decreased from being some of the world's highest to being relatively low by international standards. Yet this has been during a time when the airport has become more and more congested. In recent years, there have been calls for a change to the dual till but these have been rejected.

There is no common consensus as to the merits of single versus dual till and so consequently practice varies (Lu and Pagliari, 2003). For example the single till price cap regulation in the UK covers both the BAA London and Manchester airports (Vass, 2004; Hendriks and Andrew, 2004). A similar price cap regulatory mechanism but with the dual till was adopted when there was privatization in Mexico and Australia. In Ireland, a single till price cap exists for Aer Rianta.

Unusually for this type of regulation, Aer Rianta is under public ownership but the airports, particularly Dublin, could be considered to have significant market power. At Vienna and Hamburg a more complex dual till pricing formula is used (Niemeier, 2002).

Another important issue when airport charges and regulation are being considered is whether any pre-financing of future airport infrastructure should be allowed. Traditionally airlines have been against this as there is no guarantee that the airlines paying the charges will actually be the airlines that will benefit from the new infrastructure. Moreover, a general lack of transparent airport data means that it is difficult to prove that the airports are not abusing their market power and are actually using the charges income efficiently to provide new facilities. However, airports claim that in some cases pre-financing may be necessary to raise sufficient investment funds and that it avoids large increases in airport charges when the infrastructure comes on stream, as was experienced at Narita and Kansai airports in Japan. In reality a number of airports do use fees for pre-financing purposes. In Greece, for instance, higher passenger fees were levied, in spite of airline opposition, to pay for the financing of the new Athens airport. Elsewhere, for example in the UK, the regulator takes into account the fact that some pre-financing will take place when setting the appropriate level of charges. The appropriateness of this, particularly as regards the financing of the new terminal 5 at Heathrow, has been widely debated.

A further important aspect of regulation is service quality. When the regulation does not formally establish service standards or require quality monitoring, there may be little incentive for the airport operator to optimize quality. In reducing the service standards at the airport, the operator could be able to soften the blow of the price control. For this reason in Australia, when the initial regulatory framework was set up, some formal service quality monitoring and reporting was required. This was not the case with the UK airports until 2003 when it was established that rebates on charges could be given if certain service targets were not met (Civil Aviation Authority, 2003).

When the regulator sets the price cap, it will normally do so after assessing the accounting and other information of the airport in question. However, industry benchmarking could potentially have a much more active role as is already the case with some other European utility sectors (Civil Aviation Authority, 2000b). The adoption of such regulatory benchmarking would make the regulator's assessment much more independent but is fraught with difficulties because of extensive problems of comparability and the lack of general consensus as to the optimal method of benchmarking within the airport industry. Hence currently the contribution of benchmarking to the regulatory process is very limited.

Overall, one of the major disadvantages of price cap regulatory systems is that they can be time-consuming, bureaucratic and costly. For example, the last review of BAA took 32 months and BAA alone submitted almost 800 papers (Toms, 2003). This coupled with a great deal of uncertainty as regards the actual existence of market power and the real risks of its abuse have called for a more light-handed approach to regulation. One option is some kind of reserve regulation. Here the regulator will only become involved in the price-setting process if market power is actually abused. It is thus the threat of regulation, rather than actual regulation, which is used to provide an effective safeguard against anti-competitive behaviour. An interesting case is Australia which originally had a price cap regulation at its airports but has now moved to 'price monitoring' which in effect is reserve regulation. Elsewhere, the Scottish airports in the UK and the Bolivian airports are examples of reserve regulation practice which seems to have quite successful. However, in New Zealand, it has not stopped Auckland airport charging prices which some consider to be excessive (Forsyth, 2004; McKensie-Williams, 2004).

A possible way forward is for airlines and airports to work together and to enter into partnerships, rather than the more defensive approach through the formal regulation process. Long-term agreements have always been the practice in the United States where the airlines and airport operators sign legally binding airport use agreements. There are two key approaches used, namely the compensatory model which is similar to the dual till concept and the residual model which is closer to the single till but involves some risk-taking by the airlines. A few examples of airline–airport partnerships are now appearing elsewhere. Copenhagen airport and its airlines now have a three-year agreement concerning the level of charges. The Frankfurt airport company, Fraport, has reached a risk-sharing agreement with its airlines which replaces the requirement for government approval of the level of charges for a five-year period (Klenk, 2004). In Australia too, the movement from price regulation to price monitoring has encouraged airports and airlines to sign five-year charge agreements. Interestingly, in the UK, which has had the longest experience of airport regulation, the CAA has proposed a more light-handed approach, with more commercial negotiation taking place between the airport operators and the airlines (Civil Aviation Authority, 2004).

State aid

Whilst the discussion of airport-specific regulation tends to be largely focused on private airports, an important regulatory or legal issue for public airports is the degree of state aid which is allowed. Throughout the world, there are many loss-making publicly owned airports which in effect receive state subsidies to remain operational or to expand. In addition, indirect government subsidies may be granted when certain services such as air traffic control or maintenance are provided by the government free of charge or at less than cost. Both these direct or indirect subsidies can potentially distort competition.

Within the EU, much attention has been given to eliminating the state aid which has distorted airline competition for years, whilst airport operations have received much less consideration. One of the more controversial areas is when it is possible for airports to provide state aid for airlines as the result of being state-owned themselves. This is particularly relevant in the case of regional and secondary airports, which have provided financial support and incentives to encourage LCCs to use their airports (Barrett, 2004). In essence, according to Article 87 of the Treaty of Rome and European transport policy, aid is allowed if it encourages the development and use of currently under-utilized secondary airport infrastructure. On the other hand state aid is not allowed when it can be proved that a private airport operator would not behave in the same manner, the so-called private investor factor.

The European Commission considered these two key principles when it was investigating the incentives granted to Ryanair by Brussels South Charleroi Airport (BSCA), which is a small regional airport south of Brussels owned by the Walloon regional government. Under an agreement of 15 years, Ryanair paid reduced landing and handling charges. In addition BSCA offered some marketing support, incentive payments for each route started and covered Ryanair's costs for local crew hiring and training. Office and hangar space was also provided for a minimal cost. In 2004, the European Commission declared that Ryanair should be allowed to keep some of the aid intended for the launch of new air routes. However, certain aid such as fee discounts was not allowed because it had not been allocated in a non-discriminatory and fully transparent manner and was planned for a very long period of operation (European Commission, 2004a). Ryanair is appealing, arguing that incentives were offered to other airlines and that private sector airports offer greater discounts. Whatever the outcome, this complex decision could potentially have major implications for the relative competitive strength of private and public airports, particularly in attracting LCCs. This has created great uncertainty and the industry is calling on the European Commission to produce general guidelines to clarify the situation (Airport Business, 2004).

Within this context, it is worth noting that the public service obligation (PSO) framework within Europe, where state aid is allowed on PSO routes which typically link international airport systems to regional airports located in peripheral regions, can in effect be seen an indirect state subsidy to the regional airport. The number of PSO routes varies from country to country with the largest number being found in France, followed by Spain, UK and Portugal. In some cases, for example, in remote airports in Scotland and Ireland, subsidized PSO air services provide almost all of the traffic and can therefore be very significant to the airport operator (Cranfield University, 2002).

Slot allocation

Whilst there are greater opportunities for airport competition than in the past, there remains a number of significant obstacles that can hamper an airport's ability to compete. In some regions availability of traffic rights still largely determines the exact routes which are flown. There are also environmental constraints which restrict free access to certain airports. However, one of the most basic obstacles to airport competition is undoubtedly the shortage of slots. At many major airports, scarce slots have become important assets for the incumbent airlines and have become very difficult for new entrant or smaller carriers to acquire.

When demand for airport slots exceeds supply, as currently occurs at many airports throughout the world, a slot allocation process is needed. The mechanism, which is used virtually everywhere but in the United States, is industry self-regulation with IATA scheduling co-ordination conferences. These conferences have a number of formal procedures for allocating slots with the most important being grandfather rights. This means that any airline which has operated a slot in the previous season has the right to operate it again. This is as long as the airline operates 80 per cent of the flights – the so-called slot retention requirement or 'use it or lose it' rule.

Whilst this scheduling system has provided a relatively stable environment for allocating slots, it clearly is not the most effective in managing the scarcity of slots or in guaranteeing that the slots are used by the airlines who value them most. Nor does it encourage competition. It can be administratively burdensome and the lack of any market mechanism means that there is no guide to future investment requirements. Hence as the shortages of runway capacity continue to grow, so does the pressure for slot allocation reform. As a result the merits and drawbacks of alternative systems continue to be widely debated (for example see Boyfield et al., 2003; Debbage, 2002; Matthews and Menaz, 2003; Ross, 2003). At the heart of any discussion about slots is the controversial issue of slot ownership. The grandfather rights system, through historically giving airlines the rights to use slots for long periods of time, encourages claims of ownership by the airlines. It is certainly true that airlines view slots as financial assets which are taken into account whenever airline purchases or mergers take place. Meanwhile airports maintain that they have created and own the infrastructure which enables slots to exist, and so the airlines are, in effect, just granted usage rights.

Within the EU, legislation was introduced in 1993 which gave a legal basis to most of the voluntary scheduling committee rules. It also aimed to encourage new entrants within the slot allocation and grandfather rights process by giving them preference of up to 50 per cent of any new or unused slots. However, this legislation had very little impact on encouraging competition or lessening the influence of the major airlines primarily because the grandfather rights system was retained. At the same time delays and congestion at European airports continued to grow. Therefore the European Commission decided on a two-stage process of reform of the slot allocation rules. Some need for immediate technical amendments was identified for the first stage (PricewaterhouseCoopers, 2000) and after lengthy industry debate these became law in 2004. The most controversial issue was the EC's attempt to clarify the actual status of a slot by defining it as permission but not a property.

In the second stage of its slot reform, the European Commission is considering more radical changes and specifically whether some kind of market mechanism could be introduced (NERA, 2004). A consultation document concerning this was published late in 2004 (European Commission, 2004b). There are a number of primary or secondary trading alternatives which could be used. The simplest primary trading method would be to maintain the airport charging mechanism and to price slots at the market clearing level in order to match demand and supply. Initially it would be difficult to determine the correct price although the charges would have to be set at a considerably higher rate than the current practice to have any influence over demand patterns. Undoubtedly this would prove to be very unpopular with the airlines, particularly as the gap between airline and airport profitability, with airports outperforming the airlines, has become a very contentious issue in today's more uncertain air transport environment.

An alternative primary trading mechanism could be slot auctions (DotEcon, 2001; Gruyer and Lenoir, 2003). This has been used elsewhere with mobile telecommunications and radio frequencies. There are a number of different methods which could be adopted and the frequency of use could vary. However, whichever mechanism is chosen there would bound to be at least some upheaval and disruption for both airlines and passenger and the costs of implementation is likely to be high. There is also the issue of demand complementarities between different slots with airlines needing an appropriate combination of landing and take-off slots to operate effectively. These would be difficult to achieve through the auction mechanism and may require the slots to be auctioned in packages rather than individually. A key question would be who should benefit from the proceeds of the auctions and how the money should be used. An alternative to auctions could be slot lotteries. Whilst these might potentially be effective in encouraging competition, they could be very disruptive to services and could cause much uncertainty and again there would be the problem of demand complementarities.

Secondary trading could be operated after slots have been allocated through primary trading or combined with the established allocation system. One of the issues here would be whether it is appropriate for existing slot holders to gain financially from slots which they never actually bought. Currently such slot trading between airlines within the EU is officially illegal although airlines are allowed to exchange slots. In reality a 'grey market' in slots already exists and there have been a number of well-published cases where airlines have paid a considerable amount for additional slots. This is particularly the case in the UK since the High Court ruled in 1999 that slot exchanges with 'compensation' for less attractive slots was possible (Civil Aviation Authority, 2001b). BA is thought to have spent over £35 million buying Heathrow slots from airlines such as DAT, Virgin and Swiss since 2002 with a specific example being in October 2003 when it paid £12 million to buy four slots from United (Kane, 2003).

The only other open experience of slot trading has been in the USA since 1986 at the so-called 'high density' airports of JFK and La Guardia in New York, O'Hare in Chicago and Washington Reagan National. This led to very few outright sales of slots and very few new entrants, with the established airlines increasing their dominance (Starkie, 1998). With concerns for the competitiveness of the US airline industry, certain slots restrictions at the airports have been relaxed since 2000.

Alternatively administrative rather than market-based systems could be used to allocate slots by giving preference to certain types of traffic such as long-haul (and encouraging short-haul to transfer to surface modes) or giving priority to larger aircraft for environmental reasons. However, whilst these can be useful in pursuing some economic, social or environmental objective, they will not always ensure that a more efficient use is made of scarce airport capacity. For this, some kind of market mechanism, which ensures that slots are allocated to airlines that value them most, is needed. However such systems, as limited evidence from the United States suggest, will always tend to favour the large incumbent airlines and may well lead to greater airline concentration. In short, arguments for slot reform tend to focus on the need to make best use of scarce resources whilst at the same time encouraging competition but in reality these two aims do not seem very compatible.

Conclusion

This chapter has examined the nature of airport competition in light of the changing air transport environment. Undoubtedly there is now much more scope for airport competition and the days of airports being merely considered as public utilities have long since gone.

The evolving aviation world has brought new challenges for airports as they adapt to cope with the increasingly competitive situation. There are complicated issues related to the ownership and control of airport services, airport terminals, airport groups and international operations, which all have to be considered. In addition to remain competitive, airports need to change and be more flexible in serving the needs of their modern-day customers, such as LCCs and airline alliances.

The need for heavy-handed airport regulation seems to be decreasing and in fact it could be argued that any anti-competitive behaviour could be treated through normal competition law and litigation processes. As the airline industry becomes increasingly deregulated, less rather than more airport regulation seems the logical way forward. However, to enable this to happen, airports and airlines need to work together to improve their relationships and to develop closer links and partnerships.

Finally, slot reform remains one of the most difficult tasks which needs to be addressed. In Europe, it seems likely that market forces will play a role sometime in the future. However, whilst this may ensure that there is better use of the scarce resources, it by no means guarantees that competition is increased. Whatever happens, it is vital that this major obstacle to access to airports is removed, if a really competitive environment for airports is desired.

References

ACI-Europe (1999), Policy paper on airport competition, Brussels, ACI-Europe.

Airport Business (2004), Clarity required on government incentives to low-fare airlines, Airport Business, March, 20–21.

BA (2001), Response to competitive provision of infrastructure and services within airports, CAA, available on www.caaerg.co.uk.

BAA (2001), Response to competitive provision of infrastructure and services within airports, CAA, available on www.caaerg.co.uk.

Barrett, S. (2000), Airport competition in the deregulated European aviation market, Journal of Air Transport Management, 6, 13–27.

Barrett, S. (2004), How do the demands for airport services differ between full-service and low-cost carriers?, Journal of Air Transport Management, 10, 33–39.

Boyfield, K., Starkie, D., Bass, T. and Humphreys, B. (2003), A market for airport slots, London, Institute of Economic Affairs.

Civil Aviation Authority (2000a), The single and dual approach to the price regulation of airports, CAA, available on www.caaerg.co.uk.

Civil Aviation Authority (2000b) The use of benchmarking in airport reviews, CAA, available on www.caaerg.co.uk

Civil Aviation Authority (2001a), Competitive provision of infrastructure and services within airports, CAA, available on www.caaerg.co.uk.

Civil Aviation Authority (2001b), The implementation of secondary slot trading, CAA, available on www.caaerg.co.uk.

Civil Aviation Authority (2003), Service quality: Statement of standards and rebates, CAA, available on www.caaerg.co.uk

Civil Aviation Authority (2004), Airport regulation: Looking to the future – learning from the past, CAA, available on www.caaerg.co.uk.

Cranfield University (2002), Study on competition between airports and the application of state aid rules, Cranfield University, available on www.europa.eu.int.

De Neufville, R. and Odoni, A. (2003), Airport systems: Planning, design and management, New York, McGraw-Hill.

Debbage, K. (2002), Airport runway slots: Limits to growth, Annals of Tourism Research, 29 (4), 933–951.

Department of Transport (2003), Dublin airport – review of expressions of interest for an independent terminal, panel report to Minister for Transport, available on www.transport.ie.

DotEcon (2001), Auctioning airport slots, DotEcon, available on www. DotEcon.com.

European Commission (2004a), The Commission's Decision on Charleroi airport promotes the activities of low-cost airlines and regional development, press release IP/04/157, 3 February, available on www. europa.eu.int.

European Commission (2004b) Commercial slot allocation mechanisms in the content of a further revision of Council Regulation (EEC) 95/93 on common rules for the allocation of slots at Community airports, 17 September, available on www.europa.eu.int.

Forsyth, P. (2004), Replacing regulation: Airport price monitoring in Australia, in Forsyth, P., Gillen, D., Knorr, A., Mayer, O., Niemeier, H. and Starkie, D. (eds) The economic regulation of airports, Aldershot, Ashgate.

Graham, A. (2003), Managing airports: An international perspective, second edition, Oxford, Elsevier.

Gruyer, N. and Lenoir, N. (2003), Auctioning airport slots, Air Transport Research Society Conference, Toulouse, July.

Hendriks, N. and Andrew, D. (2004) Airport regulation in the UK, in Forsyth, P., Gillen, D., Knorr, A., Mayer, O., Niemeier, H. and Starkie, D. (eds) The economic regulation of airports, Aldershot, Ashgate.

Kane, F. (2003), BA pays £12m for four more landing slots at Heathrow, The Observer, 12 October.

Klenk, M. (2004), New approaches in airline/airport relations: The charges framework of Frankfurt Airport, in Forsyth, P., Gillen, D., Knorr, A., Mayer, O., Niemeier, H. and Starkie, D. (eds) The economic regulation of airports, Aldershot, Ashgate.

Lu, C. and Pagliari, R. (2003), New insights into the single-till versus dual till airport pricing debate, Air Transport Research Society Conference, Toulouse, July.

Matthews, B. and Menaz, B. (2003), Airport capacity: The problem of slot allocation, German Aviation Research Seminar, Leipzig, November.

McKensie-Williams, P. (2004), A shift towards regulation? The case of New Zealand, in Forsyth, P., Gillen, D., Knorr, A., Mayer, O., Niemeier, H. and Starkie, D. (eds) The economic regulation of airports, Aldershot, Ashgate.

Meincke, P. (2002), Competition of airports in Europe, Air Transport Research Society Conference, Seattle, July.

Morrell, P. (2003), Airport competition or network access? A European perspective, German Aviation Research Seminar, Leipzig, November.

NERA (2004), Study to assess the effects of different slot allocation schemes, NERA, available on www.europa.eu.int.

Niemeier, Hans-Martin (2002), Regulation of airports: The case of Hamburg airport – a view from the perspective of regional policy, Journal of Air Transport Management, 8, 37–48.

Papatheodorou, A. (2003), Do we need airport regulation? The Utilities Journal, October, 35–37.

Park, Y. (2003), An analysis for the competitive strength of Asian major airports, Journal of Air Transport Management, 9, 353–360.

Pels, E., Nijkamp, P. and Rietveld, P. (2000), Inefficiencies and scale economies of European airport operations, Air Transport Research Society Conference, The Netherlands, July.

PricewaterhouseCoopers (2000), Study of certain aspects of Council Regulation 95/93 on Common Rules for the Allocation of Slots at Community Airports, Pricewaterhouse-Coopers, available on www. europa.eu.int.

Ross, E. (2003), Airport slots: Who benefits from allocating them? In Helm, D. and Holt, D. (eds) Air transport and infrastructure: The challenges ahead, Oxford, Oxera.

SH&E (2002), Study on the quality and efficiency of ground handling services at EU airports as a result of the implementation of Council Directive 96/67/EC., SH&E, available on www. europa.eu.int.

Starkie, D. (1998), Allocating airport slots: A role for the market, Journal of Air Transport Management, 4, 111–116.

Starkie, D. (2001), Reforming UK airport regulation, Journal of Transport Economics and Policy, 35 (1), January, 119–135.

Starkie, D. (2002), Airport regulation and competition, Journal of Air Transport Management, 8, 37–48.

Toms, M. (2003), Is airport regulation fit for purpose?, In Helm, D. and Holt, D. (eds) Air transport and infrastructure: The challenges ahead, Oxford, Oxera.

Toms, M. (2004), UK regulation from the perspective of the BAA plc, in Forsyth, P., Gillen, D., Knorr, A., Mayer, O., Niemeier, H. and Starkie, D. (eds) The economic regulation of airports, Aldershot, Ashgate.

Vass, P. (ed) (2004) The development of airports regulation – a collection of reviews, Bath, Centre for the Study of Regulated Industries.

6

The market influence of tour operators on the hospitality industry

Dimitris Koutoulas

Introduction

This chapter examines the relations between tour operators and resort hotels and the latter's competitive environment. The focus is on the Mediterranean, a destination that would not have developed so rapidly over the last 50 years without the tourist flows generated by tour operators. The example of Greece is used to illustrate this relationship.

The basis of the European holiday market is the inclusive tour (or package tour) provided by tour operators. This product type is dominating the summer holiday market from the northern parts of Europe towards the warm-weather destinations of the Mediterranean basin. For instance, of the 43.8 million Germans who took a holiday trip abroad in 2002, 22.1 million chose a Mediterranean destination, while 7 million headed for Alpine countries. According to the Reiseanalyse 2003 survey, 52 per cent of those vacationing in the Mediterranean booked an inclusive tour as opposed to only 14 per cent of Alps-bound travellers (Gruner + Jahr 2004: 5). The British consumers are showing an even greater preference for the Mediterranean. Of the nearly 40 million Britons vacationing abroad in 2003 (with 27.6 million travelling on air inclusive tours – CAA 2004: 2), 25.9 million chose a holiday in one of the top seven Mediterranean destinations, i.e. in Spain, France, Greece, Italy, Portugal, Cyprus and Turkey (ABTA 2003).

Distributing hotel capacity in a tour operator-controlled market

Inclusive tour-based development of Mediterranean and Greek tourism

Hebestreit (1992: 20–21) defines the ready-made inclusive tour (as opposed to the tailor-made one) as 'a service package comprising at least two complementary travel services; it is created in advance for a yet unknown customer and is offered at a total price, with the prices of the individual services not being identifiable.'

The production and distribution system of inclusive tours comprises the following components:

- Producers of individual travel services (e.g. accommodation providers, transport companies etc.);
- Tour operators acting both as producers (by combining the individual components into a new product) and wholesalers (through brochure production and reservation systems);
- Retailers (e.g. travel agencies, travel-related websites etc.).

This system started to form in Europe in the 1950s. The 1970s saw an accelerating growth of south-bound holiday travel by Northern Europeans, as the growing use of jet planes multiplied the available airlift capacity on charter flights and decreased both the duration and the cost of travel. Mediterranean countries such as Spain, Portugal, Greece, Cyprus and Turkey responded by creating large accommodation capacities to handle the millions of sun seekers flooding their coastline each summer (see Table 6.1).

The continuous increase in bed and airlift capacity led to a huge increase in tourist arrivals. Greece, for instance, witnessed an average 349 per cent growth

Table 6.1 International tourist arrivals and total hotel bed capacity in Greece and in selected Mediterranean countries

Year	International tourist arrivals	Arrivals on charter flights as % of total arrivals	Total hotel bed capacity
Data for Greece			
1950	33,333	N/A	N/A
1960	399,438	N/A	57,022*
1970	1,609,210	N/A	118,859
1980	5,271,115	38%	278,045
1990	9,310,492	49%	438,360
2000	13,095,545	58%	593,990
2004	N/A	N/A	649,000
Data for other countries			
2000	48,200,000	Spain	1,215,290
2000	10,400,000	Turkey	404,300
2000	2,700,000	Cyprus	85,303
2000	12,100,000	Portugal	222,958
2000	5,500,000	Egypt	213,898

* Data for 1961.

Source: Greek National Tourism Organisation, Hellenic National Statistical Service, Hellenic Chamber of Hotels, AGTE 2002: 20.

per decade since 1950, with arrivals surpassing the 13 million mark in 2000. Hotel bed capacity has also grown at 84 per cent per decade on average reaching 593,990 beds in 2000 and 649,000 beds in 2004.

This development, however, would not have been possible without the charter flights employed by the major European tour operators to transport their customers. A constantly increasing share of total tourist arrivals in Greece is made on these charter flights, reaching 58 per cent in 2000. This number reveals the extent to which Greek tourism depends on tour operators (their total share is even larger considering that some inclusive tours comprise scheduled flights or other means of transportation). In contrast to other Mediterranean countries (such as Spain and Turkey), all charter flights to Greece are operated by foreign airlines as there is no Greece-based charter operator.

Dominance of the inclusive tour market by the major tour operators

The inclusive tour market of West and North European countries – especially for Mediterranean-bound holiday trips – is dominated by a few major tour operators. In Germany, for instance, the two largest operators TUI (Touristik Union International) and Thomas Cook had a combined 51 per cent share of the industry's 2003 revenues, with the top five operators controlling 79.5 per cent of the market. The market concentration is more limited in Britain, with the top five operators securing 52.4 per cent of the total air-based inclusive tour revenues (Table 6.2).

The inclusive tour market of other European countries is also highly dominated by a few tour operators. For instance, the combined market share of the five largest tour operators in the respective countries for the year 2000 is as follows (Toulantas 2001: 8): Scandinavia – 88 per cent, Austria – 83 per cent, Belgium – 80 per cent, Netherlands – 70 per cent, France – 58 per cent. This market dominance is the result of an accelerating trans-European consolidation process.

Expansion of major European tour operators

The consolidation trend among Europe's tour operators started in the late 1990s. Leading this trend is Germany-based TUI. Following the acquisition of several smaller European companies, TUI took over Thomson and Nouvelles Frontières, the leading operators of the UK and France, respectively, in 2000. These moves further strengthened TUI's position as Europe's largest inclusive tour provider. Germany's C&N also expanded in the British market by acquiring Thomas Cook and renamed its entire operation after the founder of package tours. Airtours (now MyTravel) secured a minority stake in Germany's FTI, but resold it in 2003. Another major merger is Rewe's purchase of LTU in 2001.

This horizontal expansion took place simultaneously with the vertical integration of the major European tour operators. Their portfolios include not only a

Table 6.2 Market share of Germany's and the UK's five largest tour operators, 2003

Germany's five largest tour operators	Market share for 2003
TUI	28.7%
Thomas Cook	22.3%
Rewe Touristik	17.0%
Alltours	7.2%
Öger	4.3%
Market share of top 5 operators	*79.5%*
Total revenue of Germany's large tour operators in 2003	*14 billion Euros*

UK's five largest air travel organisers	Market share for 2003
TUI UK (former Thomson)	16.9%
MyTravel (former Airtours) incl. Direct Holidays and Panorama Holiday Group	14.4%
First Choice (former Owners Abroad)	10.2%
Thomas Cook	9.0%
Trailfinders	1.9%
Market share of top 5 operators	*52.4%*
Total number of passengers carried on Air Travel Organisers' Licences in 2003	*27,800,000*

Source: Gruner + Jahr 2004, CAA 2004.

number of tour operators in several European countries but also suppliers of inclusive tour components – such as hotel chains, cruise ships and charter airlines – as well as retail networks in the form of travel agency chains. Among the international hotel brands owned by tour operators are Thomas Cook's Iberostar, MyTravel's Sunwing and Aqua Sol as well as Rewe's Calimera Aktivhotels, PrimaSol and LTI International Hotels.

Thomas Cook also owns several tour operator brands in Germany (Neckermann, Air Marin, Terramar, Aldiana, Kreutzer Reisen, Fischer Touristik, Öger Tours), Belgium (Sunsnacks), the UK (Thomas Cook, JMC, Neilson, Club 18–30) and France (Havas Voyage) as well as the airlines Condor, JMC Airlines and Sun Express. Its holdings include more than 2,000 retail travel agencies under the Neckermann, alpha, Holiday Land, Karstadt, Reise Quelle, Lufthansa City Center and Thomas Cook brands. Of similar proportions is the portfolio of MyTravel with brands and subsidiaries in Britain (Airtours Holidays, Aspro, Direct Holidays, Panorama, Bridge, Tradewinds, Manos), Scandinavia (Vingresor, Always, Saga, Globetrotter, Spies, Ombro, Premiair, Tjaereborg), France (Sunair, Voyage Conseil), Netherlands (Vakantie Toppers, Sunair, Marysol, Unitravel), an expansive network of companies in the USA as well as airline and cruise ship operations. However, the largest portfolio of tourism-related companies is the one owned and operated by TUI. The dimension of this portfolio is such that it directly affects entire destination regions and industries such as Greece and the country's hotel sector. The range of TUI's tourism-related activities will be presented in more detail below.

The accelerated trans-border growth of major European tour operators resulted in strong oligopolistic and oligopsonistic phenomena (Bastakis et al. 2004: 153). Under this situation, hotels of Mediterranean resorts are faced with powerful conglomerates that control the tourist flows not just of one but of several of their major European source markets. This control is exercised through the distribution channels as well as the airlift capacity on charter flights.

Recent developments affecting competition in the inclusive tour market

However, recent counterbalancing influences – i.e. Internet-based retail and the advent of low-cost airlines – are putting pressure on the market structure for inclusive tours that has been in a state of balance for decades. Tour operators dominated the European southbound holiday market because of the advantages of inclusive tours versus self-organised holidays, i.e. low cost, convenience and security (Middleton 1988: 275). Tour operators are achieving volume discounts on room rates and a low cost per passenger on their charter flights due to limited overhead costs and high load factors. These savings are passed on to customers.

The very same advantages – low cost and ease of booking – are now offered by online travel agencies and low-cost carriers, as well. Internet-based retail, for instance, is profiting from:

- Low-priced travel components (such as accommodation, as hotels are unloading excess and highly perishable room capacity through the Internet by offering high discounts);
- Lower cost structure as compared to conventional inclusive tour distribution (higher degree of automation, no brochure production, no city centre office rent, no travel agency commission etc.);
- User-friendly interfaces;
- Dynamic packaging allowing travellers to tailor their package of travel services to their individual needs while still enjoying low prices (Karayanni 2004).

Low-cost carriers have emerged as competitors not only to full-service carriers but also to charter flights due to their low prices. The consumer now has the choice of either buying an inclusive tour for the next summer holidays or combining a flight on a low-cost carrier with discounted accommodation arranged over the Internet. The latter option of organising a holiday trip in a 'do-it-yourself' fashion lacks the product assurance of inclusive tours such as the consumer protection provisions of the ATOL plan in the UK. This deficiency, however, did not affect the recent rapid growth of holiday trips using low-cost carriers.

The expansion of low-cost carriers' networks will potentially limit the dependency of Mediterranean-based resort hotels on charter flights operated by tour operators. It was the increase in airlift capacity on charter flights during the 1960s, 1970s and 1980s that led to the present size of the Mediterranean hotel sector. The case of Greece showcases the extent of a destination's dependency on charter flights operated by tour operators, as 75 per cent of all West Europeans – and 58 per cent of all international tourists – vacationing in Greece arrive on charter flights. According to official statistics by the Greek National Tourism Organisation and the Hellenic National Statistical Service, 78 per cent of Germans, 77 per cent of Austrians, 65 per cent of Belgians, 84 per cent of Britons and 94 per cent of Swedes visiting Greece in 2000 arrived on a charter flight (Koutoulas 2004). Tourists from Eastern Europe and overseas use charter flights on a much smaller scale.

Despite the recent commencement of several Greece-bound low-fare air services, the country still lacks the density of flights on low-cost carriers that has been witnessed in the case of Western Mediterranean countries such as Spain and Italy. The 9/11 New York attacks and the subsequent political crises as well as the weak economy in most major European source markets led to a decrease in Mediterranean-bound tourism in recent years. For instance, total inclusive tour sales in Germany for the 2002/2003 season were 4.2 per cent lower than in the previous year, with packages to Mediterranean resorts being down by 6.7 per cent (Gruner + Jahr 2003: 4; Gruner + Jahr 2004: 2 and 5), while the British market posted a 2.3 per cent loss over the same period (CAA 2004: 2). However, at the same time the online travel agencies such as Expedia, Lastminute.com and Travelocity are rapidly gaining market share at the expense of tour operators. Expedia, for instance, quadrupled its air passengers within a year, reaching 286,000 departures from the UK in 2003 (ibid.: 4).

Some of the major tour operators were quick to react to these environmental changes. TUI, for instance, has transformed some of its airlines into low-cost carriers and has created state-of-the-art Internet platforms with dynamic packaging capabilities.

Forms of competition faced by resort hotels

From the viewpoint of a Mediterranean-based, mass market-oriented resort hotel, competition takes the following forms:

* Competition from hotels and other accommodation providers located in the same destination;
* Competition from other destinations offering similar tourist products. ('The net result of these developments in tourism for the mass markets has been the establishment of destinations for particular market segments which, in all but their location, are very often remarkably similar. [. . .] These "identikit"

destinations are the result of comprehensive market research amongst various generating markets to find products with guaranteed mass demand.' Holloway 1994: 29–30);

- Competition from other members of the production and distribution chain (e.g. tour operators, travel retailers) in regard to market influence. ('The different and in many cases opposing nature, orientation and interest of all the key players provokes and maintains a complex system of co-operation, competition, conflict and inter-dependency between and among them.' Bastakis et al. 2004: 158).

Goodall and Bergsma (1990: 173) point out that there is near perfect substitutability between summer sun destinations on the inclusive tour market, a fact that has put enormous pressure on room rates offered by hotels in these destinations. However, Mediterranean resort hotels are not competing only with other hotels and destinations, but also with their wholesalers, who exercise their market power to dictate prices and product specifications. Tour operators are in the position to influence the destination choice of their Mediterranean-bound clients (Bastakis et al. 2004: 164), considering that hotels located in 'identikit' destinations and offering standardised services and facilities can easily be substituted. Thus, tour operators can manipulate the competition among individual hotels and entire destinations belonging to the same competitive set. It is, after all, the tour operators that control each destination's airlift capacity as well as the inclusive tour prices offered in the source markets. The focus of mass-market tour operators on low prices is dictated by the underlying characteristics of the inclusive tour market, considering that the market volume is directly connected to the price level of inclusive tours (Figure 6.1):

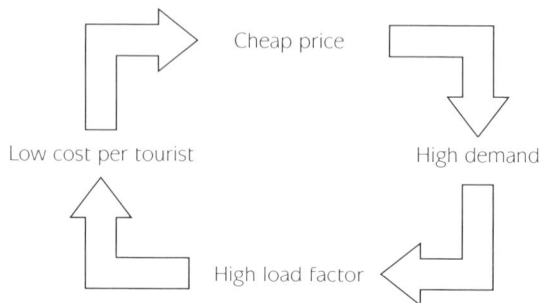

Figure 6.1 The relationship between cost, price and demand in tourism
Source: Holloway (1994: 35).

While there are many factors which motivate people to travel abroad, the most important factor will be the relative cost, compared with their income.

As greater demand also leads to lower prices, with transport and accommodation costs falling for each additional person booked, there is a direct relationship between cost, price and demand. This helps to explain the vicious price wars in the travel industry, designed to capture market share and increase numbers, especially during the difficult years of the late 1980s and early 1990s, when Britain was experiencing a severe recession.

(Holloway 1994: 35)

Hotels as well as other providers of inclusive tour components are therefore under constant pressure to lower costs.

The production and distribution system of inclusive tours has been in a state of relative stability for decades and has secured an income for all participants. Under these conditions, many resort hotels largely outsourced the marketing function to the tour operators, leaving it to the latter to sell the available room capacity. Now most of them are not prepared, or effectively, to handle two new trends:

• Decreasing business volume from tour operators combined with increasing pressure to lower prices;
• New business development opportunities through online marketing platforms.

These developments make it easier for hotels to directly sell to consumers through their own websites or through third-party online platforms, thus circumventing the traditional distribution channel, i.e. tour operators and retail travel agencies. This will increase the market power of hotels and help strengthen their competitive position, considering that they can achieve higher room rates and diversify their customer base. The prerequisite, however, is that the resort hotels will acquire the needed marketing skills to become increasingly self-reliant in the international marketplace.

TUI and Mediterranean-bound holiday travel: the case of Greece

The expansion of TUI's portfolio of companies

The current portfolio of TUI is the result of numerous horizontal and vertical expansion moves since 1968, the year the company was formed through the merger of the German tour operators Touropa, Scharnow-Reisen, Hummel Reise and Dr Tigges-Fahrten. By adding new brands and product lines to its range of inclusive tours and by expanding to other countries, TUI emerged in the 1990s as the largest among Europe's tour operators.

The acquisition of Thomson of Britain and Nouvelles Frontières of France in 2000 further strengthened TUI's position as the leading European holiday travel provider. Its portfolio of tour operators includes, among others, Arke of the Netherlands, Fritidresor of Sweden, Gulet of Austria, Scan Holidays of Poland,

Sunjets and JetAir of Belgium as well as Finnmatkat of Finland. TUI recently expanded to Russia and China, as well. This horizontal expansion resulted in dozens of inclusive tour brands being offered throughout Europe, with package sales exceeding 18 million in just twelve of TUI's major European source markets in 2003 (TUI 2004a). Some 7.1 million inclusive tours were sold in Germany, 4.5 million in Britain and 1.6 million in France, to name TUI's top three markets.

The company also expanded vertically both into the production of inclusive tour components and retail, thus allowing TUI to fully control the production and distribution chain of its inclusive tours. This expansion led to the ownership of hundreds of tourism businesses located throughout the world. Tourism-related activities of TUI (excluding its non-tourism activities) resulted in revenues of 12.7 billion Euros (representing 65 per cent of the conglomerate's turnover) and the employment of 52,000 people in 2003 (ibid.). The portfolio of TUI presently comprises: tour operator brands, retail travel agency chains, incoming agencies and tour operators operating in the destination areas, airlines, hotel chains and cruise ships. More specifically, TUI fully or partially owns 84 tour operators in 18 countries as well as 3,600 retail travel agencies in 16 countries, the latter operating under several brands such as First Reisebüro, Hapag-Lloyd Reisebüro and TUI ReiseCenter in Germany as well as Lunn Poly, Callers-Pegasus, Sibbald Travel, The Travel House and Team Lincoln in the UK. TUI also maintains a network of incoming agencies in 33 countries, with 21 of them being owned by the conglomerate. These 21 receptive operators handled 8.7 million TUI customers in 2003. Additionally, TUI is a major shareholder of TQ3, a global network of 1,200 travel agencies in 80 countries specialising in business travel management.

TUI's subsidiary TUI Airline Management operates seven carriers, i.e. Germany based Hapag-Lloyd Flug and Hapag-Lloyd-Express, Britannia Airways UK, Britannia Airways Nordic, TUI Airlines Belgium, the French carrier Corsair and the British airline Thomsonfly.com. TUI's seven airlines transported nearly 18 million passengers on their 104 aircraft in 2003. Their combined passenger kilometres make TUI the world's 17th largest airline (TUI 2004b). TUI also operates twelve hotel chains, with its TUI Hotels & Resorts division ranking as the world's 13th largest hotel group totalling 290 hotels and 76,000 rooms (Wolchuk and Scoviak 2004). These accommodations, mainly concentrated in the resort areas of the Mediterranean, achieved an average occupancy rate of 80 per cent in 2003 (Rheinsberg 2004). TUI's portfolio comprises the following hotel brands: RIU, Grecotel, Grupotel, Iberotel, Dorfhotel, Robinson, Magic Life, Paladien, Atlantica, Gran Resort Hotels, Sol y Mar and Nordotel. Finally, the TUI conglomerate includes Hapag-Lloyd Kreuzfahrten, the cruise division comprising four ships.

Greece-bound tourism traffic controlled by TUI

The Mediterranean countries are the most popular holiday destinations for TUI customers from throughout Europe. These destinations sometimes secure more than 80 per cent of TUI's clientele as in the case of holidaymakers from the UK, Ireland and the Nordic countries (TUI 2004a). Greece is among the top five holiday destinations in all of the twelve European countries under review with a weighted average market share of 14 per cent, being second in popularity only to Spain and ahead of Turkey, Italy and Cyprus (ibid.). Greece achieved its highest market share among TUI customers from the Nordic countries with 32 per cent, from Austria with 25 per cent and from Switzerland with 17 per cent. In total, 2.585 million tourists from these twelve countries visited Greece on an inclusive tour by TUI (Table 6.3). The 2.585 million TUI customers represent 29 per cent of the total tourist arrivals from the twelve countries mentioned in Table 6.3. For instance, of the 2.3 million Germans visiting Greece, 923,000 – or 41 per cent – travelled on an inclusive tour by TUI. TUI's share is even higher in the case of Austria (43 per cent of all tourists visiting Greece) and Ireland (71 per cent).

Greek hoteliers are facing a situation of oligopsony, with just one company supplying 29 per cent of their clientele from the twelve largest source markets or 17 per cent of all tourist arrivals. The dependency is more acute in mass market-oriented resort destinations (such as the islands of Crete, Rhodes and Corfu), with TUI providing an even higher share of tourists and airlift capacity to fly them into the country.

Table 6.3 Tourist arrivals in Greece, 2003: TUI customers and overall market

Origin countries	TUI customers	Total tourist arrivals	TUI customers as % of total tourist arrivals
Austria	190,000	443,595	43%
Belgium	132,000	384,793	34%
UK	630,000	3,008,382	21%
France	112,000	714,821	16%
Germany	923,000	2,267,063	41%
Switzerland	32,000	266,246	12%
Ireland	50,000	69,961	71%
Netherlands	132,000	635,882	21%
Nordic Countries (Denmark, Norway, Sweden, Finland)	384,000	1,020,805	38%
Subtotal 12 countries	*2,585,000*	*8,811,548*	*29%*
Tourist arrivals from European countries	–	*13,072,924*	*(20%)*
Total tourist arrivals	–	*14,784,560*	*(17%)*

Source: TUI 2004a, Hellenic National Statistical Service.

As part of its vertical expansion strategy, TUI has built a significant presence in Greece through several subsidiaries. TUI's Greek hotel portfolio comprises five of the twelve hotel brands belonging to TUI Hotels and Resorts, i.e. Grecotel, Robinson Club, Magic Life, Paladien and Atlantica Hotels. The largest TUI-controlled hotel chain is Grecotel, a hotel management company founded jointly by TUI and the Daskalantonakis family in 1981. Grecotel developed to become the leading Greek hotel brand totalling 31 units both in urban and resort destination with a total room count of 6,626. TUI holds equity in some of Grecotel-managed properties.

Another TUI subsidiary, Robinson Club, was among the first international hotel brands to enter Greece. Robinson presently operates three all-inclusive resorts. The acquisition of the Austrian tour operator Gulet and the French company Nouvelles Frontières secured TUI six additional resort hotels operating under the Magic Life and Paladien brands, respectively. Finally, TUI's 50 per cent stake in Cyprus-based Atlantica Hotels expanded its portfolio by three resort hotels on Rhodes. These 43 hotels comprising 9,960 rooms established TUI Hotels and Resorts as the country's largest hotel operator, controlling 0.5 per cent of all Greek hotels but 2.9 per cent of the total room inventory due to the larger-than-average size of its hotels. In addition to managing hotels, TUI also owns the largest incoming tour operator of Greece. TUI Hellas comprises a network of 22 offices located in the country's main destination areas. Founded in 1971 as Airtour Greece, the company handled 1.3 million tourists or half of TUI's total Greece-bound customers in 2003 (TUI 2004a).

Greek resort hotel survey

The other side of the equation in the inclusive tour market comprises the resort hotels acting as suppliers of tour operators. Mediterranean resort hotels are operating under a state of oligopsony in a marketplace strictly controlled by TUI and the other big players. The enormous market power of the major tour operators strongly affects the way these hotels conduct their business.

As has been previously shown, Greek incoming tourism is especially dominated by TUI and other large tour operators. These companies on the one hand secure a large flow of traffic to the country's resort hotels, but on the other hand dictate low prices and other unfavourable conditions to their suppliers. How do Greek resort hotels evaluate their cooperation with TUI and the other major tour operators? How do they perceive the advantages and disadvantages of operating in a marketplace that they do not control? The author conducted the survey presented below in order to collect primary data describing this relationship in more detail, thus shedding light on how Greek resort hotels are affected by the market influence of the large operators (Koutoulas 2005).

Methodology

An e-mail survey was conducted during the period of January–February 2005 among Greek resort hotels. The aim of the survey was to explore the relationship between resort hotels and tour operators as seen from the hotels' point of view. A 16-item questionnaire was used to collect the required data. The questionnaire comprised 14 closed questions and two open-ended ones.

The questionnaire was sent by e-mail to a sample of 2,103 hotels (out of a total of 6,373 hotels) located in resort areas of Greece in January 2005. The e-mail addresses were taken from an existing hotel database. The hotels of the sample represent half of the total room capacity in the respective areas. The questionnaire was actually received by 1,648 businesses, as there were 455 invalid e-mail addresses in the hotel database. The e-mails with the questionnaire were addressed to general managers. An introductory text stated the purpose of the survey and explained how the data provided would be used. An attached MS Word file contained the questionnaire. Respondents had the choice of returning the completed questionnaire by e-mail or by fax. The targeted response rate was 5 per cent based on the author's previous experience in similar surveys among Greek hotels (Koutoulas 2003a). The actual response rate was 6.1 per cent, with 101 out of 1,648 hotels returning completed and usable questionnaires until the cut-off date in February 2005.

Research findings

In line with experience from previous surveys, it was the larger and more upscale hotels that had a higher response rate to the present survey. This explains the significantly larger average size of the responding hotels (106 rooms) as compared to the total population of hotels located in the resort areas of Greece (41 rooms). Four and five-star hotels represent 43 per cent of the respondents but only 11.7 per cent of the total population in the selected areas.

Most respondents are from Crete and the Aegean Islands with 38 per cent and 37 per cent of the sample, respectively. The Ionian Islands and the resort areas of mainland Greece are represented with 13 per cent each. 16 per cent are part of hotel chains.

The business mix of Greek resort hotels in Table 6.5 reveals their dependency on the inclusive tour market, as tour operators supplied 60 per cent of the surveyed hotels' clientele in 2004. Another 9.7 per cent are travellers booking directly through travel agencies, while participants of meetings and incentive travel programmes constitute just 1.8 per cent of all customers (with 20 per cent being the maximum share in the sample). Independent travellers account for 22.1 per cent. Other client categories average 6.4 per cent, and include, among others, repeat guests, social tourism groups and Internet bookings. Some hotels are quite focused on these market segments, securing, for instance, up to 100 per cent of

Table 6.4 Size, category and location of hotels participating in the survey

Hotel category	5 stars	4 stars	3 stars	2 stars	1 star	All participating hotels
No. of participating hotels	7	36	20	32	6	**101**
Location:						
Crete	*3*	*18*	*3*	*11*	*3*	**38**
Aegean Islands	*–*	*12*	*12*	*11*	*2*	**37**
Ionian Islands	*2*	*3*	*1*	*7*	*–*	**13**
Mainland	*2*	*3*	*4*	*3*	*1*	**13**
Total no. of rooms	2,209	5,687	1,484	1,165	192	**10,737**
Average no. of rooms	316	158	74	36	32	**106**
Hotels of the sample that are members of hotel chains	*4*	*10*	*2*	*0*	*0*	**16**

their clientele through social tourism programmes, up to 20 per cent through Internet bookings and up to 65 per cent through repeat business.

Of the sample's 101 hotels, eight work exclusively with tour operators, while 14 do not accept tour operator clients at all. Five hotels accepted only independent travellers in 2004. When calculating the average business mix only for those hotels accepting tour operator clients, then the share of tour operator-generated business reaches 69.9 per cent. The highest degree of dependency on tour operator-generated business is registered in the case of one-, four- and five-star hotels, with up to 76.5 per cent of all guests being tour operator customers in the case of four-star hotels. Above-average travel agency bookings characterise three-star hotels with 19.6 per cent, whereas five-star hotels are the only ones to secure a significant amount of business through the meetings and incentive travel market (9.4 per cent of all customers). Three out of ten guests of one- and two-star hotels are independent travellers, with two-star hotels securing another 11.6 per cent of customers from other market segments.

Table 6.5 also reveals some regional differences among Greek resort hotels. For instance, Cretan hotels depend to a much larger extent on tour operator-generated business (78 per cent of all customers) as opposed to just 42 per cent of properties located on the Aegean islands. The share of independent travellers among the clientele of Cretan hotels is only a third of the one secured by hotels in other resort areas. Properties belonging to hotel chains also have a significantly higher dependency on the inclusive tour market with 71.9 per cent of their clientele coming through tour operators. The share of independent travellers is less than 10 per cent as is also the case with travel agency bookings.

Table 6.5 Business mix of hotels participating in the survey for the year 2004

	N	Tour operator clients	Clients booking through travel agencies	Meeting and incentive travel participants	Independent travellers	Other hotel clients	Total
All hotels of the sample	**99**	**60.0%**	**9.7%**	**1.8%**	**22.1%**	**6.4%**	**100%**
5-star	7	66.3%	10.0%	9.4%	10.1%	4.1%	100%
4-star	34	76.5%	6.9%	1.0%	11.7%	3.9%	100%
3-star	20	49.6%	19.6%	2.1%	23.7%	5.1%	100%
2-star	32	45.8%	8.1%	1.2%	33.4%	11.6%	100%
1-star	6	69.5%	1.7%	0%	28.8%	0%	100%
Crete	37	78.0%	6.7%	1.9%	9.5%	3.9%	100%
Aegean Islands	36	42.0%	14.0%	1.7%	32.1%	10.2%	100%
Ionian Islands	13	61.2%	5.8%	1.6%	24.8%	6.5%	100%
Mainland	13	57.3%	10.5%	2.0%	27.3%	2.8%	100%
Accepting tour operator clients	85	69.9%	8.3%	1.7%	15.0%	5.2%	100%
Belonging to hotel chains	15	71.9%	9.5%	4.2%	9.9%	4.5%	100%

N: number of hotels completing the respective question of the questionnaire (some of the respondents did not complete all questions).

The main nationalities of the sample's hotel guests are presented in Table 6.6. The leading nationality is Greeks with 23.6 per cent of all hotel guests, followed by Germans (19.6 per cent), Britons (16.5 per cent) and citizens of the Nordic countries (8 per cent). Other major source markets include the French, the Belgians, the Dutch, the Austrians, the Swiss, the Italians, the East Europeans, the Turks and the Americans.

It is interesting to compare the preferences of each nationality according to hotel category and region with its overall average. Greeks, for instance, favour mid-scale and economy hotels, with Germans preferring four-star hotels but avoiding two-star hotels. Britons, on the other hand, tend to go either to the high or to the low end of the hotel supply. Nordic travellers frequent budget accommodation, while French show a clear preference for four-star hotels. It is also worth mentioning the preference of East Europeans for luxury accommodation. Greeks command only a small share among the clientele of Cretan hotels (9.7 per cent) as opposed to other regions. Germans have a strong presence on Crete (24.2 per cent) and the mainland (31.9 per cent), with Britons commanding a 41.5 per cent share among hotel guests of the Ionian Islands. Cretan hotels also have a significant number of Nordic and French guests.

The hotels of the sample achieved an average room occupancy rate of 68.7 per cent in 2004 (see Table 6.7). Four-star hotels had the highest occupancy with 72.5 per cent. The sampled hotels from the Aegean Islands trailed the others with a low 61 per cent occupancy in 2004, while Cretan hotels topped the list with 74.4 per cent. Table 6.7 also includes data on room rates charged by the sample hotels in 2004. The room rate charged to tour operators averages 59.60 Euros and ranges from a minimum of 9 Euros to a maximum of 650 Euros. Five-star hotels command a high average room rate of 224.40 Euros, however, when excluding the maximum value of 650 Euros, the average drops to 118 Euros.

The room rate charged to individual guests in 2004 averages 71.96 Euros and ranges from a minimum of 15 Euros to a maximum of 872 Euros. Five-star hotels command a high average room rate of 301.40 Euros, however, when excluding the maximum value of 872 Euros, the average drops to 158.75 Euros. Room rates charged to tour operators are on average 25.7 per cent lower than the ones charged to individual guests and travel agencies. The maximum discount among the sample's hotels is 67.1 per cent. The lower the hotel category, the higher the room rate discount provided to tour operators (up to 35.8 per cent for one-star hotels). Members of hotel chains – predominantly upscale hotels – achieved better-than-average results in 2004 according to the findings presented in Table 6.7. Their occupancy reached 72.5 per cent, while room rates charged to both tour operators and individual guests were twice as high than the sample's average.

Hotel managers were asked how tour operator-generated business developed over the last three years. Only one-third (34.8 per cent) of the sample's hotels mentioned that the room rates they charge to tour operators were actually raised (see Table 6.8). The average increase was 5.8 per cent during the period

Table 6.6 Main nationalities of hotel guests for the year 2004

	N	Greeks	Germans	Britons	Nordic	French	Belgians +Dutch	Austrians + Swiss	Italians	East Europe + Turks	Americans
All hotels	**94**	**23.6%**	**19.6%**	**16.5%**	**8.0%**	**6.6%**	**5.6%**	**2.7%**	**2.6%**	**2.6%**	**1.4%**
5-star	6	14.2%	21.8%	18.7%	3.3%	2.5%	2.2%	3.5%	1.7%	10.3%	0.7%
4-star	34	14.4%	25.8%	16.6%	1.5%	12.6%	8.9%	3.5%	2.1%	1.3%	0.6%
3-star	19	30.2%	19.1%	14.6%	5.3%	3.8%	4.5%	1.3%	5.8%	3.5%	1.8%
2-star	29	33.1%	12.6%	16.1%	17.0%	3.5%	1.7%	2.7%	1.9%	2.3%	2.6%
1-star	6	19.2%	18.5%	21.0%	14.3%	0.3%	12.7%	2.5%	0.0%	0.8%	0.3%
Crete	36	9.7%	24.2%	16.4%	13.3%	12.9%	5.9%	2.3%	1.5%	2.0%	1.5%
Aegean Islands	37	34.8%	14.5%	10.9%	6.1%	4.2%	4.5%	3.8%	4.8%	0.8%	2.2%
Ionian Islands	10	29.5%	9.0%	41.5%	4.0%	0.0%	5.3%	2.7%	0.5%	2.2%	0.0%
Mainland	11	26.6%	31.9%	12.6%	0.5%	0.2%	8.4%	0.8%	1.1%	11.1%	0.0%

N: number of hotels completing the respective question of the questionnaire (some of the respondents did not complete all questions).

Table 6.7 Occupancy and average room rates for the year 2004

	N	Average room occupancy for the year 2004	N	Average room rate charged to tour operators in 2004 (in Euros)	N	Average room rate charged to individual guests and travel agencies in 2004 (in Euros)	N	Average room rate discount for tour operators
All hotels of the sample	*97*	*68.7%*	*85*	*59.60*	*91*	*71.96*	*83*	*25.7%*
5-star	6	69.7%	5	224.40	5	301.40	5	25.0%
4-star	36	72.5%	34	56.12	34	70.38	33	20.5%
3-star	20	66.0%	18	42.67	18	58.72	17	25.9%
2-star	31	65.9%	24	30.79	29	47.45	24	31.1%
1-star	4	67.8%	4	26.00	5	43.00	4	35.8%
Crete	37	74.4%	34	64.88	34	86.50	32	24.9%
Aegean Islands	36	61.0%	32	46.66	36	63.61	32	25.5%
Ionian Islands	12	70.9%	10	52.80	11	66.09	10	29.1%
Mainland	12	72.0%	9	46.00	10	59.00	9	25.3%
Belonging to chains	15	72.5%	15	106.30	14	144.60	14	21.1%
Working with TUI	40	71.5%	39	70.00	39	92.70	39	25.3%
Working with Thomas Cook	24	74.0%	24	54.92	24	74.33	24	25.7%
Working with Rewe	13	76.3%	11	50.73	11	71.18	11	29.0%
Working with MyTravel	10	76.7%	9	66.89	8	89.75	8	18.9%

N: number of hotels completing the respective question of the questionnaire (some of the respondents did not complete all questions).
Comment: The average room rate discount for tour operators (see last column above) is calculated by dividing the difference between the room rate charged to individual guests and travel agencies and the room rate charged to tour operators with the room rate charged to individual guests and travel agencies.

2002–2004, i.e. below inflation. 44.6 per cent kept the same prices, while 20.6 per cent of the surveyed hotels had to lower their room rates by an average 9.9 per cent. Almost all five-star and half of the four-star hotels managed to increase their room rates, while Cretan and mainland hotels were also more likely to increase their room rates than the average hotel. It seems that one- and two-star hotels as well as the ones based on the Ionian Islands are in the worst position, with about 40 per cent being forced to lower the room rates provided to tour operators. 23.9 per cent of the sample's businesses witnessed an increase in tour operator-generated traffic over the last three years. The average increase in customers was 18.3 per cent during the period 2002–2004, with four- and five-star hotels as well as hotels from Crete and the mainland performing better than the average hotel. However, 31.5 per cent of surveyed hotels saw a drop in inclusive tour travellers averaging 22.4 per cent. Low-category accommodation and hotels from the Aegean Islands lost the most in tour operator business.

As is evident from the data of Table 6.8, the surveyed Greek resort hotels are facing an unfavourable balance in their cooperation with tour operators. The tour operator-controlled distribution system represents a shrinking market both in terms of visitor volume and income for most of the hotels. Members of hotel chains are in a much more favourable position than the sample's average hotel, with twice as many hotel chain members – or 66.7 per cent – posting an increase in the room rates charged to tour operators. However, tour operator-generated business is shrinking faster in the case of hotel chain members.

Despite the shrinking inclusive tour market, Greek hoteliers seem to be rather optimistic in their expectations regarding tour operator-generated traffic (see Table 6.9). Only 14.8 per cent of the surveyed resort hotels expect that tour operator clients staying with them over the next years will decrease. 42 per cent are counting on an increase, while 43.2 per cent are forecasting a steady flow of tour operator-generated business. Most optimistic are members of hotel chains as well as five-star hotels with 62.5 per cent and 57.1 per cent expecting an increase in inclusive tour business, respectively. One-star and two-star hotels tend to be more pessimistic, with 33.3 per cent and 22.2 per cent expecting a decrease, respectively. Hotel managers were asked whether tour operators usually request lower prices, higher quality in services and facilities provided or other concessions. The large majority of Greek hotel resorts – or 91.6 per cent – are faced with a demand for lower prices. Only 37.9 per cent of hotels were asked by tour operators to provide services and facilities of a higher quality. Among other concessions demanded, the request for added value offers was mentioned by 3.2 per cent of surveyed hotels. This finding is an indication of the commoditisation of inclusive tours to the Mediterranean and the constant pressure put on accommodation providers to lower costs.

Some 82 of the sample's 101 hotels provided specific details on the tour operators they work with. Over half of them – 51.2 per cent – accept guests from TUI and its subsidiaries such as Thomson and Nouvelles Frontières (Table 6.10).

Table 6.8 Variations of tour operator-generated business over the last three years

	Share of hotels mentioning that room rates charged to tour operators over the last three years:				Share of hotels mentioning that number of customers from tour operators over the last three years:			
	N	Increased	Remained steady	Decreased	N	Increased	Remained steady	Decreased
All hotels	92	34.8% (average increase of 5.8%)	44.6%	20.6% (average decrease of 9.9%)	92	23.9% (average increase of 18.3%)	44.6%	31.5% (average decrease of 22.4%)
5-star	7	85.7%	14.3%	0.0%	7	42.9%	28.6%	28.6%
4-star	35	48.6%	40.0%	11.4%	35	28.6%	48.6%	22.9%
3-star	18	22.2%	61.1%	16.7%	18	22.2%	38.9%	38.9%
2-star	27	14.8%	48.1%	37.0%	27	18.5%	44.4%	37.0%
1-star	5	20.0%	40.0%	40.0%	5	0.0%	60.0%	40.0%
Crete	36	38.9%	38.9%	22.2%	36	30.6%	44.4%	25.0%
Aegean Islands	32	31.3%	56.3%	12.5%	32	18.8%	43.8%	37.5%
Ionian Islands	12	25.0%	33.3%	41.7%	12	8.3%	58.3%	33.3%
Mainland	12	41.7%	41.7%	16.7%	12	33.3%	33.3%	33.3%
Belonging to chains	15	66.7%	20.0%	13.3%	16	25.0%	37.5%	37.5%
Working with TUI	41	46.4%	39.0%	14.6%	41	31.7%	43.9%	24.4%
Working with Thomas Cook	24	54.2%	25.0%	20.8%	23	34.8%	34.8%	30.4%
Working with Rewe	13	53.8%	23.1%	23.1%	12	50.0%	33.3%	16.7%
Working with MyTravel	10	10.0%	60.0%	30.0%	10	10.0%	70.0%	20.0%

N: number of hotels completing the respective question of the questionnaire (some of the respondents did not complete all questions).

Table 6.9 Expectations regarding tour operator-generated business and requirements of tour operators towards hotels

	Share of hotels mentioning that they expect their tour operator clients over the next years to:				Tour operators usually request from hoteliers to provide:*			
	N	Increase	Remain steady	Decrease	N	Lower prices	Higher quality	Added value
All hotels	88	42.0%	43.2%	14.8%	95	91.6%	37.9%	3.2%
5-star	7	57.1%	28.6%	14.3%	7	100.0%	14.3%	0.0%
4-star	35	48.6%	40.0%	11.4%	35	91.4%	45.7%	0.0%
3-star	16	31.3%	62.5%	6.3%	17	100.0%	35.3%	5.9%
2-star	27	37.0%	40.7%	22.2%	29	86.2%	41.4%	6.9%
1-star	3	33.3%	33.3%	33.3%	6	100.0%	16.7%	0.0%
Crete	35	40.0%	54.3%	5.7%	35	88.6%	40.0%	0.0%
Aegean Islands	29	48.3%	37.9%	13.8%	34	94.1%	35.3%	2.9%
Ionian Islands	12	25.0%	25.0%	50.0%	13	92.3%	46.2%	0.0%
Mainland	12	50.0%	41.7%	8.3%	12	100.0%	33.3%	16.7%
Belonging to chains	16	62.5%	31.3%	6.3%	16	93.8%	43.8%	6.3%
Working with TUI	41	46.3%	39.1%	14.6%	–	–	–	–
Working with Thomas Cook	23	30.4%	65.2%	4.4%	–	–	–	–
Working with Rewe	13	38.5%	46.1%	15.4%	–	–	–	–
Working with MyTravel	10	40.0%	50.0%	10.0%	–	–	–	–

N: number of hotels completing the respective question of the questionnaire (some of the respondents did not complete all questions).
* Multiple replies.

Table 6.10 Tour operators contributing most customers

Tour operator	Share of surveyed hotels cooperating with the tour operator	Average contribution of the tour operator to overall overnight stays in 2004	Source markets
TUI (incl. Thomson and Nouvelles Frontières)	51.2%	30%	Germany, UK, France, Austria, Netherlands, Belgium, Nordic countries, Poland
Thomas Cook	29.3%	34%	Germany, Netherlands, UK, Belgium, Austria, Hungary, France
Rewe (incl. ITS and LTU)	15.9%	25%	Germany, Austria
MyTravel	12.2%	55%	UK, Nordic countries
Alltours	9.8%	30%	Germany
Apollo	8.5%	38%	Nordic countries
First Choice	7.3%	29%	UK
Attika Reisen	4.9%	24%	Germany
Vacances Heliades	4.9%	23%	France
Med Hotels	4.9%	27%	UK
Esco	3.7%	12%	Switzerland
Olympic Holidays	3.7%	47%	UK
Kuoni	3.7%	9%	Switzerland
Alpitour	2.4%	40%	Italy
Columbus Viaggi	2.4%	18%	Italy
Fram	2.4%	65%	France
Helvetic Tours	2.4%	20%	Switzerland
Reiseladen	2.4%	15%	Austria
N			*82*

N: number of hotels completing the respective question of the questionnaire (some respondents did not complete all questions).

The average contribution of TUI's tour operators to the total overnight stays of the surveyed hotels in 2004 was 30 per cent. The second most frequently mentioned tour operator is Thomas Cook (by 29.3 per cent of the sample's hotels) contributing on average 34 per cent of total overnight stays, followed by another German company, Rewe, being mentioned by 15.9 per cent of the hotels. MyTravel of UK, Alltours of Germany and Apollo of Sweden occupy places four to six on the list.

The hotels surveyed were asked to evaluate their cooperation with tour operators (Table 6.11). The main advantage of working with tour operators is that hotels secure a large part of their guests that way, as was mentioned by 68.3 per cent of participating resort hotels. Other advantages include securing significant traffic during the shoulder and low season (mentioned by 56.4 per cent of the sample) and getting payment in a timely fashion (47.5 per cent). Only 11.9 per cent of respondents are satisfied with the room rates they charge to tour operators. Five- and four-star hotels as well as hotels on Crete have a far more positive evaluation of their cooperation with tour operators than do other hotels.

The main disadvantage of working with tour operators is the constant pressure to lower room rates, as was mentioned by 76.2 per cent of surveyed hotels. 48.5 per cent of respondents feel that tour operators are channelling their clients to other destinations, 33.7 per cent have had trouble in getting paid on time, while only 6.9 per cent complain that they get just a small number of clients through tour operators. Mid-scale and economy hotels are most critical in regard to their cooperation with tour operators.

Half of the hotels participating in the survey posted a profit in 2004, while 26 per cent had a loss (Table 6.12). One-, four- and five-star properties fared the best among the sample's hotels. However, hotels based on the Aegean Islands achieved the worst results, with 43.3 per cent making a loss last year.

There are significant differences between the sample's average hotel and the hotels belonging to chains as well as of those working with the four major tour operators. Respondents belonging to hotel chains secured 71.9 per cent of their customers through tour operators in 2004, thus having a higher-than-average dependency on the inclusive tour market as compared to just 60 per cent for the total sample (Table 6.5). Nevertheless, these hotels appear to fare better than the average by achieving higher room occupancy and higher room rates, increasing room rates charged to tour operators during the last three years, being more profitable and more optimistic in their expectations regarding cooperation with tour operators.

Hotels working with the four major tour operators – i.e. TUI, Thomas Cook, Rewe and MyTravel – are far more profitable than the overall sample. They also achieve a higher-than-average room occupancy ranging between 71.5 per cent for TUI partner hotels and 76.7 per cent for MyTravel partner hotels as compared to the overall 68.7 per cent average (see Table 6.7). TUI leads the list of the highest room rate charged to tour operators, paying on average 70 Euros as compared

Table 6.11 Positive and negative aspects of working with tour operators as seen from the hotels' point of view

	Positive aspects of working with tour operators*				Negative aspects of working with tour operators*			
	Large number of clients	Getting paid on time	High traffic out of high season	Good room rate	Small number of clients	Not getting paid on time	Pressure for low prices	Sending our clients to other destinations
All hotels	**68.3%**	**47.5%**	**56.4%**	**11.9%**	**6.9%**	**33.7%**	**76.2%**	**48.5%**
5-star	85.7%	57.1%	85.7%	14.3%	0.0%	28.6%	57.1%	28.6%
4-star	83.3%	61.1%	69.4%	11.1%	0.0%	27.8%	75.0%	50.0%
3-star	60.0%	40.0%	45.0%	15.0%	10.0%	30.0%	80.0%	35.0%
2-star	59.4%	37.5%	43.8%	12.5%	12.5%	46.9%	78.1%	65.6%
1-star	33.3%	33.3%	50.0%	0.0%	16.7%	33.3%	83.3%	16.7%
Crete	92.1%	65.8%	68.4%	13.2%	2.6%	23.7%	78.9%	50.0%
Aegean Islands	51.4%	35.1%	43.2%	10.8%	13.5%	48.6%	78.4%	43.2%
Ionian Islands	53.8%	30.8%	46.2%	15.4%	7.7%	46.2%	69.2%	61.5%
Mainland	61.5%	46.2%	69.2%	7.7%	0.0%	15.4%	69.2%	46.2%
Working with TUI	83.3%	57.1%	78.6%	11.9%	0.0%	23.8%	81.0%	52.4%
Working with Thomas Cook	87.5%	66.7%	54.2%	12.5%	0.0%	16.7%	91.7%	37.5%
Working with Rewe	84.6%	69.2%	76.9%	15.4%	0.0%	7.7%	92.3%	38.5%
Working with MyTravel	100.0%	20.0%	60.0%	20.0%	0.0%	70.0%	70.0%	80.0%

* Multiple replies.

Table 6.12 Financial results for the year 2004

	N	Profit	Zero profit	Loss
All hotels of the sample	*96*	*49.0%*	*25.0%*	*26.0%*
5-star	6	83.3%	16.7%	0.0%
4-star	35	54.3%	25.7%	20.0%
3-star	20	45.0%	20.0%	35.0%
2-star	29	37.9%	27.6%	34.5%
1-star	6	50.0%	33.3%	16.7%
Crete	37	64.9%	21.6%	13.5%
Aegean Islands	37	27.0%	29.7%	43.3%
Ionian Islands	9	66.7%	11.1%	22.2%
Mainland	13	53.8%	30.8%	15.4%
Belonging to chains	14	64.3%	21.4%	14.3%
Working with TUI	39	61.5%	18.0%	20.5%
Working with Thomas Cook	24	66.7%	20.8%	12.5%
Working with Rewe	12	83.3%	16.7%	0.0%
Working with MyTravel	10	70.0%	30.0%	0.0%

N: number of hotels completing the respective question of the questionnaire (some of the respondents did not complete all questions).

to 66.89 Euros charged to MyTravel, 54.92 Euros charged to Thomas Cook and 50.73 Euros charged to Rewe, with the overall average being 59.60 Euros (the average room rate also reflects the hotel categories used by each operator). Hotels working with TUI, Thomas Cook and Rewe reported significantly better results than the total sample in regard to room rates charged to tour operators and tour-operator generated traffic (see Table 6.8). However, hotels working with MyTravel did not as well as their counterparts. TUI partner hotels also were more optimistic in their expectation of tour-operator generated business than the other surveyed hotels (see Table 6.9). The partner hotels of TUI, Thomas Cook, Rewe and MyTravel made a more positive evaluation of their cooperation with tour operators than the overall sample (see Table 6.11). The large tour operators get high marks in regard to volume of traffic, paying on time (in the case of the three German companies) and generating significant traffic during the shoulder and low seasons. However, hotels are especially critical in regard to the pressure to lower prices and to not paying on time in the case of MyTravel partners. Many hoteliers working with the large tour operators also think that the latter are routing their clientele to other destinations.

The survey sheds some light on regional differences among Greek resort hotels. Despite their large dependency on tour operator-generated business accounting for 78 per cent of total overnight stays, Cretan hoteliers seem to be faring better than their colleagues in other parts of the country. They achieved the highest room occupancy and were more likely to raise prices charged to tour operators and to attract more inclusive tour customers. They also have a more positive stance towards tour operators than hotels in other parts of the country. Hotels based on the Aegean and to a lesser extent the Ionian Islands seem to be faring worse than the sample's average. Upscale hotels reported better-than-average results in regard to room occupancy and profitability. They managed to raise business volume and prices charged to tour operators and to offer lower room rate discounts. They are also more favourable towards the inclusive tour market, while mid-scale and economy hotels are more critical in regard to their cooperation with tour operators.

Research limitations

The conclusions drawn from the present survey reflect the following limitations:

*   The hotels participating in the survey represent 1.6 per cent of the total population in the selected resort areas or 4.1 per cent of the total hotel room capacity.
*   There is a bias towards larger-than-average and upscale hotels in the sample.
*   The large majority of the hotels located in resort areas are seasonal operations. Most of the hotels were actually closed at the time the survey was conducted. Therefore, some bias towards 12-month operations should be expected.
*   The subject of the survey was the relation of hotels with tour operators. Hotels not working with tour operators may have been less interested in participating in the survey.

Discussion

Tour operators greatly contributed to the development of tourism in Mediterranean resort areas over the last half century. Thousands of local businesses were formed throughout the Mediterranean basin to cater for the huge tourist flows created mainly by operators from Northern Europe. Recently, however, the Mediterranean-bound inclusive tour market has become increasingly dominated by a handful of large tour operators following their accelerating horizontal and vertical expansion of the last ten years. The large market power gained by these operators is putting pressure on the providers of inclusive tour components such as the accommodation sector, with this pressure aiming especially at lower prices. This policy of tour operators is based on their need to offer the lowest possible prices but ignores the viability of their providers, the latter facing a vicious cycle of declining quality and depreciated prices (Bastakis et al. 2004: 153, 162).

Additional pressure stems from the constantly expanding accommodation capacity of both established and emerging destinations throughout the Mediterranean basin, especially from countries outside the European Union such as Turkey, Croatia, Bulgaria and North African countries. Both individual hotels and entire destinations have become highly substitutable due to the commoditisation of Mediterranean-bound inclusive tours which constitute a price-sensitive mass market (Gilbert 1990: 25; Kreilkamp 1993: 298).

The intense price competition among Mediterranean destinations was particularly strongly felt by Greek hoteliers after the introduction of the Euro in 2002. Greek resort hotels are now forced to compete against destinations with more favourable currency exchange rates and lower operating costs. This has led to a decline in inclusive tour business for these hotels over the last three years as has been shown in the aforementioned survey. There are, however, alternatives to competing on the price-sensitive mass market. The example of Southern France shows that a destination can be differentiated from low-cost offerings, thus allowing the region's hotels to charge room rates that are much higher than in other parts of the Mediterranean (Gilbert 1990).

Greek resort hotels are predominantly orientated towards the inclusive tour market as they secure 60 per cent of their clientele through tour operators. Most of these hotels actually outsourced their marketing function to tour operators, thus lacking the ability to market themselves in an efficient way on the international marketplace. This has not been a problem for decades, as tour operators supplied a steady flow of business to resort hotels. However, the recent drop in Greece-bound inclusive tour traffic and the increasing pressure applied by tour operators to lower room rates is now forcing Greek hoteliers to explore other markets and distribution channels.

The dependency of Greek resort hotels on tour operator-generated business is the result not only of their limited direct access to the European market but also of the lack of sufficient Greece-bound airlift capacity other than charter flights. Major European tour operators control these charter flights that are used by 58 per cent of all foreign tourists arriving in Greece. Despite the growing market influence of tour operators and the recent decline in Greece-bound inclusive tour traffic, hotels working with the major operators appear to achieve better results than the average hotel according to the aforementioned survey. These hotels also evaluate their cooperation with the tour operators more positively and are more optimistic in their expectations regarding tour-operator generated business in the near future when compared to the sample's average hotel. However, the outlook in regard to inclusive tours is one of growing competition among Mediterranean destinations combined with a clear cost disadvantage in the case of Greek resort hotels.

Strategies for hotels and government policies towards destinations

The increasingly price-focused competition of the Mediterranean-bound holiday market combined with a drop in inclusive tour arrivals in the case of Greece makes it necessary for both the hotel sector and government agencies in charge of tourism development to pursue strategies that will enhance the competitive position of the destination's businesses.

The main target of resort hotels should be to limit their dependency on mass-market inclusive tour traffic, which is dominated by a few powerful tour operators. Holiday packages to the Mediterranean have to a large extent become commodities with the emphasis by both tour operators and consumers being on low prices. In order to avoid direct price competition with businesses from lower-cost countries, Greek resort hotels should employ the following strategies (Krippendorf 1971: 122; Gilbert 1990: 24; Hebestreit 1992: 227–228; Freyer 1999: 403):

(a) diversification of markets by attracting new market segments,
(b) product differentiation, and
(c) diversification of distribution channels.

The first strategy aims at tapping an unexploited market potential found both in the major source markets of Western Europe and the emerging markets of Eastern Europe. For instance, Greece has not yet succeeded in attracting its fair share of independent Western European travellers, as in the case of Germans, considering that half of them travel independently to the Mediterranean. The constantly growing arrival numbers from East European countries also reveal that these source markets still have a considerable potential for further growth. In addition, there are numerous special-interest travel niches representing a significant market size such as sports-related, travel, nature activities, cultural itineraries etc. These market niches have the added advantage of a different seasonal pattern that is complementary to the one of mainstream sea-and-sun holiday travel.

The second strategy aims, first, at achieving higher room rates through added-value offerings and, second, at catering to the needs of special-interest travellers such as people interested in sports, health and beauty treatments etc. An upgrade of room amenities, a special hotel design, the addition of spa and sports facilities and other enhancements allow hotels to charge higher room rates to both their inclusive tour customers and independent travellers. The third strategy is based on the new business development opportunities offered by online marketing platforms. Resort hotels can now sell directly to the end consumer by utilising either their own or third-party e-commerce platforms, thus circumventing the traditional distribution channel comprising tour operators and retail travel agencies. For instance, some of the surveyed hotels reported that they already secure up to 20 per cent of their total business through the Internet. The prerequisite for implementing these three strategies is that resort hotels develop the marketing skills needed. This, however, seems to be a challenge due to the fact that most resort hotels neglected their marketing skills, as for decades tour operators have secured them a constant flow of business.

The role of governmental tourism agencies and cooperative destination-marketing organisations is crucial in making a destination's resort hotels more competitive. The large majority of Greek hotels are small businesses employing on average less than thirty employees (Koutoulas 2003a), thus lacking the market power, the funds and the expertise to influence the market with their own means. These organisations should, therefore, promote policies to strengthen the competitive position of the hotel sector such as:

- Enhancing the marketing skills of individual hotels;
- Creating or supporting macro-marketing and distribution platforms that are open to individual businesses (such as product clubs, convention bureaux, e-commerce platforms etc., Koutoulas 2003b);
- Conducting destination-marketing activities targeted at specific market segments and at repositioning the destination;
- Supporting a quality enhancement policy for upgrading hotels;
- Supporting cost control measures for hotel operations;
- Creating a close working relationship with tour operators themselves (for promoting less-developed parts of the country, for a better presence in the special-interest travel programmes, for expanding charter flights and travel programmes into the low season etc., Koutoulas 2004);
- Providing incentives for new air services from European countries (especially by low-cost carriers) and for setting up charter airlines based in the destination country.

The last policy is especially crucial for Greece to maintain its market share among major European source markets. The Greek government's tourism policy is to blame for the lack of transportation alternatives to the charter flights of the major tour operators, the latter flying in over half of the country's total foreign tourists.

Finally, there is the issue of regulating the conduct of tour operators. Their vast control of the inclusive tour market has created an oligopsony situation which allows them to negotiate with individual hotels under conditions of dependency and even coercion (Bastakis et al. 2004: 153). This issue can only be dealt with at the European Union level. Any national policy on this matter may lead to a loss in competitiveness for the country trying to impose rules and measures aimed at controlling the huge market power of tour operators. These strategies and policies will help resort hotels to be less dependent on tour operators and achieve a more profitable business mix. Full disengagement from tour operators, however, does not seem to be realistic for most hotels and it even may not be advisable, considering the huge market size and the considerable shoulder season traffic these companies represent.

References

ABTA, 'We know where you're going this summer?' (London, Press release of 2 June, 2003). Found at http://www.abtamembers.org/press/.

AGTE, Greek Tourism 2010: Strategy and Goals (Athens, 2002).

Bastakis, Constantinos, Buhalis, Dimitrios and Butler, Richard, 'The perception of small and medium sized tourism accommodation providers on the impacts of the tour operators' power in Eastern Mediterranean', Tourism Management xxv (2004), 151–170.

CAA, ATOL Business (London, 2004).

Freyer, Walter, Tourismus-Marketing: Marktorientiertes Management im Mikro- und Makrobereich der Tourismuswirtschaft, 2. Auflage (München and Wien, 1999).

Gilbert, David, 'Strategic marketing planning for national tourism,' Revue de Tourisme 1 (1990), 18–27.

Goodall, Brian and Bergsma, Jan, 'Destinations – as marketed in tour operators' brochures', in Ashworth, Gregory and Goodall, Brian (eds), Marketing Tourism Places (London, 1990).

Gruner + Jahr, Veranstalterreisen: Branchenbild (Hamburg, 2003).

Gruner + Jahr, Veranstalterreisen: Branchenbild (Hamburg, 2004).

Hebestreit, Dieter, Touristik Marketing: Grundlagen, Ziele, Basis-Informationen, Instrumentarien, Strategien, Organisation und Planung des Marketing von Reiseveranstaltern, 3. Auflage (Berlin, 1992).

Holloway, J. Christopher, The Business of Tourism, 4th ed. (London, 1994).

Karayanni, Ada, 'Dynamic Packaging: I nea tasi sta paketa diakopon', TravelDailNews (29 October 2004). Found at: http://www.traveldailynews.gr/makeof.asp?central_id=562&permanent_id=2.

Koutoulas, Dimitris, 'Characteristics of employment of Greek hotels,' International Scientific Conference 'Educating for Tomorrow's Tourism', (Ohrid, 10–12 October 2003a).

Koutoulas, Dimitris, 'Creating marketing organisations for sustainable tourism products', International Scientific Conference 'Sustainable Tourism Development and the Environment' (Chios, 2–5 October 2003b).

Koutoulas, Dimitris, 'Stratigikes Epiloges gia tin Amvlynsi tis Exartisis apo tous Tour Operators', TravelDailyNews (8 September 2004). Found at: http://www.traveldaily news.gr/makeof.asp?central_id=512&permanent_id=40.

Koutoulas, Dimitris, 'The 2005 Greek Hotel Branding Report' (Athens, 2005).

Kreilkamp, Edgar, 'Produkt- und Preispolitik', in Haedrich, Günther, Kaspar, Claude, Klemm, Kristiane und Kreilkamp, Edgar (Hrsg.), Tourismus-Management: Tourismus-Marketing und Fremdenverkehrsplanung, 2. Auflage (Berlin and New York, 1993).

Krippendorf, Jost, Marketing im Fremdenverkehr (Bern and Frankfurt, 1971).

Middleton, Victor T.C., Marketing in Travel and Tourism (Oxford, 1988).

Rheinsberg, Thies, 'Change is the Challenge is the Chance', International WTO Conference (Larnaca, 22 October 2004).

Toulantas, George, 'Valuing Tour Operators during Volatile Times', Deloitte & Touche Leisure Review 4 (2001), 5–11.

TUI, Geschäftsbericht 2003 (Hannover, 2004a).

TUI, TUI AG – The integrated tourism group (Hannover, 2004b).

Wolchuk, Sally and Scoviak, Mary, 'Hotels 325', Hotels (July 2004).

7

Competition in the travel distribution system
The US travel retail sector

Dimitri Ioannides and Evangelia Petridou Daughtrey

Introduction

For over four decades, US-based travel providers (e.g., airlines, hotels, and the cruise industry) have depended significantly on intermediaries to distribute their products to consumers. These intermediaries, including tour wholesalers, traditional 'bricks and mortar' travel agencies, and Global Distribution Systems (GDS), form part of the travel distribution channel of the tourist industry. In recent years, the advent of the Internet, and specifically e-commerce, plus platforms like mobile devices have enabled the appearance of online agencies and a range of other electronic distribution channels, which increasingly allow customers to bypass traditional travel intermediaries. Coupled with these changes has been the emergence of a small number of giant corporations, especially within the travel retail sector, whose market share is constantly expanding.

Travel agencies are one component of the tourism distribution system in the USA that has seriously been affected by industry consolidation and the advent of new technologies. It appears that the number of independent travel agencies has already witnessed a sharp decline and some analysts offer a pessimistic outlook concerning the industry's hopes for survival (Petridou Daughtrey 2004). Other commentators, by contrast, are more optimistic, arguing that talk of the travel agent's death have been seriously exaggerated (Abels 2004). Whatever the situation within the travel retail sector, it is obvious that there exists very little academic research concerning its structure and organization and the manner in which it has been affected by growing industrial concentration and new technologies. This contrasts sharply to the surge in interest in certain parts of the European travel distribution system, especially tour operators (Buhalis 2000, 2001; Buhalis and Licata 2002; Bastakis et al. 2004; Papatheodorou 2003).

The purpose of this chapter is to offer an in-depth examination of the travel distribution system in the USA, focusing specifically on the travel retail sector. We investigate recent changes that have taken place in the travel agency business resulting from enhanced industrial concentration. We also offer insights of how new information technologies have directly and indirectly affected travel agencies, and offer our thoughts concerning the future of travel retail services. We also speculate briefly on the possible effects that deregulation of global distribution system may have on this sector.

Travel distribution channels

Although academics now pay considerable attention to sectors that constitute part of the supply-side of the tourist industry, in-depth examinations of the structure and organization of intermediary businesses like inbound and outbound tour wholesalers and retail travel agencies have remained rare. These sectors together with other components of the travel distribution channel such as global distribution systems (GDS) or computer reservation systems (CRS), and destination-marketing organizations play a pivotal role in distributing travel services from suppliers like airlines to consumers (Buhalis and Laws 2001; Kotler et al. 1996) (see Figure 7.1).

A handful of useful comprehensive reports and articles concerning travel distribution channels, especially tour operators, made their appearance as early as the 1970s and 1980s (R. Britton 1978; Dunning and McQueen 1982; Sheldon 1986; Touche Ross 1975). However, much of the existing research on this topic has only been published over the last decade. In response to Stephen Britton's (1991) argument that tour operators can easily 'shift tourist flows from one destination to another or one supplier to another through the travel products they construct and promote' (457–458), Ioannides (1998) provided a detailed account of the structure and composition of the tour operating industry. Specifically, he paid attention to the manner in which tour operators interact with other players in the travel industry like travel agents, airlines, hoteliers, and destination management organizations.

Ioannides argued that mass market tour operating businesses are in a controlling position because their emphasis on selling product type as opposed to specific places means they can easily substitute one destination with another, especially in cases where destinations offer a similar product to each other (see also R. Britton 1978; S. Britton 1991; Goodall and Bergsma 1990). This argument has been reinforced more recently in studies by Baloglu and Mangaloglu (2001), Bastakis et al. (2004), Buhalis (2000), Medina-Muñoz et al. (2003), and Papatheodorou (2003). It is obvious that in instances where the tourist landscape is dominated by small-scale accommodation facilities, these players regularly find themselves in a weak bargaining position with tour operators based in key market countries and rarely reach agreements on favourable terms (Bastakis et al. 2004).

Since the tour wholesaler industry, especially within Europe, has continually experienced further market consolidation with large companies taking over competitors but also expanding vertically through the acquisition of airlines and other components of the tourist production system, the competitive position of small and medium tourism enterprises in many destinations will likely continue to

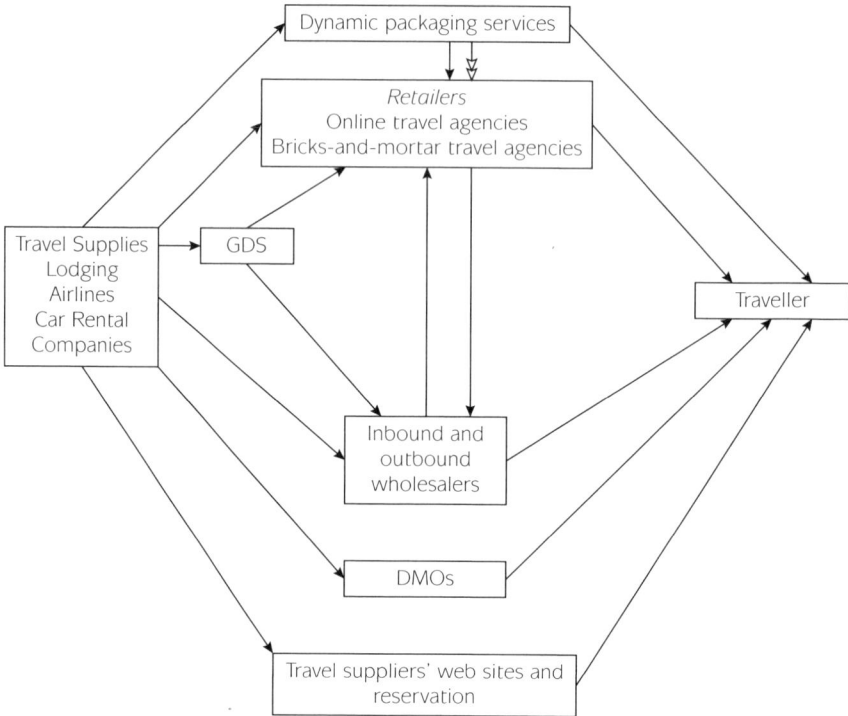

Figure 7.1 Travel distribution channels

be undermined. The situation appears particularly grim for the numerous undiffer-entiated sun and sand destinations of the Mediterranean, which continue to depend heavily on major tour operators in northern European countries.

Not surprisingly, much of the recent literature relating to travel intermediaries has explored the surge towards a highly oligopolistic market structure in countries like Germany and Britain. Among others, Papatheodorou (2003) points out that in 2000 the market share of the four largest British tour operators amounted to 44 per cent, a share which has now risen even further as the largest company Thomson was acquired by the German company Preussag, the parent company of TUI, one of the major global players in the industry. By 2002, just three companies MyTravel UK, TUI UK, and Thomas Cook UK controlled 72 per cent of the British market in terms of total receipts and 68 per cent of the market in terms of clients served (Marcussen 2004; TUI 2004). Certain destinations, like the Greek islands, remain highly dependent on arrivals participating on packaged tours suggesting 'the creation of potential neo-colonial relationships and the resulting low tourism multipliers' (Papatheodorou 2003: 282).

The literature on travel distribution channels has concentrated heavily on outbound tour operators, especially major European companies, which target mass travellers. This attention has a lot to do with the fact that statistical infor-mation on major European outbound tour wholesalers is readily available, whereas it is much harder, if not outright impossible, to acquire such data for other parts of the world, including the United States. No doubt the attention on major European tour operators also has to do with the sheer size of these companies compared to their counterparts in North America, which makes them a highly visible sector in the travel distribution system and key gatekeepers in determining the rise and fall of individual destinations (R. Britton 1978).

By contrast, studies relating to other parts of the travel distribution system, including travel agencies, niche tour specialists and inbound tour operators have not been as prominent. Exceptions include Ioannides' (1998) analysis of specialized tour operating firms based in the USA and Yamamoto and Gill's (2002) in-depth study of the Japanese tourism production system, which included an investigation of inbound tour operators in Whistler, British Columbia. March (2000) has examined so-called business-to-business links between origins and destinations by exploring the relationships of Australian inbound tour operators to key local suppliers, consumers and foreign-based wholesalers.

Internet-based intermediaries and e-commerce in general are also areas of the travel distribution channel that have increasingly become the focus of aca-demics' attention (Buhalis 2000). Buhalis and Licata (2002) argue that traditional e-Mediaries, namely information technologies like CRS and GDS, which in recent years have supported parts of the distribution system such as travel agen-cies and tour operators, now face increasing competition from a new generation of e-Mediaries, which in addition to the Internet are based on interactive digital television and mobile devices. According to Buhalis and Licata, these new technologies enable suppliers like airlines to bypass traditional intermediaries by selling through dedicated websites, directly to consumers who are increasingly technologically savvy (March 2000). The new technologies have also prompted the creation of e-companies including web-based travel agencies like Expedia.com and auction sites like Priceline.com, which attract price-sensitive customers (Tsai et al. 2004).

Naturally, given the proliferation of new technologies and their use to develop new forms of travel distribution channels there has been much debate as to whether or not traditional travel intermediaries like 'bricks and mortar' travel agencies, tour wholesalers, and pioneer e-Mediaries (e.g., GDS) will survive. Certain authors paint a gloomy picture for the future of these players (Tsai et al. 2004) while others, including travel trade representatives, believe that it is highly unlikely the Internet will entirely wipe out high street vendors (Abels 2004). Regardless of their outlook, however, there is widespread agreement that for players to survive the onslaught of new technologies and the increasing consolidation of the travel industry into giant corporations they must adapt to the Internet and other distribution technologies and become adept at offering tailor-made packages for various market niches.

How then do these issues, namely increasing market concentration and the advent of new technologies, play out in the North American travel distribution system, which presents certain characteristics setting it aside from the situation in Europe? The next section seeks to offer answers to this question by focusing on one aspect of the travel distribution system, namely travel agencies.

Travel distribution systems in the United States

A fundamental difference between the American and European travel distribution system is displayed in the tour operating industry. Travel wholesalers in the USA have never achieved the dominant presence of their counterparts in Britain and Germany, where a handful of gigantic companies control a major portion of the market. In 2002–3, TUI Deutschland was Germany's number-one tour wholesaler with 28.68 per cent of the market in sales while the second largest company was Thomas Cook with 22.32 per cent of the market (Quandt 2003). TUI AG, the parent company of TUI Deutschland, has now consolidated its position as the largest tourism group both in Europe and worldwide (see Chapter 6).

Though it is harder to obtain data on market shares of European travel agencies it is obvious that this sector has also witnessed consolidation. In Britain the largest travel agencies have been taken over by vertically integrated tour operators like Thomson and later TUI, meaning the industry has become increasingly oligopolistic. In 1996 the four largest travel retailers in Britain accounted for 57 per cent of foreign package sales by travel agents (Competition Commission 1997). More recently, the largest three agencies in Germany had approximately 60 per cent of the package market share while independents accounted for just 10 per cent of the market and 5 per cent of turnover (FVW International 2002). TUI and Rewe Touristik, the latter having bought out DER, dominate the German travel retail sector.

In the USA the tour operating industry does not reflect the extreme levels of market concentration witnessed in Europe nor does it demonstrate the highly vertically integrated structure exhibited by companies like TUI. Generally, American travel wholesaling companies are far smaller than their European counterparts. This situation is best highlighted by the fact that while TUI Deutschland alone had earnings of 4 billion euros and accounted for almost 7 million tourists (Quandt 2003), the entire membership of the United States Tour Operators' Association (USTOA) (a total of 56 companies) generated combined sales of $8 billion and carried 10 million passengers (USTOA 2004).

In 2001 there were approximately 3,200 tour operating establishments in the USA (businesses listed under NAICS Code 561520) (US Census Bureau 2004). Of these, only two had over 1,000 employees while almost 1,900 companies employed fewer than five persons. These statistics highlight the extremely fragmented nature of the US tour operating sector. The dominance of numerous small companies can be largely explained by the industry's exceedingly low entry barriers (Euromonitor 2004). In fact, many tour operators in the United States are small niche specialists compared to the mass tour operators seen in Europe (Ioannides 1998). A possible explanation for this is that Americans are far less eager than Europeans to purchase a full travel package:

> In Europe the concept of selling a package is the norm, with air often provided by charter operators or vertically integrated tour operators . . . The US is almost the mirror opposite. Consumers have been trained to buy à la carte travel products with air provided by scheduled service providers. They are concerned that the retailer may take advantage of the pricing opacity and gouge the consumer. They are also concerned that the component pieces may not be of equal quality.
>
> (Fitzgerald, in Lenhart 2004: 27)

To complicate matters, in the USA 'there is also a significant grey area' since various components of the travel industry other than tour operators also engage in packaging holidays. These include but are not restricted to 'airlines, travel agencies and hotels, which may offer products ranging from full package tours to daily or overnight all-inclusive excursions' (Euromonitor 2000: 36). This complex situation makes it impossible to derive meaningful statistics relating to the tour operating sector alone. Since most companies in this sector are privately owned and operated they are not obliged to release their financial information and few do. Additionally, the larger publicly owned companies are often not comparable with each other since it is hard to disentangle their tour operating component from their overall business. According to Euromonitor (2004) it is impractical and highly unreliable to assign market shares to individual companies, thus explaining why it is impossible to obtain updated statistics on the state of the tour operating sector. The last report that provided market share statistics on US-based tour operators was published more than two decades ago (Sheldon 1986).

The US travel agency sector – a profile

Because it is virtually impossible to obtain reliable statistics, including market share information, concerning the size of the US tour operating business, and since this sector does not reflect the degree of market concentration witnessed in other components of the travel industry, the rest of the chapter focuses on the travel retail industry, which has seen significant changes in the last few years. Most important has been the trend towards consolidation, since the nation's top agencies (those earning over $100 million annually) increasingly account for a larger share of the market. In 1999 the leading five players claimed 20.2 per cent of total value while in 2003 their share had increased to more than 30 per cent (Euromonitor 2004; Travel Weekly 2004) (Table 7.1).

To be sure, the US travel agency industry does not display the same degree of market concentration witnessed in the software sector where Microsoft dominates, but one indisputable fact is that the larger companies are becoming larger, 'the many are becoming the few and the simple have become the complex' (ibid.: 20). A close examination of the Travel Weekly's 'Power List,' a special report published annually on the state of the travel agency industry, reflects two interesting trends. First, the impressive growth of the largest companies (the top 50), which include both 'bricks and mortar' and online agencies, has been fuelled by mergers and acquisitions. Second, in order to survive these companies, especially the traditional agencies, are changing the way they are doing business, mainly because of new distribution technologies.

Today, each of the top 50 travel agencies in the United States reports annual retail earnings of $100 million and over. The top 13 companies have earnings above $1 billion and altogether bring in more than $60 billion. A number of these top companies have enhanced their power even further over the last few years because they have absorbed some of their closest competitors. In 2003, American Express, the largest company with $16 billion in sales (11.6 per cent market share) bought out another travel retail giant Rosenbluth International. Similarly, the second largest company Carlson Wagonlit with sales of $12.3 billion acquired Maritz. An important reason behind American Express' decision to expand was its determination to consolidate its position as the leading corporate travel company. By inheriting a major portion of the business that was once Rosenbluth's, American Express will be in a position to generate significant economies of scale in servicing their clients on a global level. It is worth mentioning that American Express is not

Table 7.1 US travel agencies with sales more than $1 billion

2000	2002	2003
American Express Travel Related Services, Inc/ $14.6 billion	American Express/ $15.5 billion	American Express Travel/ $16 billion*
Carlson Wagonlit Travel/ $12 billion	Carlson Wagonlit Travel/ $12.5 billion	Carlson Wagonlit Travel/ $12.7 billion
Rosenbluth International/ $4.8 billion	Navigant International/ $5.34 billion	Interactive Corp/ $10.7 billion
Worldtravel BTI/ $4.3 billion	Expedia/$5.3 billion	Worldtravel BTI/$4.2 billion
Navigant International, Inc/$3.8 billion	Rosenbluth International/ $5.2 billion	TQ3 Navigant/$4 billion
Travelocity.com, Inc/ $2.5 billion	Worldtravel BTI/$4.2 billion	Travelocity/$3.9 billion
Expedia, Inc/$1.79 billion	Travelocity/$3.5 billion	Orbitz/$3.4 billion
TQ3 Maritz Travel Solutions/$1.66 billion	AAA Travel/$3.16 billion	AAA Travel (AAA Inc)/ $3 billion
Liberty Travel/$1.39 billion	Orbitz/$2.5 billion	Cendant Travel/$1.66 billion
Satotravel/$1.2 billion	TQ3 Travel Solutions/ $1.6 billion	Liberty Travel/$1.45 billion
	Cendant Retail Travel Services/$1.4 billion	Omega Travel/$1.1 billion
	Liberty Travel/$1.39 billion	Priceline.com/$1.1 billion
	Omega World Travel/ $1 billion	Total Travel Management/ $1.06 billion

* The revenue reported by American express does not reflect the Rosenbluth acquisition because it was not completed until October 2003.
Source: Travel Weekly (2001, 2002, 2003). Retrieved November 11, 2004 from http://travelweekly.com.

just a travel agency but also includes a tour operating division, American Express Vacations and a luxury cruise wholesaler, Golden Bear (Travel Weekly 2004).

One of the most interesting companies, which just makes the top ten of the Power List is Cendant Travel Distribution Services (TDS), which in 2003 employed 5,000 workers and had sales amounting to $1.66 billion. In October 2004, Cendant completed one of the most amazing coups of the travel industry in recent years by acquiring the online agency Orbitz, which just a year earlier was listed number 7 on the Power List (Schaal 2004a). By doing so, Cendant TDS has now surpassed Travelocity to emerge as the number two online travel business.

What makes Cendant TDS truly stand out is that it is a subsidiary of what has arguably become one of the world's largest travel-related companies, Cendant Corporation. This huge parent company, which originally began as Hospitality Franchise Systems, has become the world's largest hotel franchiser-controlling 5,400 properties, which amounts to 500,000 units. Other businesses under the Cendant group include a number of vacation home rental agencies including the Danish company Novasol, prominent car rental agencies (e.g., Budget and Avis) and real estate brokerage firms (Table 7.2). Cendant TDS itself is rapidly becoming a major player in the travel distribution business offering both online and offline services. Among its holdings it lists one of the world's most important global distribution systems, Galileo International, Travelwire, a software package for travel agencies, Cheap Tickets an online seller of leisure travel products, Lodging.com an online listing of discounted hotel rooms, and Travel 2/Travel 4 a British-based tour wholesaler. Further, in December 2004, Cendant announced the pending acquisition of e-Bookers and UK-based tour operator Gullivers Travel Associates (Schaal 2004b).

Table 7.2 Cendant Holdings

Hotel Franchises	Amerihost Inn, Days Inn, Howard Johnson, Knights Inn, Ramada, Super 8, Travelodge, Wingate
Vacation Ownership Group	Trendwest, Fairfield Resorts, RCI
Consumer Travel Americas	Cendant Travel, Orbitz.com, CheapTickets.com
Hospitality and Leisure Services	Lodging.com, Neat Group
Supplier Services	Shepherd Systems, Trust International, WizCom
Car Rental Group	Avis, Budget
Vacation Rental Group	Cuendet, Holiday Cottages Group, Novasol, Welcome Holidays, Holiday Network, Landal Green Parks
Corporate Travel Solutions	Travelport, Galileo GDS, Orbitz for Business
International Markets	Travelwire, Travel 2/Travel 4, HotelClub.com, RatesToGo.com
Pending Acquisitions*	e-Bookers, Gullivers Travel Associates

*as of December 16, 2004.

Sources: Cendant (1999–2000) 'About Cendant', retrieved December 6, 2004, from http://cendant.com/about-cendant. Schaal, Dennis (2004b, Travel Weekly, retrieved January 16, 2004 from http://www.travelweekly.com/articles.aspx?articleid=44673.

Despite being companies that are fairly complex in their structure by way of the services they offer, American Express, Carlson, Worldwide BTI and TQ3 Navigant all still fit the profile of traditional 'bricks and mortar' travel agencies. Unlike travel agencies in Britain, however, (e.g., Lunn Poly) most of these giant American companies concentrate heavily on the business/corporate travel sector. Indeed, only one traditional leisure-oriented travel agency, Liberty Travel (Liberty Travel 2004), which packages and retails tours to places like Florida, the Caribbean and Mexico, is listed in the top ten of the Power List with sales of approximately $1.5 billion (Travel Weekly 2004).

The focus of most major 'bricks and mortar' agencies on corporate travel as Euromonitor (2004) explains, stems from 'the relative ease of serving businesses. Rates are often negotiated in advance and sales are steady, as there are ongoing needs for travel in any sizeable business.' By contrast, leisure travellers who are price-sensitive do not require the services of travel agents on a steady basis and are likelier than their business counterparts to seek bargain fares through Web-based intermediaries. And, it could be argued, it is the growth of Internet-based travel agencies that provides one of the most significant forces that have transformed the travel industry in recent times.

In a matter of just a few years, Internet-based intermediaries have consolidated their position in the top ten group of the Power List (Travel Weekly 2004). Orbitz and Travelocity, which have already been mentioned, feature in the top ten. By 2003, Expedia Inc. had witnessed its share of the market rise to 6.2 per cent from just 2.1 per cent a couple of years earlier. Expedia together with two other popular internet travel sites, Hotwire.com and Hotels.com is now under the control of the third largest travel agency in the USA, namely Interactivecorp, which last year generated more than $10 billion in sales. Another significant player, Priceline.com, is excluded from this list even though it is in its own right a major player in Internet-based travel sales because, according to Euromonitor (2004), owing to the way it operates by inviting bids for tickets it does not really fit the profile of a travel agency.

According to the Office of Advocacy (2001), e-commerce will likely continue having a major impact on travel agencies. Back in 2000 over 90 million individuals accessed online travel businesses and eventually almost 25 million actually bought a travel product from the Internet. Although this number reflects a small percentage of the travel market (7 per cent of overall travel sales in 2000), the Office of Advocacy estimated that by 2005 sales over the Internet would reach 30 per cent and continue to rise.

Assessing the influence of the Internet

The advent of the Internet has meant that ever-improving travel distribution technologies can now provide most if not all the value-added services once associated with travel agencies, namely recommendation, research, reservations, reporting and relationship (the 5 R's of travel agencies). Thus, today's travellers, especially leisure travellers with time on their hands, can confidently bypass the 'bricks and mortar' agency and access websites to obtain services like airline-related information on fares, routes and schedules or information about hotel location, services and prices. It takes only a few key-strokes to make e-ticket airline reservations, and it is just as simple to enrol for frequent flyer programmes and cash accumulated miles for tickets. Bookings and changes to reservations for hotel rooms, rental cars, theatre tickets and tours can also be made over the Internet.

One of the most significant outcomes of the growth of online distribution channels is that travel providers such as airlines no longer have to depend on traditional travel agencies to provide information about and sell off their inventory. Instead, through their online sites these providers can sell their product direct to the traveller, thus diminishing the 'perceived value of intermediaries such as travel agencies' (Office of Advocacy 2001: 1). The advantage to these providers is that given their ability to quickly access the market place via the Internet they no longer need to pay commissions to 'bricks and mortar' travel agencies and, thus can derive a huge saving.

The gradual erosion of commissions paid by airlines in the USA to travel agents over the last decade has arguably had the single most important negative effect on traditional travel agencies, especially smaller, independent companies. Whereas at one time airlines provided generous commissions (usually 10 per cent with no cap), and commission overrides, to travel agents as a reward for protecting their respective market shares, since the mid-1990s they have sought to find ways to eliminate this expense, a step facilitated through the advent of information technologies.

As seen in Figure 7.2, the trouble for the agents first started in 1995 when Delta and then other major carriers instituted a domestic commission cap of $50 on the sale of a roundtrip ticket. By 1997 commissions had been reduced from 10 per cent to 8 per cent of the ticket price with a commission cap and in 1998 a cap of $100 was implemented on the sale of round-trip international tickets. In 1999 commissions were further cut to a maximum of 5 per cent with an upper cap, which by 2001 was reduced from $50 to $20. The total elimination of commissions by airlines on all domestic flights was finally announced in March 2002 and with the high probability that sooner or later other travel providers including hotels and cruise companies may follow suit, the travel agency industry has been plunged into turmoil (Joselyn 2002; Office of Advocacy 2001).

Because of the elimination of commissions agencies have been forced to institute fees for their services. This step has proved costly, since consumers who once flocked to travel agencies for the provision of what was essentially a free service have now discovered they must pay an extra charge when purchasing a ticket or booking a hotel room through an intermediary. By contrast, more and more Internet-savvy individuals recognize that they can access the websites

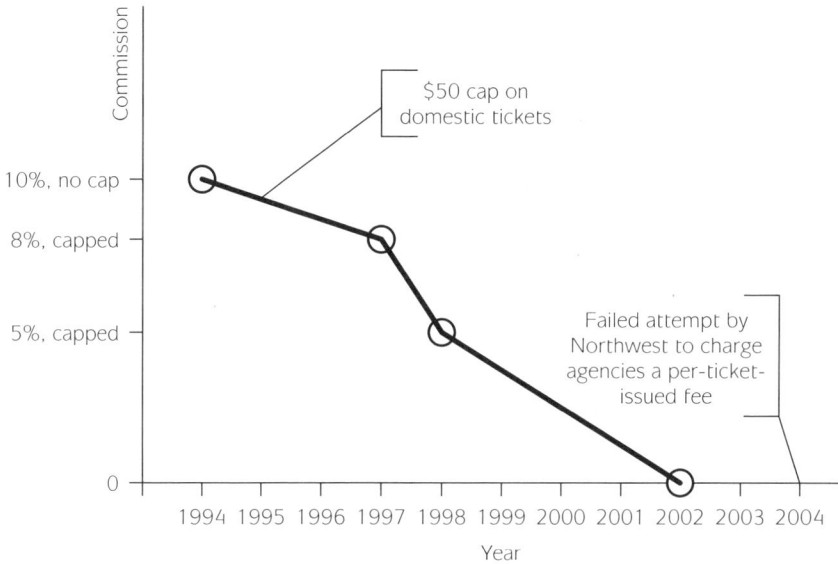

Figure 7.2 Commission cut timeline

Source: Las Vegas Review Journal, Travel Weekly.

of airline companies and other travel product providers and make their travel arrangements without been slapped with extra fees.

Recognizing their passengers' aversion to paying extra fees beyond the regular ticket price US-based airlines have made further efforts to steer their customers to make reservations from their dedicated websites. Carriers now charge a fee if someone attempts to buy a ticket by telephoning the airline or visiting its airport ticket counter. Northwest Airlines recommended in 2004 that travel agencies should pay the airline a per-ticket-issued fee in an attempt to further inspire consumers to bypass intermediaries and buy directly from the Web. Even though Northwest's attempt failed it shows the degree to which airlines have gone to eliminate their mounting costs over the last few years (Schaal 2004c).

The future of the travel agency industry in the US

The elimination of commissions and the rising significance of Internet-based distribution technologies have drastically transformed the face of the US travel agency business. What then does the future hold in store for this portion of the travel distribution industry? What will happen to the numerous small players, specifically the mom and pop travel agencies who have already seen their share of the market severely eroded as major players have consolidated their position in the market?

Many of the smallest companies will soon close their doors if they have not done so already. These businesses, which once emerged simply because of low entry barriers, are the ones that are the most threatened from recent changes. The Office of Advocacy (2001) offers a number of suggestions for small agency survival including: setting up a home office instead of operating from a main street store; adding other services such the retailing of travel-related apparel; and offering services to specialty niche markets. Agencies may also be able to survive by adapting to new technologies or allowing themselves to be bought out by larger players. Some of these smaller players have already taken advantage of off-the-shelf e-commerce website tools developed by GDS vendors and travel agency consortia, which provide 'agencies the ability to offer customers online information and reservation capabilities similar to large online agencies' (ibid.: 21).

One recent technological innovation that could still benefit innovative travel agencies, regardless of their size, is dynamic packaging. This is 'the technological capability to quickly assemble a single-priced travel package involving multiple components such as air, hotel, car and activities all in real time and culled from a wide variety of suppliers and third party sources' (Lenhart 2004: 20). In a few seconds dynamic packaging allows the creation of a complete multi-element travel package, reflecting a combined price. Because of the flexibility associated with dynamic packaging, creating a travel package no longer remains the domain of a tour wholesaler. Rather, travel retailers and suppliers (e.g., hotels), among others, can take advantage of dynamic packaging to create in real-time a tour package based on up-to-date prices and availability that fits a customer's particular specifications. Internet-based travel agencies like Expedia and Travelocity already offer dynamic packaging to consumers who want to build their own travel package. But, as Lenhart argues, this should not stop a whole host of other industry players, including travel agencies and tour operators, from taking advantage of these new technologies.

An important advantage that dynamic packaging programmes like NeatAgent/ Galileo NeatAgent and JurniCustomtrip convey to the travel agencies is the ability to set their own mark-up price for the product demanded by the client (NeatAgent 2004). For agencies that have suffered from dwindling commissions this is certainly welcome news. Dynamic packaging providers like the JurniNetwork, a travel agency consortium owned by Sabre, even pay agents commissions for using their Customtrip product. This means that the agent using this particular product earns a commission over and above the mark-up that has already been set for the travel package. Yet another benefit from dynamic packaging is that the technology can be used to create travel packages to any destination, as opposed to the traditional packages that were put together by wholesalers mostly for leisure travellers (e.g., ski resorts and beach destinations). 'If someone is going to Detroit, you can package air, hotel, transfer, a spa visit, theatre tickets all together. People can get the same benefit of discounted prices in a package regardless of the destination' (Quinby, quoted in Lenhart 2004: 22).

Whether steps like market niche and increased use of dynamic packaging will help over time smaller players in the travel distribution system like travel agents and specialized tour wholesalers stay in business remains unclear. On a pessimistic note, considering the point made earlier, that relatively few Americans buy travel packages, what guarantee is there that demand for dynamic packages will ever grow to become a major portion of the travel agency business? In the short run, it seems likelier that for every travel agency that adopts new technologies such as dynamic packaging there are hundreds of others that will cease to exist. Moreover, given that information technologies, including those enabling dynamic packaging, can also be used by many other players in the tourist industry there is no guarantee that consumers will seek the services of travel intermediaries. After all, these consumers can on their own access websites maintained by one of these players and create their tailor-made travel package (Lenhart 2004).

There is yet another reason to be cautious. Although more dedicated web-based products are now available, a number of these are produced and/or controlled by subsidiaries of existing giant conglomerates, including some of the biggest players in the travel distribution system. Last year, Cendant Corporation, bought out NeatGroup the company that created the NeatAgent dynamic packaging tool. Since then, Cendant has added a new product called Galileo NeatAgent, to specifically target subscribers of its Galileo International GDS. 'Both NeatAgent products are web-based, enabling users to access net-rate inventory and set up their own mark-up on vacation packages created from at least two components of discounted air, hotel and car rates. Participating suppliers include but are not limited to the hotel and car rental brands owned by Cendant Corp' (ibid.: 22). This situation, where one super-company like Cendant controls various suppliers plus elements of the travel distribution system reinforces the image of an increasingly oligopolistic industry. In turn, this means that although some of the new technologies like NeatAgent may help certain small travel agencies stay in business these players are, in fact, competing for an ever-shrinking slice of the pie.

The impact of GDS deregulation

A final point must be made about the recent deregulation of global distribution systems, which was implemented in the USA in July 2004. Specifically, questions arise concerning the effect of deregulation on travel agencies' competitive position. While it is perhaps early to assess the full impact of GDS deregulation, here we offer our own perspective as to what this event may mean for the industry's future.

Travel Distribution Report described the possible changes arising from deregulation as 'evolutionary, not revolutionary' (2004). This was reflected recently after Northwest Airlines attempted to penalize travel agents who booked travel through

GDSs by charging a per-ticket fee (Schaal 2004c). SABRE, one of the leading GDS companies, responded with the threat of litigation since they stood to lose substantial revenue if agencies shifted to non-traditional means of travel distribution to curb their costs and maintain their profit margins. Demonstrating that they wield considerable power, which has been enhanced through deregulation, the GDSs adopted measures against Northwest by refusing to list the airline's product on the first page of their availability display, something that in the regulated GDS environment would have been prohibited. This demonstrates a bias by the GDS against the airline since travel agents, all things being equal, will book a carrier from the first page of their availability display. Faced with this response, Northwest eventually backed down and rescinded the fee.

While it could be argued that the stance of the GDSs against Northwest was self-serving, it boosted the position of travel agencies since they stood to lose the most if additional fees had been added on the ticket sale price. Travel agencies may benefit even further, since under deregulation the low cost carriers like Southwest Airlines may be drawn to list their itineraries on the GDSs for the first time, thus providing more pricing options for customers. In the past, low cost airlines chose not to be listed on GDSs because of excessive booking fees, and instead marketed their own proprietary software allowing participating agencies access to real time inventory. Now, because of deregulation, GDSs are no longer obliged to implement a uniform pricing model for all airlines (US Department of Transportation 2004). This means that the GDS can negotiate different rates with different airlines, and develop more favourable terms from the low cost carriers' standpoint. This, in turn allows one or more low cost carriers the flexibility to use yet another distribution channel, namely a GDS (as long as the latter chooses to negotiate with the said carriers); this means that travel agencies may now be in a position to provide more options for customers in search of discounted fares.

Under the old regulated environment, even though efforts had been made to protect travel agencies from unfair GDS contracts, the agencies had to honour costly and exclusive contracts prohibiting them from using their own equipment or any other third party software or distribution channels. Now, both the GDSs and the travel retailers are free to engage in negotiations governed by changing market forces and emerging technology. This will make GDS be accountable when it comes to researching and developing new products, and will give additional choices of distribution channels to retailers who no longer have to be bound by prohibitive terms favouring the distribution systems (ibid.).

GDS deregulation seems to be the most recent natural step in a general trend that has affected the travel retailing sector following rapid technological advances and increasing market concentration through mergers and acquisitions. Indications, at least for the short term, are that it may actually provide the necessary agility for certain entrepreneurs in this sector to survive. This is certainly welcome news for an industry that has recently been plagued by bad news.

Conclusion

The travel agency, a key component of the travel distribution system within the USA, has witnessed considerable upheaval over the last decade, a result of a combination of forces including growing industry consolidation, changing technologies, the gradual erosion of the sector's customary source of income through commissions and, recently, the deregulation of GDSs. Today, despite the continued presence of thousands of small-scale agencies, the industry has increasingly become dominated by a few giant corporations, the largest generating annual sales over $1 billion. What's more, there is continuous movement in the top ten list of largest agencies since certain corporations continue to expand by taking over their closest rivals.

Nationwide, the top companies in the travel agency business include both 'bricks and mortar' agencies like American Express and Liberty Travel plus online based companies like Travelocity and Expedia. Also, the market share of online businesses is constantly becoming larger-reflecting the increasing domination of the Internet in the travel distribution system. Indeed, the impact of the Internet has been such that even the 'bricks and mortar' agencies have had to adapt their operations by embracing existing online technologies and, in some instances, developing their own.

Market consolidation in the travel agency business has led to increasingly diffuse businesses offering far more than the retailer's customary services to travellers. Certain companies like American Express, for instance, are not pure travel retailers but also are involved in tour packaging and financial services. Cendant Distribution Systems, a subsidiary of Cendant – itself, a global player in many aspects of the tourism production system, including accommodation and car rental – is a diffuse company, which includes online and 'bricks and mortar' services, GDS and new dynamic packaging systems.

The trend towards further horizontal integration in the travel agency business will likely continue in the near future and although highly vertically integrated companies such as the ones in Europe are unlikely to develop, it is clear that in the future the successful players in this sector will be ones involved in more than one step of the travel distribution system. What then, does this spell for the thousands of smaller agencies around the country? Perhaps a handful will remain fairly successful if they have a steady stream of corporate clients or if they offer services to specific specialized niches. No doubt, the majority will cease to exist, especially if they continue to insist on acting as mere booking agents for airline companies, hotels and car rental agencies. It seems certain that the travel agency of tomorrow, whether a pure online business or a 'bricks and mortar' company, will have to constantly adapt to new technologies like the ones allowing instantaneous creation of specialized travel packages for increasingly demanding travellers. Finally, on a brighter note early indications are that GDS deregulation may have already created a more favourable environment for travel agencies, allowing a number of these to survive in the near future.

References

Abels, Joel M. (2004). 'What's the future of agent killers versus killer agents?' Travel Trade. http://www.traveltrade.com/editorial.jsp?articleID=5197 (website accessed September 27, 2004).

Baloglu, S. and Mangaloglu, M. (2001). 'Tourism destination images of Turkey, Egypt, Greece and Italy as perceived by US-based tour operators and travel agents'. Tourism Management 22: 1–9.

Bastakis, C., Buhalis, D. and Butler, R. (2004). 'The perception of small and medium sized tourism accommodation providers on the impacts of the tour operators' power in Eastern Mediterranean'. Tourism Management 25: 151–170.

Britton, R.A. (1978). 'International tourism and indigenous development objectives: a study with special reference to the West Indies'. PhD dissertation, University of Minneapolis, MN.

Britton S.G. (1991). 'Tourism, capital and place: towards a critical geography of tourism'. Environment and Planning D. Society and Space 9(4): 451–478.

Buhalis, D. (2001). 'Tourism distribution channels: practices and processes'. In D. Buhalis and E. Laws (eds) Tourism Distribution Channels: Practices, Issues, and Transformations. London: Continuum, 7–32.

Buhalis, D. (2000). 'Relationships in the distribution channel of tourism: conflicts between hoteliers and tour operators in the Mediterranean region'. International Journal of Hospitality and Tourism Administration 1(1): 113–139.

Buhalis, D. and Laws, E. (eds) (2001). Tourism Distribution Channels: Practices, Issues and Transformations. London: Continuum.

Buhalis, D. and Licata, M. (2002). 'The future of eTourism intermediaries'. Tourism Management 23: 207–220.

Cendant (2004). About Cendant. http://www.cendant.com/about-cendant (website accessed December 6, 2004).

Competition Commission (1997). 'Foreign package holidays: A report on the supply in the UK of tour operators' services and travel agencies services in relation to foreign package holidays'. http://www.competition-commission.org.uk/rep_pub/reports/1997/412foreign.htm (website accessed January 19, 2005).

Dunning, J.H. and McQueen, M. (1982). 'Multinational corporations in the international hotel industry'. Annals of Tourism Research 9: 69–90.

Euromonitor 2004. Travel and Tourism: Market Direction Report. London: Euromonitor PLC.

Euromonitor 2000. Travel and Tourism: Market Direction Report. London: Euromonitor PLC.

FVW International (2002). 'Consolidation continues in German travel distribution market'. http://www.fvw.com/index.cfm?ID=594 (website accessed January 17, 2005).

Goodall, B. and Bergsma, J. (1990). 'Destinations as marketed in tour operators brochures'.

In G. Ashworth and B. Goodall (eds) Marketing Tourism Places. London: Routledge, 170–192.

Ioannides, D. (1998). 'Tour operators: The gatekeepers of tourism'. In D. Ioannides and K. Debbage (eds) The Economic Geography of the Tourist Industry: A Supply-side Analysis. London: Routledge, 139–158.

Joselyn, R.W. (2002). Testimony for the National Commission to Ensure Consumer Information and Choice in the Airline Industry. Scottsdale, AZ: Joselyn, Tepper and Associates.

Kotler, P., Bowen J. and Makens, J. (1996). Marketing and Hospitality for Tourism. Upper Saddle River, NJ: Prentice Hall.

Lenhart, M. (2004). 'Dynamic packaging: the next big thing.' Travel Professional: The Official Journal of the Travel Institute (August/September): 19–27.

Liberty Travel (2004). www.libertytravel.com, accessed on October 26, 2005.

March, R. (2000). 'Buyer decision-making behavior in international tourism channels'. In J. Crotts, D. Buhalis, and R. March (eds) Global Alliances in Hospitality Management. Binghamton, NY: The Haworth Press, Inc., 11–25.

Marcussen, C.H. (2004). 'Package tours versus self-organized holidays to Madeira – from Northern Europe'. Internal working report. Bornholm, Denmark: Centre for Regional and Tourism Research.

Medina-Muñoz R.D., Medina-Muñoz, D.R., and Garcia-Falcon J.M. (2003). 'Understanding European tour operators' control on accommodation companies: an empirical evidence'. Tourism Management 24: 135–147.

NeatAgent (2004). http://www.neatgroup.com/neatagent.htm (website accessed November 15, 2004).

Office of Advocacy, US Small Business Administration (2001). E-Commerce's Impact on the Travel Agency Industry (contract number: SBAHQ-00-M-0797). Washington, DC: Small Business Administration.

Papatheodorou, A. (2003). 'Corporate strategies of British tour operators in the Mediterranean region: an economic geography approach'. Tourism Geographies 5(3): 280–304.

Petridou Daughtrey, E. (2004). The effect of information technology on travel agencies and a feasibility analysis of the industry. Unpublished paper. Ozark Technical Community College, Springfield, MO.

Quandt, B. (2003). 'Das Jahr der Spezialisten.' Beilage zur FVW International 31 (18/12/2003).

Schaal, D. (2004a). 'Cendant buys Orbitz for $1.25 B'. Travel Weekly (October 4, 2004). http://www.travelweekly.com (website accessed October 21, 2004).

Schaal, D. (2004b). 'It's a Cendant world: Firm to make third major buy in 3 months'. Travel Weekly. http://www.travelweekly.com (website accessed January 16, 2005).

Schaal, D. (2004c). 'Under the gun, NWA rescinds $7.50 GDS fee'. Travel Weekly (September 6, 2004). http://www.travelweekly.com (website accessed January 17, 2005).

Sheldon, P.J. (1986). 'The tour operator industry: an analysis'. Annals of Tourism Research 13: 349–365.

Touche Ross and Company (1975). Tour Wholesaler Industry Study. New York: Touche Ross.

Travel Distribution Report (2004). 'What does the new, free, market GDS look like'. May 10: Vol. 12: 81–83.

Travel Weekly 2004. 'Travel Weekly's Power List: a special report.' Travel Weekly. http://www.travelweekly.com/specialreports/powerlist/index.html (website accessed December 16, 2004).

Travel Weekly 2003. 'Top 50 travel agencies.' Travel Weekly. http://www.travelweekly.com/specialreports/Top50_2003.htm (website accessed December 16, 2004).

Travel Weekly 2001. 'Top 50 travel agencies.' Travel Weekly. http://www.travelweekly.com/specialreports/top50/index.html (website accessed December 16, 2004).

Tsai, H., Huang, L. and Lin, C. (2004). 'Emerging e-commerce development model for Taiwanese travel agencies'. Tourism Management 25.

TUI (2004). http://www.tui.com/en/konzern/companies_brands/ (website accessed November 19, 2004).

United States Census Bureau (2004). County Business Patterns. http://www.census.gov (website accessed November 1, 2004).

United States Department of Transportation (2004). Computer Reservation System (CRS) Regulations. Washington, DC: Office of the Secretary.

United States Tour Operators' Association (2004). http://www.ustoa.com/ (website accessed November 18, 2004).

Yamamoto, D. and Gill, A.M. (2002). 'Issues of globalization and reflexivity in the Japanese tourism production system: The case of Whistler, British Columbia'. Professional Geographer 54(1): 83–93.

8

The impact of information technology on tourism competition

Dimitrios Buhalis

Introduction

Since the mid-1990s a wide range of digital tools has emerged, changing best practice in both business functions and processes. Information Communication Technologies (ICTs) and the Internet in particular have revolutionised the tourism industry. The development of eBusiness and eTourism has changed not only the best operational and strategic practices for organisations on a global level but also the competition conditions in the marketplace. The Internet introduced opportunities for promotion of products to consumers. It also provides a mechanism for interconnectivity (ability to connect electronically between organisations supporting Business to Business [B2B] solutions) and interoperability (ICT enabled automatic collaboration between partners using heterogeneous hardware and software components that work together conveniently and inexpensively) between partners, and this is changing the competitiveness of all tourism enterprises and regions around the world. Transparency of both product characteristics and prices as well as the development of a number of new intermediaries in the marketplace forced organisations around the world to prove to their consumers the value they add to their products and services as well as forced them to justify their profit margins. Innovative organisations that took advantage of the emerging technologies managed to improve their product and enhance their communication with consumers and stakeholders (Buhalis, 2003; O'Connor, 1999).

This chapter explores the impact of ICTs and the Internet in particular on the competitiveness of tourism organisations as well as on the levels of competition in the marketplace. The chapter illustrates the complexity of the various types of systems and demonstrates how they fit together in the production, distribution and delivery of tourism products as well as their strategic implications. It demonstrates the different levels of competition and explains how technology is changing the different competition layers and provides a discussion on managerial action required for tourism organisations.

Information communication technologies and Internet revolution

Buhalis (2003) concluded that ICTs include 'the entire range of electronic tools, which facilitate the operational and strategic management of organisations by enabling them to manage their information, functions and processes as well as to communicate interactively with their stakeholders for achieving their mission and objectives'. Thus, ICTs emerge as an integrated system of networked equipment and software, which enables effective data processing and communication for organisational benefit in transforming organisations into eBusinesses.

The emergence of the Internet empowered the global networking of computers, enabling individuals and organisations to access a plethora of multimedia information and knowledge sources, regardless of their location or ownership, often free of charge (Smith and Jenner, 1998). Rapid enhancements in ICT capabilities, in combination with the decrease of the size of equipment and ICT costs, have improved the reliability, compatibility and inter-connectivity of numerous terminals and applications, and have changed the way that tourism organisations manage their operations. The pace of Internet adoption globally demonstrates that ICTs and the Internet in particular restructure the way we live, work, shop and play. Millions of people worldwide rely on the Internet for home-shopping, tele-entertainment, tele-working, tele-learning, tele-medical support and tele-banking. The electronic/interactive/intelligent/virtual home and enterprise emerge gradually, facilitating the entire range of communications with the external world and supporting all functions of everyday personal and professional life through interactive computer networks.

Synergies emerging from the use of these systems effectively make information widely available and accessible through a variety of media and locations. Inter-connectivity has supported organisations in connecting with their partners in their value chain and 'plug and play'. This in turn has supported the automation of business to business (B2B) interactions and transactions through the development of ontologies and interoperability methodologies. Both consumers and business users can use mobile devices such as portable computers, mobile phones and PDAs as well as digital television and self-serviced terminals/kiosks to interact and perform several functions. This convergence of ICTs effectively integrates the entire range of hardware, software, groupware, net-ware and human-ware and blurs the boundaries between equipment and software (Werthner and Klein, 1999; Buhalis, 2003).

Business Process Re-engineering was employed by many tourism businesses to reconfigure all their business processes to take advantage of the emerging opportunities and to avoid the new challenges. ICTs and the Internet introduced a second industrial revolution in the late 1990s. Although the predictions and assumptions made for the Internet revolution were challenged by the NASDAQ crash and what is now known as the 'Internet bubble burst' in early 2000, organisations that had a solid product proposition and value for consumers managed either to survive and develop into significant organisations (e.g. Expedia.com and Hotels.com) or to be acquired by larger organisations (e.g. Orbitz, OctopusTravel. com and eBookers, all purchased by Cendant in 2004). Hence, ICT applications in tourism accelerated rapidly, affecting both operational and strategic functions and raising the levels of competition for almost everybody in the marketplace.

Competition, competitiveness strategy and ICTs

Tourism organisations compete primarily to increase their market share (and consequently the volume of their sales) and also to increase their profit margin (by maximising their final price and also their share of the total margin generated throughout the chain). They do that by offering value for money (sufficient value for the price paid) as well as value for time (sufficient value for the time spent) to their consumers.

Cooper and Buhalis (1998) demonstrated that competition in tourism is multi-level. However the tourism industry players are often myopic with regard to the competition as they tend to concentrate on their immediate rivals and primarily local tourism product service providers. For example, hotels are primarily concerned about competition from other neighbouring properties. Hence, most tourism players fail to understand the magnitude and the global nature of the competitive environment of tourism, or to appreciate that they compete against all the alternative leisure options for consumers' time and money, as well as within distribution channels in order to attract a larger share of the profit margin generated by the entire chain. Five different levels of competition can be observed therefore and ICTs have implications for all of those as demonstrated in Table 8.1.

Porter (2001) suggests that the greatest impact of the Internet has been the reconfiguration of existing industries that have been constrained by the high costs of communications, gathering information or accomplishing transactions. He reassures that whether the industry is new or old its structural attractiveness is still determined by the five underlying forces of competition, namely the intensity of rivalry among existing competitors, the barriers to entry for new competitors, the threat of substitute products or services, the bargaining power of suppliers and the bargaining power of buyers. Table 8.2 demonstrates that the Internet has had both positive and negative impacts on the competitive position of a wide range of players in the marketplace. In particular the Internet has enabled organisations to strengthen their position by disintermediating the channel and going directly to the final consumer whilst expanding the overall size of the market. However, at the same time, the Internet provides buyers with easier access to information about products and suppliers, thus bolstering buyer bargaining power.

Although the Internet can assist the expansion of the market, this can come at the expense of average profitability. Perhaps most importantly Porter explains that 'the great paradox of the Internet is that its very benefits–making information

Table 8.1 Competition levels, tourism challenges and ICT solutions

Level of competition	Tourism challenge	Technology solution
Level 1: Competition from similar products and service providers	Tourism organisations compete with similar organisations in their proximity. For example, a hotel will be competing with other accommodation establishments at the destination. However, tourism organisations should not focus their competitive efforts against their neighbouring business but rather develop co-opetition strategies, to take advantage of collaboration at the destination.	Extranets facilitate this initiative and provide electronic tools for facilitating this process.
Level 2: Competition from similar or undifferentiated destinations	Many destinations have established an image with the consumer which is easily substitutable by alternative destinations. The most obvious example is the sun and sea products in the Mediterranean coast. It seems that for some consumer segments, sun, sea and a reasonable accommodation establishment are all that are required, independent of the location of the destination and the socio-cultural surroundings. Therefore, tourism organisations need to collaborate to establish their brand and develop their collective differentiation.	Internet representation helps tourism destinations to reinforce their image nationally and internationally and to promote their uniqueness.

Level 3: Competition from differentiated destinations	Unique tourism destinations and products take advantage of their natural and socio-cultural resources and add unique value. Tourism products in these areas are regarded as unique as they are not easily substitutable.	Internet can reinforce uniqueness and Extranets can bring together all partners to develop suitably themed experiences.
Level 4: Competition within the distribution channel	Competition within the distribution channels reflects the effort of each channel member to increase their own profit margin. This is against the profit margin of the other channel members, since consumers are willing to pay up to a certain price before switching provider or channel.	Technology enables disintermediation, giving the opportunity to suppliers to reach their customers and strengthen their position. When intermediation is inevitable, interoperability tools can reduce the distribution cost allowing a higher margin to be share by all partners.
Level 5: Competition with alternative leisure activities or purchases	Alternative activities might have an element of training and education, or might be purely recreational. The development of rural tourism, sophisticated leisure activities and theme parks at the tourists' place of origin might effectively reduce the need for consumers to travel to particular destinations in order to enjoy tourism products. In addition, alternative substantial purchases such as a new house or a new car may result in a postponement of a holiday effectively acting as competition to the entire industry.	Many leisure and recreation alternatives emerge as ICT applications, including virtual reality and computer games which might encourage people to stay at home and discover the destination from the convenience and safety of their armchair. However in reality many of these activities take place at destinations and hence Internet representations can be used to promote a variety of alternative leisure and recreational activities at the destination.

Table 8.2 How the Internet influences industry structure

Bargaining power of suppliers	Rivalry among existing competitors	Threat of substitute products or services	Buyers	Barriers to entry
(+/–) Procurement using the Internet tends to raise bargaining power over suppliers, though it can also give suppliers access to more customers	(–) Reduces differences among competitors as offerings are difficult to keep proprietary	(+) By making the overall industry more efficient, the Internet can expand the size of the market	(+) Eliminates powerful channels or improves bargaining power over traditional channels	(–) Reduces barriers to entry such as the need for a sales force, access to channels and physical assets – anything that Internet technology eliminates or makes easier to do reduces barriers to entry
(–) the Internet provides a channel for suppliers to reach end users, reducing the leverage of intervening companies	(–) Migrates competition to price	(–) The proliferation of Internet approaches creates new substitution threats	(–) Shifts bargaining power to end consumers	(–) Internet applications are difficult to keep proprietary from new entrants
(–) Internet procurement and digital markets tend to give all companies equal access to suppliers, and gravitate procurement to standardised products that reduce differentiation	(–) Widens the geographic market, increasing the number of competitors		(–) Reduces switching costs	(–) A flood of new entrants has come into many industries
(–) Reduced barriers to entry and the proliferation of competitors downstream shifts power to suppliers	(–) Lowers variable cost relative to fixed cost, increasing pressures for price discounting			

Source: Porter, 2001

widely available; reducing the difficulty of purchasing, marketing and distribution; allowing buyers and sellers to find and transact business with one another more easily – also make it more difficult for companies to capture those benefits as profits' (Porter, 2001: 66).

It is evident, therefore, that tourism organisations will find it more difficult to compete in an increasingly globalised, concentrated and fiercely competitive environment. Although it seems only natural to compete against enterprises of the same sector within destinations, tourism organisations should appreciate the entire range of competition forces and to deal with the different levels of competition. Vertical and horizontal co-opetition within destinations and within value systems will be increasingly important for the survival and profitability of organisations. Gradually we will observe independent organisations sharing the same destiny (co-destiny). Co-opetition should improve the collective competitiveness of destinations or value chains against rival systems and substitute products or factors which reduce their profitability. Technology assists destinations and value systems to develop links between all the nodes of the network and to operationalise an interactive and intelligence system to enhance wealth creation and distribution between partners.

eTourism and competition in the tourism industry

Poon (1993) predicted that 'a whole system of ICTs is being rapidly diffused throughout the tourism industry and no player will escape ICTs impacts'. The technology revolution has already had profound implications for the tourism sector. Information is the life-blood of tourism and so technology is fundamental for the ability of the industry to operate. Unlike durable goods, intangible tourism services cannot be physically displayed or inspected at the point of sale before purchasing. They are normally bought before the time of their use and away from the place of consumption. They therefore rely almost exclusively upon representations and descriptions by the travel trade and other intermediaries, for their ability to attract consumers. Timely and accurate information, relevant to consumers' needs, is often the key to successful satisfaction of tourism demand. Few other activities require the generation, gathering, processing, application and communication of information for operations. ICTs and the Internet have enabled innovative tourism organisations to develop their processes and adapt their management to take advantage of the emerging digital tools and mechanisms to:

- Improve the operation, structure and strategy of organisations. Not only do they reduce both communication and operational costs, but they also enhance flexibility, interactivity, efficiency, productivity and competitiveness.
- Increase their internal efficiency and manage their capacity and yields better. By incorporating sophisticated yield management systems they support

organisations to adjust their pricing to demand fluctuations in order to maximise their profitability. They can also manage their inventory and reservations systems more efficiently and improve occupancy levels.

- Enhance the operational and geographic scope by offering strategic tools for global expansion. A number of international organisations use technology to manage their operations 'by wire' and often at a great distance.
- Use portals for interacting effectively with consumers and personalising the product. For example, British Airways has launched a strategy to enable passengers to undertake a number of processes, including booking, ticketing, check-in and seat and meal selection on BA.com.
- Revolutionise tourism intermediation and increase the points of sale. For example, Expedia, Travelocity, Lastminute, Orbitz and Opodo have emerged as the most dominant electronic travel agencies, offering an one-stop shop for consumers.
- Empower consumers to communicate with other consumers. For example www.virtualtourists.com or www.igoyougo.com supports the exchange of destination information and tips. Moreover, www.untied.com or www. alitaliasucks.com enable dissatisfied customers to make their views available.
- Use interoperability tools to support efficient cooperation between partners in the value system. For example Pegasus enables independent hotels to distribute their availability through their web sites and other partners online.

Each of these trends modifies the competitive forces and changes the conditions of competition. The Internet provided a globally distributed infrastructure for inexpensive delivery of multimedia information, promotion and distribution of tourism. It empowered the provision and marketing of tailor-made products to meet the needs of individual tourists and hence, it bridged tourism demand and supply in a flexible and interactive way. ICTs are becoming pivotal for tourism and it is evident that ICTs have a dramatic impact on the travel industry because they force this sector as a whole to rethink the way in which it organises ICT business, ICT values or norms of behaviour and the way in which it educates the ICT workforce (Sheldon, 1997; Poon, 1993; Buhalis, 1998). Consequently the rapid development of both tourism supply and demand makes ICTs an imperative partner for the marketing, distribution, promotion and co-ordination of the tourism sector.

By the year 2005, only 10 years after the general public used the first browser, there was a certain degree of maturity evident in the marketplace. This was particularly the case for organisations in well-developed economies, such as North America, Europe, Australia and North Asia (Marcussen, 2003). This was demonstrated by a number of indicators, namely:

- Most suppliers had established comprehensive and fully functional web sites.
- Tourism was already one of the most successful areas of eCommerce and the sector that attracted the highest expenditure online.

- An estimated 18% of all airline bookings were made on the Internet, often reaching more than 90% for no-frills carriers.
- The top three agencies in the USA accounted for 74% of the online market.
- Most hotel chains and international car rental firms were reporting a significant increase in their direct sales through their web sites.
- Several key travel intermediaries emerged as global players through a number of mergers and acquisitions.
- Increasingly travellers search online before booking holidays either online or offline.
- Practically all tourism destinations around the world have some sort of web site providing information for their region.
- Advanced destinations have developed comprehensive systems supporting itinerary building and reservations for all their suppliers.

Although ICTs are not a panacea and cannot guarantee financial success on their own, ignoring, under-utilising or over-utilising ICTs can be disastrous for the competitiveness of most tourism enterprises and destinations. This is because ICTs are instrumental in ensuring efficient internal organisation, effective communication with partners and interactivity with consumers. Failure to address these issues can jeopardise the competitiveness, prosperity and even existence of tourism organisations. To the degree that ICTs can contribute to the value chain of products and services, by either improving their cost position or differentiation, they reshape competitiveness and thus have strategic implications for the prosperity of the organisation (Porter, 2001). The competitiveness of both tourism enterprises and destinations should be therefore reassessed, according to organisational need, in the utilisation, development and application of ICTs.

The impact of the Internet and ICTs on competition for each of the sector industry

Developments in the Internet and ICT have propelled dramatic changes in the competition forces for each sector of tourism and its members. Not only have a number of new players emerged and gained a significant market share, but existing players also had to develop defensive strategies to protect their position as well as aggressive strategies to capitalise on the emerging opportunities. The proliferation of low-cost airlines and the emergence of intermediaries such as Expedia and Lastminute.com epitomise these changes. In essence, Internet developments have forced each organisation in the tourism system to try hard to increase both their market share and profit margin. Competition for market share emerged through promotions and directed communications based on Customer Relation Management (CRM) systems for existing customers. Expansion into new markets was facilitated through specialised web sites known as vortals (either for geographical markets or for specialist markets such as ski), supported by calling centres that could support the language of the new market or had expertise in that specialised form of tourism. Using technology to communicate with remote locations allowed organisations to outsource many of these functions to low-cost locations such as India and Mauritius, significantly reducing their cost base.

As demonstrated in Figure 8.1, on the one hand suppliers had the opportunity to partly disintermediate their distribution channels and communicate directly with the consumers, increasing customer loyalty, volume of sales and profit margins. For example British Airways increased their direct bookings through BA.com to almost 50% for short-haul flights. However, as the low-cost carriers used different business models and a much lower cost basis, BA had to redesign its service and pricing strategies to meet the new conditions of the marketplace. Direct customer service provides a wide range of new challenges, and innovative tourism organisations can enjoy the opportunities and the intelligence that such contact avails.

On the other hand, re-intermediation in the marketplace meant that both new intermediaries emerged, whilst existing intermediaries changed their practices to adjust to the new realities. Almost everybody that had access to consumers,

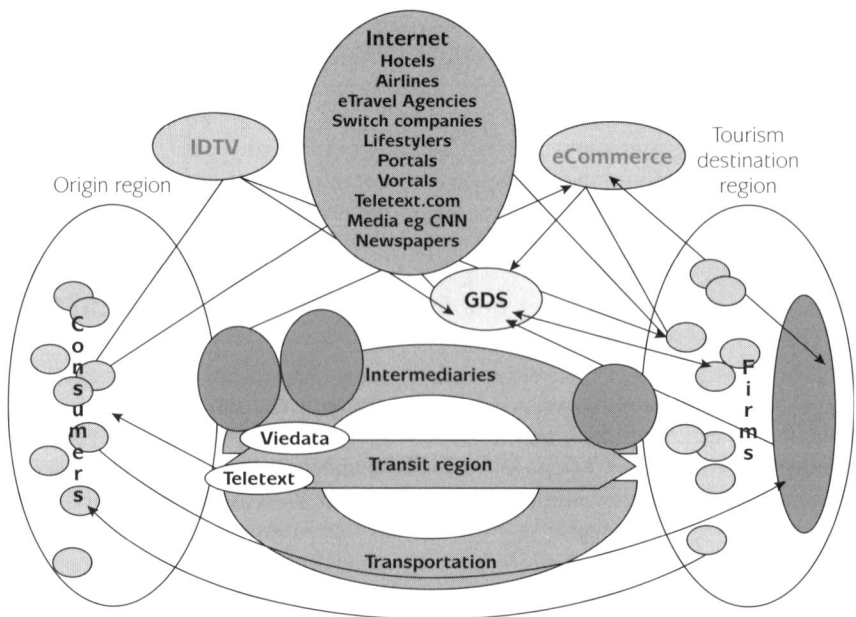

Figure 8.1 Internet impacts on the tourism industry

Source: Buhalis and Licata, 2002.

Note: OTA: Outgoing Travel Agency, TO: Tour Operator, ITO: Incoming Tour Operator, DMO: Destination Management Organisation.

including search engines (e.g. Yahoo and MSN), newspapers (e.g. *The Times* and *Telegraph*), TV channels (e.g. CNN), guide books (e.g. Lonely Planet) and many others emerged as tourism intermediaries, using their web sites to attract customers. Organisations such as OTC (Online Travel Corporation) fulfil these services through while-label solutions for a commission; i.e. they provide travel content and reservation capabilities on the web site of a third party whilst maintaining the look and feel of the hosting site. Commission capping and the gradual abolition of commissions forced intermediaries to identify new methods to maintain their profitability. This created incredible competition on profit margins as each member of the channel struggled to maintain or increase their profit margin. New models emerged in the marketplace such as service charges for each transaction made by intermediaries and dynamic packaging which enabled consumers to purchase a bundle of products for a comprehensive price without knowing the individual price of each component. This was based on the merchant model which allowed intermediaries to buy a product at agreed prices and then add their desired profit margin on top, according to market conditions, competition and commercial priorities. This created pressure on the suppliers' brand integrity, whilst it confused consumers as they could find the same product at many different prices. Price comparison services such as Cheapflights.com, Kelkoo.com, Mobissimo.com, Kayak.com or FareChase.com search about 150 travel sites, including low-cost airlines which rarely show up on Global Distribution Systems, and travel portals made pricing very transparent (Buhalis and Ujma, 2005). This forced each tourism organisation to justify the exact value that they offer to the public and to demonstrate value for money and for time.

A thorough analysis of the various sectors of the tourism industry demonstrates the key Internet-propelled developments in the marketplace and the emerging relationships between partners and the consumers and stakeholders.

Airlines

ICTs have been used extensively in airlines due to the scale of operations and the intensity of their functions. Airlines realised quite early the need for efficient, quick, inexpensive and accurate handling of their inventory and internal organisation, due to the complexity of their operations. As early as 1962, American Airlines introduced the SABRE Computerised Reservations System instead of expanding its Boeing 707 fleet by 50% (from eight to twelve aircraft) (Archdale, 1991: D.15). During the deregulation years prices, schedules and routes were liberalised, airlines could change them indefinitely, while new airlines entered the market, making technology critical in both operational and strategic terms.

Distribution remains a crucial element of airlines' strategy and competitiveness, as it determines the cost and the ability to access consumers. Nowadays ICTs and internal CRSs are used heavily to support the Internet distribution of airline seats. These systems are in the heart of airline operational and strategic agendas (Buhalis,

2004; O'Toole, 2004). This is particularly the case for smaller and regional carriers as well as no-frills airlines which cannot afford GDS fees and aim to sell their seats at competitive prices. This has forced even traditional/full-service/flag airlines to recognise the need for re-engineering the distribution processes, costs and pricing structures. Hence, they use the Internet for:

- Enhancing interactivity and building relationships with consumers and partners;
- On-line reservations;
- Electronic ticketing;
- Yield management;
- Electronic auctions for last-minute available seats;
- Disintermediation and redesign of agency commission schemes; and
- Maximising the productivity of the new electronic distribution media (Buhalis, 2004).

The emergence of the Internet had a number of implications for the competition forces in the industry. Firstly, new no-frills airlines (such as Southwest, Ryanair and easyJet) emerged with a low-cost business model facilitated by Internet-based direct distribution. Having about 20–30% savings on their distribution costs, as they did not pay for GDS fees, travel agency commissions and ticketing administrative costs, they could offer much more competitively priced flights to consumers and still ensure profitability. Flag airlines had to react as they were haemorrhaging market share to the newcomers. A very painful adoption process of both prices and ticketing rules allowed more flexibility and transparency but reduced profit margins and forced them to readdress their cost basis. Unable to compete with the low-cost base of the no-frills airlines they were effectively forced to maintain a number of loss leaders as feeders to long-haul flights. Nevertheless airlines are investing heavily in direct sales which, coupled with 'customer relations management' and 'revenue management systems', will enable them to better control their distribution and strategic marketing.

O'Connor (2003) explained that: 'one of the reasons that travel suppliers have not been successful at diverting significant amounts of business to their own web sites remains that in many cases consumers want a one-stop-shop offering both brand choice and the ability to cater for all their travel booking requirements – something that is clearly not available on a single company's branded web site.' As a result, suppliers have been trying to extent their product online. For example SouthWest.com, British Airways, easyJet and most other innovative airlines extent their value chain online and offer hotel and car rentals. Similarly, Hyatt.com provides air and car booking facilities and Dollar.com air and hotel reservation capabilities. Yet despite the attempts to expand the value chain to offer a broader product selection, supplier sites cannot offer as wide a choice of alternative brands as travel agencies.

The rapid expansion of online travel agencies such as Expedia and Travelocity threatened to dominate the distribution of suppliers. To reduce the power of emerging online agencies, many leading travel suppliers have formed industry alliances in order to divert business away from the existing major agencies and to develop alternative one-stop shops. For example, it is generally accepted that 'T2' – the original name for Orbitz – stood for 'Terminate Travelocity' and was conceived as a way for the airline suppliers to unseat Travelocity, which at the time was the largest online travel company. Three major companies have emerged as a co-opetition between airlines to sell their tickets – Orbitz (US), Opodo (Europe) and Zuji (Asia), whilst Hotwire and TravelWeb brought together different hotel corporations. Unlike supplier direct web sites, online-agency-killers can offer the broad range of both brands and products demanded by online consumers, and their ownership by consortia of suppliers rescue them from claims of bias or unfavourable practices. For suppliers, the benefits of such co-operation are clear – no agency commission and in many cases reduced transaction fees, as many of these new sites bypass the traditional GDSs by connecting directly with supplier databases. Currently the airlines pay $15 to $17 in booking fees to the GDSs for each ticket sold – about $1.7 billion a year for all airlines in the United States. With these new systems, the airlines get some of the booking fees back in the form of rebates, cutting their transaction costs by 30%, or $10.50 to $12 per ticket, a saving that can then be passed on to consumers. By bonding together, travel suppliers are able to get the best of both worlds – scale to be able to effectively compete with the mega-agencies, but at a lower cost (O'Connor, 2003). However, airlines have had several difficult years following September 11th and were reluctant to continue supporting those agencies. As a result, in 2004, Orbitz was sold to Cendant, which also owns Galileo and several other supplier brands, for $1.2bn, whilst Amadeus acquired the majority of shares of Opodo, enabling both GDSs to develop their consumer interface and expanding their distribution.

Global distribution systems

In 1978, the deregulation of the US air transportation boosted the usage of CRSs, as it enabled airlines to compete fiercely by adapting their schedule and fares to demand (Levine, 1987). As the barriers of entry within the USA airline transportation collapsed, everybody could fly one route and abandon another (Copeland and McKenney, 1988). To increase competitiveness, airlines developed the 'hub and spoke' systems, while the fare structure became complex and unstable. As the prices, schedules and routes were liberated, airlines could change them indefinitely, while new airlines entered the markets. 'Fare wars' multiplied the fares available and increased the computing and communication needs (Hopper, 1990). The sophistication of airline CRSs had to expand in order to distribute up-to-date information to all potential customers worldwide and to support the operation and administration of airlines. This development also resulted in the promotion of CRSs to marketing and distribution systems as they contributed significantly to the competitiveness of vendor/host airlines. Gradually CRSs evolved to become global distribution systems (GDSs) and became strategic business units (SBU) in their own right, due to their ability to generate income and boost airlines' sales at the expense of their competitors.

As far as competition practices are concerned, GDSs helped vendor airlines to benefit from incremental revenues by increasing their load factors. Incremental revenues can be defined as the added revenues an airline receives from increased passenger volumes on its flights, due to the use of its CRS or GDS by travel agents. They resulted from screen bias (defined as the inclusion of parameters in software packages to favour the services of the airline vendor over other carriers) and the 'halo effect' (the close business relationship that emerged between travel agencies and vendor airlines, due to the subscription of an agency to an airline's CRS). This incremental revenue proved very profitable as airlines estimated that between 40% and 80% of incremental revenues translate directly into increased net earnings (House of Commons, 1988). Whenever a connection flight is requested between a 'city pair' CRSs utilise a set of criteria to display the eligible flights and to rank them on the screen accordingly. In the early days of GDSs vendor airlines deliberately influenced the information retrieval algorithms, by including favourable parameters for their own airline. Similarly to accessing an airline web site, an individual CRS enables access to a particular airline's system and hence they carry a natural and legitimate bias. However, in single-access GDSs, where all participating airlines, users and consumers anticipate an equally unbiased treatment, bias is against both the public interest and the anti-monopoly regulations (ibid.). There are four major types of bias in favour of vendor/host airlines, namely, display or screen bias, incentive policies, distorted information and vendor system bias, as demonstrated in Table 8.3.

Screen bias is the presentation of information in a preferable way for the vendor airline and to a lesser degree other carriers willing to pay fees in return for preferential displays (called co hosts) (Truitt et al., 1991). Screen bias refers to the screen a particular flight appears on, while display bias corresponds with the location of a particular flight on the screen (Boberg and Collison, 1985). It is widely argued that the display position of the flights on the terminal influence significantly the possibility of being chosen, as between 70% and 90% of all bookings are made from the first screen and 50% from the first line of the first page (House of Commons, 1988). Therefore the criteria of the display priority for each flight drastically determine the possibility of a flight sale. Secondary screen bias refers to secondary display which can be overtly biased towards one particular airline, as demonstrated in multi-access systems. 'In response to a consumer's known airline preference or a travel agent's incentive scheme a separate (secondary) display can be selected which will focus on selected airlines only, or give certain airlines priority' (ibid.; Adam, 1990).

Table 8.3 Typologies of incremental revenues in airline CRSs

A. SCREEN DISPLAY BIAS	
Ia. Display bias	*II. Distorted information*
• Carrier bias	• Code sharing
• Structural bias	• Funnel flights
• Screen/display bias	• Elapsed time
• Airport/connection/point bias	• Unrealistic time
• Route bias	• Default time
• Categorisation	• Not update competitors
• Screen padding	information
	• Fare bias (maximum only)
Ib. Secondary screen bias	
• Incentive policies for travel agencies	
III. Vendor/system bias	B. HALO EFFECT
• Fee bias/commission overrides?	• Travel agencies' tendency to book on vendors' airline rather than competing carriers
• Subscriber contracts (travel agency prohibited from having second CRS)	
• Restricted entry	
• Market intelligence	

Source: Boberg and Collison, 1985: 179; House of Commons, 1988; Adam, 1990.

Distorted information contained in airline CRSs and GDSs also causes bias towards host/vendor airlines as information is arranged in order to deceive a CRS's algorithms and get priority in the flight display. Hence, distorted information eventually creates display/screen bias without being illegal. Numerous sources of distorted information can be identified which affect the competitiveness of smaller carriers as well as consumers' convenience, such as code sharing, when two different airlines share the same code; reduction of elapsed time and thus, display of a technically shorter trip; default timing, which favours vendors' airlines departure times; funnel flights showing a single flight number for a connecting flight; and delaying market intelligence information or passing on up-to-date information less rapidly (House of Commons, 1988; Adam, 1990). Although CRSs were expected to facilitate bargain fare identification, most CRSs had a fares bias towards the dearest full fares as they could not display unofficial rates, these being available exclusively through consolidators.

System or vendor bias is the bias exercised by vendor carriers' CRSs on their contracts with their suppliers (airlines) and customers (outgoing travel agencies), which aims to weaken demand for both competing carriers and CRSs. Negotiable fees for reservations and market intelligence, with unfavourable fees for competitors; CRSs restricted access, service or ticket distribution capabilities on competing carriers; subscriber contracts eliminating the usage of other CRSs systems in travel agencies and finally market intelligence capabilities by the vendor airlines, are some of the commonly described types of vendor/system bias (House of Commons, 1988; Truitt et al., 1991).

Finally, halo effect is the tendency of travel agencies to book flights on a vendor airline's system even if these services are inconvenient and more expensive. Although the reasons causing the 'halo effect' are unknown, travel agencies seem to have higher confidence that information on a vendor's schedules and tariffs are updated and accurate, while appreciating an extensive range of support services provided by the host/vendor airline. It may also be generated by the fact that travel agencies usually join the CRS of the dominant carrier in their geographical region, and thus, they may use this carrier more frequently. Additionally, numerous specific requests from a customer such as specific meals or seating can be better accommodated by the host/vendor's airline. It is suggested that the 'halo effect' has great benefits for the host/vendor airline which are estimated to be between 6% and 30% of CRS vendor revenues (House of Commons, 1988). Thus, incremental benefits have been used as resources of power and 'information based strategies' (Boberg and Collison, 1985; Levine, 1987; Truitt et al., 1991).

These practices distorted airline competition and forced public authorities to introduce legislation and regulations for airline CRS, as bias in favour of one particular airline is against public interest. However, some vendor airlines defend their right to bias their own systems, as a reasonable return from their investment. 'Airlines did not deny this bias, arguing that it was appropriate given the financial risks incurred by host carriers which develop the systems' (Mietus, 1989). Nevertheless, antitrust laws and consequently commercial pressures inevitably led to regulation by both American and European bodies. As early as 1984 the American Civil Aeronautics Board (CAB) and the Department of Transport (DOT) identified a number of practices which appeared to affect airline competition (Mietus, 1989). Consequently, the DOT issued regulations governing the operation of carrier-owned systems which promoted the equal treatment of CRSs and prevented the screen connection point, fee, business, information, barriers to entry and subscriber contract bias (House of Commons, 1988). The International Civil Aviation Organisation (ICAO) also proposed a number of suggestions for a more fair display of non-vendor airlines and partners (Feldman, 1988). Most of the displayed bias problems were solved by the First Regulation Act but the DOT came back in 1988 to fight the difference in fees charged as well as the tie-in policies. In Europe, regulation measures have been taken by three separate organisations, i.e. the European Civil Aviation Conference (ECAC), the European Community (EC, 1993) and thirdly the International Civil Aviation Organisation (Wheatcroft and Lipman, 1990). However, discrimination problems for non-host airlines were hardly solved. Despite regulations, non-vendor airlines claimed that substantial bias still existed and that passengers rarely were able to book their optimal flights. Many discovered that 'CRS operations are undemocratic' and that the competition gap between the owners and the non-owners was increasing. 'In the USA, despite the fact that airlines competed for passengers, airlines that did not own a share of a CRS depended on, and pay money to competitors for their livelihood', whilst CRS ownership was described as the 'key to survival in the airlines business' (Feldman, 1988).

Since the early 1990s however, GDSs emerged as strategic business units (SBU) in their own right. The newly founded (at that time) European GDSs Amadeus and Galileo and the American Sabre and Worldspan belonged to a consortium of airlines, and hence uncompetitive practices were not commercially and strategically acceptable. Gradually, as demonstrated in Table 8.3, through mergers and acquisitions most GDSs were owned by more than one airline or by independent companies. Hence, GDSs emerged as fairly neutral in the marketing and distribution process and airlines had to co-opete, compete and collaborate at the same time. By 2004 many airlines sold their interests in GDSs to generate cash in order to finance their operational losses, enabling GDSs to operate as independent distribution companies. Airlines and other suppliers input data into all five GDSs which displayed information to agents who made bookings on behalf of consumers. Effectively every travel agency had access to all airlines. The introduction of the Internet enabled airlines to sell tickets directly to consumers. This is particularly the case for no-frills and charter carriers. Increasing use of travel Internet web sites did not necessarily change the number of bookings processed by GDSs (Table 8.4) as they also powered the inventory and reservation capability

Table 8.4 GDS worldwide bookings comparison

	2000	2001	2002	2003	2004(e)
(Bookings in millions)					
Amadeus[1]	393.9	386.1	395.6	383.1	402.3
Galileo[2]	350.9	306.2	286.0	267.4	276.7
Sabre	466.6	430.8	397.4	364.3	376.5
Worldspan[3]	172.6	195.6	191.8	194.0	205.6
Total bookings	1,384.0	1,318.7	1,270.8	1,208.8	1,261.1
Growth in total bookings (%)		(1.5)	(3.6)	(4.9)	4.3

Source: CIBC World Markets.

1 Does not include Germany's Start Leisure Bookings.

2 Cendant acquired Galileo in late 2001. Estimates prior to 2001 are based on Galileo public filings.

3 Worldspan was sold in mid-2003. Estimates are for 2002 and 2003 based on public filings and CIBC estimates.

Table 8.5 GDS profiles

	Galileo	Sabre	Worldspan	Amadeus
Founded	1993	1960	1990	1987
Headquarters	Parsippany, New Jersey USA	Southlake, Texas, USA	Atlanta, Georgia, USA	Madrid, Spain
Original owners	11 North American and European airlines; floated in 1997 on NY and Chicago stock exchanges	American Airlines and IBM	Delta Airlines, Northwest Airlines and Trans World Airlines combining the companies' existing reservation technologies that has been developed since 1968	Air France, Iberia, Lufthansa
Current ownership	Acquired by Cendant in 2001 for US$ 1.8bn after bidding battle with Amadeus	Sabre Holdings is the New York listed parent of Sabre Travel Network, Travelocity and Sabre Airline Solutions; owns 50% of Travelocity Europe	Worldspan was sold in June 2003 to Transaction Processing Corp, a vehicle set up by Citigroup Venture Capital and Teacher's Merchant Bank for ($745m) €900m; in April 2004 the company announced plans for an IPO, which has subsequently been aborted.	Quoted on the Madrid, Paris and Frankfurt stock exchanges. In February 2004, Lufthansa reduced its stake to 5.1% from 18.3% in a move that, analysts suggested, the company could herald sector consolidation. Air France (23.36%) and Iberia (18.28%) remain the largest shareholders

2003 revenues	Not known	$2.05 billion; full year net earnings were $83m compared to $214m for 2002. Bookings processed through the Sabre GDS were 8% down on 2002 at $366 million.	$896.9m down 2% on 2003; full year net earnings were $13.7m, down 87% compared to 2002	€1.9bn and net income of €148.6m
Customer base	44,000 travel agents	56,000 travel agents	16,000 travel agencies	65,250 travel agents; 10,500 airline offices
Inventory	470 airlines; 56,000 hotels; 24 car rental agencies; 430 tour operators, and all major cruise lines	400 airlines; 60,000 hotels; 53 car rental agencies; 9 cruise lines, 36 rail companies, 232 tour operators	465 airlines, 55,000 hotels; 40 car rental agencies; 40 tour & cruise lines	469 airlines; 58,000 hotels; 50 car rental agencies; ferry, rail, cruise and insurance providers

Source: Adapted from Griffin, 2004.

of many of the online travel sites on the background. However, it did change the power base and relative profitability of the various channels. With less reliance on agents, airlines have been able to slash commissions and in the case of the low-cost carriers, some of whom only sell through their web sites, deprive GDS and agents of product and commission altogether (Griffin, 2004). Griffin cites the following data:

Ward et al. (2003) demonstrate clearly that change is on the cards again. The anticipated deregulation in 2005 will resolve the regulatory controls on GDSs and enable them to reconfigure their activities.

The deregulation is expected to allow carriers that own a GDS to change or eliminate their previous business models; permit the GDS to create price discrimination packages, sell booking data and access others' data; eliminate agency booking thresholds and volume incentives and allow agencies to cancel contracts. As a result, airlines and GDSs will be negotiating direct deals that will include fees, display position and other privileged services.

This will inevitably mean that some carriers will choose not to distribute their inventory through some of the GDSs if the conditions in the marketplace are not suitable. With deregulation virtually eliminating mandatory GDS participation, suppliers will consolidate volume in exchange for discounts; each GDS will likely have fewer subscribers. Not all airlines will be distributing through all GDSs, forcing travel agencies to either install and learn how to use more than one GDS or to find alternative ways to access airline inventory. Given that no-frills airlines distribute almost their entire inventory through their Internet portals, scheduled airlines are expected to follow suit and also to use their accommodation and car rental partners to expand their value chain. Equally, these changes will increase competition, forcing GDS players to differentiate more sharply and to enhance the number and types of value-added services they offer. The proposed elimination of regulatory barriers, a cost structure that is predominately fixed in nature, the existence of several undifferentiated competitors and the real threat of substitution from direct connect will put considerable pressure on the GDSs to alter pricing and to negotiate with airlines fees according to volume of business and access to all their fares. For example, Amadeus at the end of 2004 was offering a discount from the normal fee of €4.9 per segment to €2.67 per segment if an airline was distributing all its content, including their web fares, on the GDS. Amadeus claimed that this would also support airlines and intermediaries, as agencies would no longer have to go through the time-consuming and costly process of logging on to an airline's web site to book on the lowest fares. As suppliers negotiate prices for individual contracts, deregulation will increase the advantages to be gained by suppliers through economies of scale, especially for larger players. Smaller carriers will probably have a hard time distributing through GDSs unless they operate feeder services and code sharing with larger players. These impacts of deregulation, in conjunction with opportunities and threats of direct distribution, are expected to change travel distribution dramatically once again, affecting all members of the channel.

Hospitality

ICTs enable hotels to improve their productivity, as well as strategic and operational management. They use Property Management Systems (PMSs) to co-ordinate front office, sales, planning and operational functions by administrating reservations and managing the hotel inventory. Moreover, PMSs integrate the 'back' and 'front' of the house management and improve general administration functions such as accounting and finance; marketing research and planning; forecasting and yield management; payroll and personnel; and purchasing (Beldona et al., 2001). One of the most promising developments in hospitality is 'application service providers' (ASPs) which host a number of business applications for hospitality organisations (Paraskevas and Buhalis, 2002). Hotel chains use Central Reservation Offices (CROs) to manage their collective inventory and maximise their profitability. Smaller and independent properties either undertake direct distribution or participate in hotel consortia and/or representations companies (Go and Welch, 1991). Their systems facilitate both in-house management and distribution through electronic media to provide easy, efficient, inexpensive and reliable ways of making and confirming reservations. Global presence and distribution in a wide range of outlets is essential in order to enable both individual customers and the travel trade to access accurate and up-to-date information on availability and rates.

The Internet empowered the promotion of hotels through individual web sites that enable properties to show their amenities and promote direct bookings. Even small accommodation establishments can take advantage with a modest web site and promote themselves in the electronic marketplace (Morrison et al., 1999; Van Hoof et al., 1999). Online bookings provide a range of benefits including an expansion of accessible markets as well as a dramatic reduction of operational costs. For example the cost per individual booking can be reduced from US$10–15 for voice-based reservations, to US$7.50–3.50 for reservations through GDSs, to US$0.25 through the WWW. Savings can also be achieved in printing, storing, administrating and posting promotional material. In addition, hotel chains have the opportunity to establish comprehensive portals to promote their properties as well as to support their brands. Switch companies, such as THISCO and WIZCOM, expanded their operations to provide an interface between the various systems and property management systems and enable a certain degree of transparency. This reduces both set-up and reservation costs, whilst facilitating reservations through several distribution channels (Emmer et al., 1993; Connolly et al., 1998; O'Connor and Frew, 2000; Murphy et al., 1996).

On the one hand, the Internet has strengthened the competitive position of hotels by providing unprecedented tools for hotels to promote their inventory and to expand their market by using both direct distribution and a much wider range of distributors than before. On the other, it intensified competition as not only prices were transparent for all to see online but also because it provided the ground for several hotel aggregators (such as hotels.com, allhotels.com) to emerge and sell the hotel product almost exclusively on price. The oversupply of accommodation, combined with the limited demand after September 11th, intensified competition and forced hotels to negotiate minimal rates with aggregators. As in most are small and medium-sized, independent, seasonal and family properties, they find it extremely difficult to utilise ICTs fully.

The merchant model emerged, where aggregators were agreeing a fixed price per room and had the right to sell at any price that was suitable for their needs. This was in contrast to the commission model where the hotel was determining its price and was offering a commission of about 10%. Expedia in particular were successful in using the merchant model and used it extensively to build dynamic packaging where they were offering a combined price with the air tickets. As airlines were not paying commissions any more, online agencies hoped that a combined sale would enable them to compensate for the loss of revenue from airlines. Consumers were able to find cheaper hotel prices on aggregator and travel agency sites than from hotels themselves, reducing the direct distribution prospects and damaging relationships with consumers. Not only hotels were selling their rooms for less money, but they were paying commission and administrative fees to distributors and also were attracting clientele that had lower expenditure in the property, jeopardising their Revenue per Available Room (RevPAR), profit margins and profitability. In addition, hotel chains were losing the commission charged (8–10%) to individual properties for reservations.

Hence, the commoditisation of the hotel properties, the damage to hotel brands and the price guarantees offered on hotel chain portals forced hotel chains to regain some of their distribution powers. They introduced extensive terms and conditions that restricted aggregators to sell accommodation at pre-agreed prices and to respect a number of rules that reinforce their brands. Lastminute. com for example has agreed favourable terms and conditions with Hilton and Intercontinental hotels. In addition, Hilton, Hyatt, Intercontinental, Marriott and Starwood launched Travelweb as a 'co-opetition' portal.

Intermediaries: tour operators and travel agencies

Tourism intermediation is affected by ICT and Internet developments. Tour operators have been arranging packages consisting of charter flights and accommodation, for leisure travellers. ICTs are used widely for organising, promoting, distributing and co-ordinating their packages, improving their productivity and capacity management. Most tour operators use databases to reduce their information-handling costs and increase the speed of information transfer and retrieval. Links with Travel Agencies who retail these packages are also facilitated by ICTs (Kärcher, 1996).

The Internet is gradually transforming the competition forces in the marketplace. Several tour operators in Germany, Scandinavia and the UK are moving towards electronic brochures and distribute their products electronically, enhancing direct distribution. Already a number of successful operators report up to 25% of their packages being booked directly by consumers online. There are major benefits in direct distribution, including: the ability to offer customised packages; update brochures and prices regularly to meet market conditions; save the 10–20% commission and reduce the costs of incentives, bonus and educational trips for travel agencies; and save the cost for developing, printing, storing and distributing conventional brochures, which is estimated to be approximately £20 per booking. In this sense they have improved their competitive position. However, the Internet developments and dynamic packaging allow consumers to package their own packages and threatens the dominance of tour operators. As ICTs will determine the future competitiveness of the industry, the distribution channel leadership and power of tour operators may be challenged. Although a partial disintermediation seems inevitable, there will always be sufficient market share for tour operators who can add value to the tourism product and deliver innovative, personalised and competitive holiday packages. As other channel members or online travel agencies utilise ICTs effectively to package and distribute either unique or cheaper tourism products, they challenge the leadership of tour operators in packaging. In response, many key players including TUI have started disintegrating their packages and selling individual components directly to the consumers. In this sense they will be able to re-intermediate, by offering their networks of suppliers through their channels.

ICTs and the Internet have radically changed the competitive forces for travel retailing. Travel agencies operate various reservation systems, which mainly enable them to check availability and make reservations for tourism products. ICTs, and particularly GDSs, have been critical for business travel agencies to access information and make reservations on scheduled airlines, hotel chains, car rentals and a variety of ancillary services. GDSs help construct complicated itineraries, while they provide up-to-date schedules, prices and availability information, as well as an effective reservation method. In addition, they offered internal management modules integrating the 'back office' (accounting, commission monitor, personnel) and 'front office' (customers' history, itinerary construction, ticketing and communication with suppliers). Multiple travel agencies in particular experience more benefits by achieving better co-ordination and control between their remote branches and headquarters. Transactions can provide invaluable data for financial and operational control as well as for marketing research, which can analyse the market fluctuations and ameliorate tactical decisions. ICTs are therefore irreplaceable tools for travel agencies as they provide information and reservation facilities and support the intermediation between consumers and principals.

The Internet has revolutionised the travel agency industry as, for the first time ever, agencies had the ability to reach travel inventory directly without having to invest in time and costs for acquiring GDSs. They are able to search and book suppliers such as airlines and hotels online, increasing their bookable inventory.

They also have the tools to sell their own services and to promote their organisations. The Internet developments in theory could have allowed established travel agencies to build their online presence and to capture the market that was migrating from offline to online. In reality the vast majority of players failed to see the opportunity and prepare suitable solutions, damaging their competitiveness. Travel agencies have been reluctant to take full advantage of the ICTs, mainly due to their limited strategic scope; deficient ICT expertise and understanding; low profit margins, which prevents investments; and focus on human interaction with consumers. This has resulted in a low level of integration of ICTs and capitalisation on the Internet's potential. As a result many agencies lack access to the variety of information and reservation facilities readily available to consumers and their credibility in the marketplace is reduced. This may jeopardise their ability to maintain their competitiveness and consequently, they may be threatened by disintermediation. Forces that intensify this threat include the fact that consumers increasingly search information and make reservations online; principals aim to control distribution costs by communicating directly with consumers and by developing customer relationship management; commission cutting forces consumers to pay upfront for service charges; and often many travel agencies have limited expertise as they employ inadequately trained personnel who cannot compete with knowledgeable consumers.

However, newcomers emerged to capture the online market. The development of major eTravel Agencies such as Expedia, Travelocity, Lastminute, Orbitz and Opodo has created powerful 'travel supermarkets' for consumers. They provide integrated travel solutions and a whole range of value-added services, such as destination guides, weather reports and insurance. By adopting dynamic packaging, i.e. the ability to package customised trips based on bundling individual components at a discounted total price, they effectively threaten the role of tour operators and other aggregators. New players have demonstrated a spectacular growth and marketplace penetration, as demonstrated in Table 8.6. As location becomes less significant electronic travel agents will dominate global travel retailing. Already in the USA more than 80% of online travel retailing is concentrated in the top five players. These players invested heavily in 2004 in purchasing online agencies such as eBookers and Opodo in order to get access to the European market.

Table 8.6 Online majors travel bookings revenue (US$ million)

Provider	2001	2002	2003
Expedia	3600	5300	8200
Travelocity	3100	3500	3890
Orbitz	818	2566	3440

Source: Clarke, 2004.

As a result, traditional travel agencies have been losing both market share, as consumers migrated to online intermediaries or suppliers directly, as well as profit margin as suppliers reduced commissions to minimal amounts. Despite the fact that many introduced service charges for each transaction undertaken many offline players find it difficult to compete in the marketplace. This is in contrast with online players who have seen their market to grow and are gradually raising their profitability. Therefore, the future of travel agencies will depend on their ability to utilise ICTs in order to reach their customers to increase the added value to the final tourism product and to serve their customer. Agencies which simply act as booking offices for tourism products will jeopardise their competitive position and face financial difficulties in the future. In contrast, knowledgeable and innovative agencies which utilise the entire range of technologies in order to provide suitable integrated tourism solutions will add value to the tourist experience and increase their competitiveness.

Horizontal and vertical integration in tourism intermediation

It is becoming increasingly evident that both horizontal and vertical integration emerge as key strategies in tourism intermediation. Emerging organisations use horizontal integration to expand their market share and market coverage as well as to compete with other online and offline intermediaries. Vertical integration is used for expanding value chains and propositions through a comprehensive portfolio of both intermediaries and principals. A wide range of principals that operate as SBUs ensure that there is adequate inventory to cover the entire range of market needs, even at times of product shortage. A comprehensive and inter-linked range of intermediaries enable vertically integrated organisations to build a comprehensive value system through layers that enable them to control the entire distribution channel.

The best example of horizontal integration can be observed on Lastminute.com which has used mergers and acquisitions for developing a comprehensive B2C, B2B, B2B2C travel portal. Lastminute.com has relationships with over 9,300 suppliers, including international scheduled airlines, hotels, package tour operators, theatre, sports and entertainment promoters, restaurants, speciality service providers, gift suppliers and car hire, both in the UK and internationally. Working with these suppliers in the travel, entertainment and gift industries it brings to its customers a comprehensive range of products and services. The company has developed a distinctive brand, which communicates spontaneity and a sense of adventure, attracting a loyal community of registered consumers that use the Lastminute.coms web site and have submitted their email addresses and other data to receive weekly emails. Lastminute.com carries almost no inventory risk, selling perishable inventory for its suppliers, and, where appropriate, protects suppliers' brand names until after purchase. Lastminute.com aims to create a one-stop shop for all last-minute needs and to develop its competitiveness as a global player. To expand its market base and also to enable their B2B and B2B2C distribution Lastminute.com purchased a number of companies, including HolidayAutos and Medhotels. This gave Lastminute.com a larger inventory basis and also enabled the company to move to the wholesale market by encouraging travel agencies to book on those web sites for suitable commissions. This growing multinational presence has developed and further strengthened the Lastminute. com brand. Lastminute.com is currently Europe's most visited travel and leisure web site. With 9.8m unique users per month across Europe, 100m page impressions per month and 7.5m newsletter subscribers in Europe, Lastminute.com has developed its European market share to an estimated 13%. This has been achieved by attracting consumers from traditional travel agencies and by expanding the market basis by encouraging consumers to take more last-minute and spontaneous holidays. As far as competition is concerned Lastminute.com has created competition for other intermediaries, as consumers have often shifted to online purchasing whilst at the same time it provides collaboration on a B2B2C basis, when intermediaries use Lastminute.com for sourcing inventory to build products and experiences for their customers. Suppliers benefit by increasing their market share and global reach although they effectively compete with Lastminute. com for their profit margins and have to ensure that they maintain their brand integrity.

The best example of the emerging vertical integration can be observed through the Cendant's Travel Distribution Services Division. As the world's largest hotel and car rental supplier/franchiser Cendant has developed a comprehensive and vertically integrated distribution structure that drives distribution value for principals and vice versa. They leverage technology investment in infrastructure across a broader spectrum to provide highly efficient connectivity between principals and distributors. Although each organisation remains independent, creating an integrated distribution mechanism and strategy ensures cost-effective distribution alternatives for franchisees in a world where distribution is becoming more concentrated. A number of high-profile acquisitions in 2004, including Orbitz ($1.25bn), eBookers.com (£209m), Gulliver and OctopusTravel.com ($1.1bn) have clearly demonstrated that Cendant has effectively bought a considerable global distribution network. The acquisitions provided Cendant with a vast hotel, tour and packaged travel content and expanded their global footprint in the travel distribution business.

These strategies have a wide range of competition implications in the marketplace. On the one hand, they generate direct competition for similar companies and demonstrate that increasingly barriers to entry will make it considerably difficult for new comers to penetrate. They also demonstrate that a comprehensive value system will enable vertically integrated organisations to trade their margins between companies of the same corporation and at the same time keep them within the corporate, maximising their collective yield. Competitors of any of those businesses will be at a disadvantage in distributing their products or accessing inventory at competitive terms. Hence, vertical integration enhances the collective competitiveness of the entire value system, against other companies and systems. Vertically integrated organisations will gradually move to other markets including tour operating by using dynamic packaging. As a result, they will have major implications for all tourism organisations in the marketplace.

Synthesis

ICTs stimulate radical changes in the operation and distribution of the tourism sector, whilst empowering consumers to identify and access specialised products which satisfy their specific requirements. Hence the ICT and Internet developments propel a paradigm shift in the tourism industry. The competition forces have changed dramatically as the Internet has provided opportunities for all players to develop direct interaction with consumers, altering value chains. Best business practices have been changed and new models are essential to take advantage of the opportunities and reflect the challenges in the marketplace. The competitiveness of all tourism enterprises and destinations continues to change rapidly as new tools emerge to support interoperability and interconnectivity, making a combination of distribution mechanisms that include B2C, B2B and B2B2C 'plug and play' the new industry paradigm. Although ICTs can introduce great benefits, especially in efficiency, co-ordination, differentiation and cost reduction, they are not a panacea and require a pervasive re-engineering of business processes, as well as strategic management vision and commitment in order to achieve their objectives. Only those creative and innovative principals and destinations which rationalise their utilisation of ICTs through their management vision and use intellect as a major asset will enhance their future competitiveness.

References

Adam, R., 1990, A licence to steal? The growth and development of airline information systems, Journal of Information Science, Vol.16(1), pp.77–91.

Archdale, G., 1991, Computer reservation systems: The international scene, Part 1, Insights, November, pp.D15–D19.

Beldona, S., Beck J., and Qu, H., 2001, Implementing enterprise resource planning in a hotel: towards theory building, International Journal of Hospitality Information Technology, Vol.2(1), pp.9–22.

Boberg, K. and Collison, F., 1985, Computer reservation systems and airline competition, Tourism Management, Vol.6(3), pp.174–183.

Buhalis, D., 1998, Strategic use of information technologies in the tourism industry, Tourism Management, Vol.19(3), pp.409–423.

Buhalis, D., 2003, eTourism: information technology for strategic tourism management, Pearson (Financial Times/Prentice Hall), London.

Buhalis, D., 2004, eAirlines: Strategic and tactical use of ICTS in the airline industry, Information & Management Journal, Vol.41(7), pp.805–825.

Buhalis, D. and Licata, C., 2002, The eTourism intermediaries, Tourism Management, Vol.23(3), pp.207–220.

Buhalis, D. and Ujma, D., 2005, The future of intermediaries, in Buhalis, D. and Costa, C. (eds), Tourism Business Frontiers: Consumers, Products And Industry, Butterworth-Heinemann, Oxford.

Clarke, R., 2004, Value proposition, Airline Business, March 2004, pp.44–45.

Connolly, D., Olsen, M. and Moore, R., 1998, The internet as a distribution channel, Cornell Hotel and Restaurant Administration Quarterly, Vol.39(4), pp.42–54.

Cooper, C., and Buhalis, D., 1998, Competition or co-operation: Small and medium sized tourism enterprises at the destination, in Laws, E., Faulkner, B. and Moscardo, G. (eds), Embracing and Managing Change in Tourism, Routledge, London, pp.324–346.

Copeland, D., 1991, So you want to build the next SABRE System, Business Quarterly, Vol.55(33), pp.56–60.

Copeland, D. and McKenney, J., 1988, Airline reservation systems: lessons from history, MIS Quarterly, Vol.12, pp.535–370.

EC, 1993, Proposal for a Council Regulation (EEC) amending Regulation (EEC) No.2299/89 on a code of conduct for Computerised Reservation Systems, Official Journal of the European Communities, No. C58/28, 26/2/1993, pp.28–33.

Emmer, R., Tauck, C., Wilkinson, S. and Moore, R. (1993) Marketing hotels using Global Distribution Systems, The Cornell Hotel Restaurant Administration Quarterly, Vol.34(6), pp.80–89.

Feldman, J., 1987, CRS in the USA: determining future levels of airline competition, Travel and Tourism Analyst, No.3, pp.3–14.

Feldman, J., 1988, CRS and fair airline competition, Travel and Tourism Analyst, No.2, pp.5–22.

Go, F. and Welch, P., 1991, Competitive strategies for the international hotel industry, The Economist Intelligence Unit, Special report No.1180, London.

Griffin, D., 2004, Carrying the load–how deregulation will impact the GDS heavyweights, Deloitte&Touche Reports, 2004, Tourism, Hospitality & Leisure Review, London, http://www.hospitalitynet.org/file/152001651.pdf.

Hopper, L., 1990, Rattling SABRE: New ways to compete on information, Harvard Business Review, Vol.68(3), May–June, pp.118–125.

House of Commons, 1988, Airline competition: computer reservation systems, Transport Committee, Session 87–88, Minutes of proceedings and appendices.

Kärcher, K. (1996) Re-engineering the package holiday business, in Klein, S. et al. (eds), Information and Communication Technologies in Tourism, Conference proceedings ENTER'96, Springer-Verlag, Wien, pp.221–233.

Levine, M., 1987, Airline competition in deregulated markets: theory, firm strategy and public policy, Yale Journal of Regulation, Vol.14, pp.393–494.

Marcussen C. 2003, Internet distribution of European travel and tourism services, Research Centre of Bornholm, Denmark. http://www.crt.dk/uk/staff/chm/trends.htm.

Mietus, J., 1989, European Community regulation of airline computer reservation systems, Law and Policy in International Business, Vol.21(1), pp.93–118.

Morrison, A., Taylor, S., Morrison, A. and Morrison, A., 1999, Marketing small hotels on the world wide web, Information Technology & Tourism, Vol.2(2), pp.97–113.

Murphy, L., Forrest, E., Worthing, C., Brymer, R., 1996, Hotel Management and marketing on the internet, Cornell Hotel and Restaurant Administration Quarterly, Vol.37(3), pp.70–82.

O'Connor, P., 1999, Electronic Information Distribution in Tourism and Hospitality, CAB, Oxford.

O'Connor, P. 2003, Online Intermediaries – Revolutionizing Travel Distribution, EIU Travel and Tourism Analyst, London.

O'Connor, P. and Frew, A. (2000). Evaluating electronic channels of distribution in the hotel sector: A Delphi study, Information Technology and Tourism, Vol. 3(3/4), pp. 177–193.

O'Toole, K., 2004, IT trends survey 2003, Airline Business/SITA, August.

Paraskevas, A. and Buhalis, D., 2002, Outsourcing IT for small hotels: The opportunities and challenges of using application service providers. Cornell Hotel and Restaurant Administration Quarterly, Vol.43(2), pp.27–39.

Poon, A., 1993, Tourism, Technology and Competitive Strategies, CAB International, Oxford.

Porter, M., 2001, Strategy and the Internet, Harvard Business Review, March, Vol.103D, pp.63–78.

Sheldon, P., 1997, Information Technologies for Tourism, CAB, Oxford.

Smith, C. and Jenner, P., 1998, Tourism and the Internet, Travel and Tourism Analyst, No.1, pp.62–81.

Truitt, L., Teye, V. and Farris, M., 1991, The role of computer reservation systems: international implications for the tourism industry, Tourism Management, Vol.12(1), pp.21–36.

Van Hoof, H., Ruys, H. and Combrink, T., 1999, Global hoteliers and the Internet: use and perceptions, International Journal of Hospitality Information Technology, Vol.1(1), pp.45–63.

Ward, M., Lin, S. and Iverson, B., 2003, Travel distribution 2007: the profitability constellation: effective new patterns of travel distribution, An IBM Institute for Business Value Future Series report, IBM Business Consulting Services, Chicago.

Werthner, H. and Klein, S., (1999) Information Technology and Tourism – A Challenging Relationship, Springer, New York.

Wheatcroft, S. and Lipman, G., 1990, European liberalisation and world air transport: towards a transnational industry, Economist Intelligence Unit, Special Report, No.2015, London.

9

Competition in visitor attractions

Stephen Wanhill

Introduction

The taxonomy of markets within the discipline of economics depends on the number of firms or businesses in the marketplace and the nature of the product offer, whether it is uniform or differentiated, the latter enabling the supplier to brand the product so as to encourage customer loyalty. In turn, the market structure influences how the enterprise conducts itself through its pricing strategy in the narrow sense, to non-price competition in the broader sense, namely promotion, mergers, acquisitions and alliances, and innovative development. Creating barriers to entry allows firms to charge high prices and reap excess profits. In modern economies, the market conduct of businesses is hedged about with legal requirements and codes of good practice. The wisdom in economics is that competition is better than the exercise of monopoly power. Firms should provide consumers with goods and services that meet their demands at the lowest possible prices. Hence, the presumption of the law is against anti-competitive practices, save where they can be shown to improve production or distribution, or result in technical progress. Governments do not condemn monopolies, per se, for recognising that profits are an incentive to innovate, and as such innovation promotes economic development and growth, most countries have patent laws to allow businesses to exploit the profit potential of new ideas. It is the abuse of monopoly power that they legislate against.

The nature of visitor attractions

A visitor attraction may be broadly defined as a focus for amusement, recreation and, in part, educational activity undertaken by both day and stay visitors that is frequently shared with the local resident population. Within any society, the range of visitor attractions is extensive – every municipality and rural district boasts at least one attraction, adding to its appeal as a destination. Thus the market structure may be considered as competition amongst the many, which is near to the economist's ideal of perfect with a large number of sellers who exert negligible influence on price. On the other hand, there are numerous variations in terms of the product concept or creativity of the design and its appeal, which may be termed the 'imagescape' to match the term 'imagineers' used by the Disney Corporation to describe its designers (Kirsner, 1988). This concept is based on the fact that all attractions, in some part, measure their performance by the number of visitors, for which the output is the visitor experience. To enhance the latter, the modern approach is to place tangible objects, say, a thrill ride or a collection of artefacts, within the context of a specific theme or image in a particular setting or environment; hence the word 'imagescape'.

The accepted thesis in the 'post-Fordist' society is that to retain market position, suppliers should no longer sell goods with attached services but rather services with attached goods, so that each customer receives a bespoke package (Pine and Gilmore, 1999). Figure 9.1 presents an abstract construction of an attraction product where the core is the imagescape, the purpose of which is to convey the essence of the visitor experience to the potential market. To complete the attraction product, the core is surrounded by commodities and services such as retailing, catering, cloakrooms, first aid, special needs access, internal transport and car parking, as well as an augmented imagescape designed to ensure that all customer

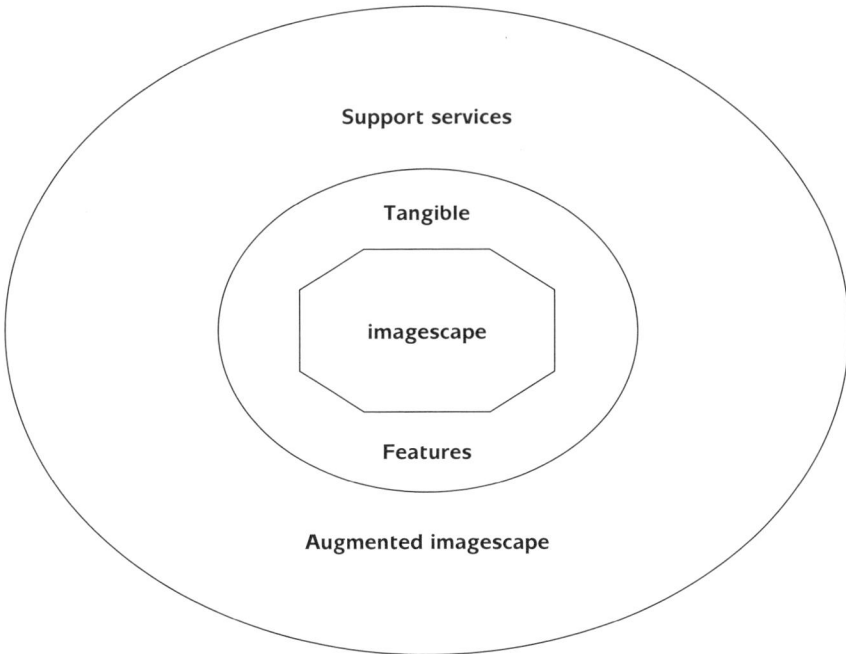

Figure 9.1 The attraction product

experiential requirements are met, for example, visitor orientation, queue entertainment, complaints handling, puppet characters, shows, presentations, and so on. The object is to generate memorable mood benefits for the visitor, and in consequence attachment. It is commonly argued that 'word-of-mouth' recommendation is the best promotion of all, and a well-known tag line in the amusement business is: 'If I have a good experience I will tell ten people; if I have a bad one, I will tell fifty!'

The right imagescape portrays, through the functional aspect of theming, all four realms of the visitor experience, namely, entertainment, education (which have been combined in the word 'edutainment'), aesthetics and escapism. Only then does a location become a distinctive place to stage an experience, which is what is embodied in truly successful visitor attractions, be they theme parks in the private domain or heritage attractions in the non-commercial sector. As indicated in Table 9.1, the range of imagescape themes for visitor attractions is beyond doubt extensive, but quintessentially there is very little new in what draws visitors: the main attractions are still the wonders of the natural and physical world and the endeavours of human society, including, but to a much smaller extent, dark subjects that deal with what are considered to be behaviour inversions, such as the grim consequences of war (Smith, 1998), crime and punishment (Foley and Lennon, 1996), and the erotic.

The acceptance of the content and style of production of the imagescape is determined by fashion, which has its own dynamic that is born out of the spirit of enquiry and competition within society to alter its patterns of consumption and value systems. Thus animals in captivity in the form of zoos or safari parks are no longer acceptable to many people and there is a marked decline of interest in static attractions and object-oriented museums, unless they are national collections or they are best presented in this way, as for example jewellery. Fashion exists and

Table 9.1 The variety of imagescapes

– Armed forces	– Industry
– Art & media	– Miscellaneous
– Built environment	– Myths & fantasy
– Childhood	– Natural world
– Civilisations	– Physical world
– Dark subjects	– Politics
– Entertainment	– Religion
– Famous & notorious	– Retailing
– Food & drink	– Science & discovery
– Future	– Society & culture
– History & heritage	– Sport
– Hobbies & pastimes	– Transport
– Human body	– War & conflict

is encouraged in the branding of everything that is purchased; if it were not so the world would be cluttered with masses of still usable commodities and there would be little change in the nature of service provision. The closer the intrinsic qualities of the product, the more importance becomes branding to define market position. Undoubtedly, the Disney brand gives the corporation substantial market power even though the technology of most amusement rides is available to everyone.

The business concept of branding is a subset of a more general feature of visitor attractions identified by MacCannell (1989), in which the intrinsic value is functionally related to increasing the level of attraction differentiation through signs and symbols (semiotic separation) and the content of the imagescape, which he interprets as the sacralisation process. The apex of this process is when the attraction turns into a point of pilgrimage for visitors: a tourist 'must see'. For example, amongst LEGO enthusiasts, a trip to Legoland in Denmark, which is the home of LEGO, has infinitely more prestige than a trip to similar parks in America, England and Germany. Though, as Seaton (1999) observes from the historical study of the Waterloo campaign, sacralisation is never complete, since it too is subject to changing fashions and values with time, so that it is no longer appropriate to look at the battlefield in strident partisan terms.

Monopolistic competition

The sheer variety of imagescapes and the number of attractions suggests that the market as a whole falls into Chamberlain's definition (1933) of monopolistic competition. This is similar to perfect competition in which many firms compete and entry and exit is relatively easy, but each is protected by a differentiated product and, in the case of service products, geographical location, for unlike commodities, the imagescape of an attraction has to be consumed at the place of production, which highlights the importance of market boundaries or catchment areas. For example, major cultural attractions in world-class cities have a market that spans the entire globe, which is technically infinite in size, as there is always a new generation of potential visitors coming along.

The behaviour of firms under monopolistic competition is illustrated in Figure 9.2. There is normally not one admission charge, but a regular or published price panel of admission rates reflecting corporate strategies, such as maximisation of profitability or growth, as well as communicating chosen positioning and the imagescape to target market segments, through expectations about the value of the experience. The generic market segments for attractions are: local residents, same-day visitors, domestic and foreign tourists travelling independently, and groups, which include coach parties, schools, and people using the facilities for meetings and conferences. Usually, price panels offer concessions from the full adult rate for children, seniors and groups, with inclusive family tickets for attractions focusing on that market.

Admission charge

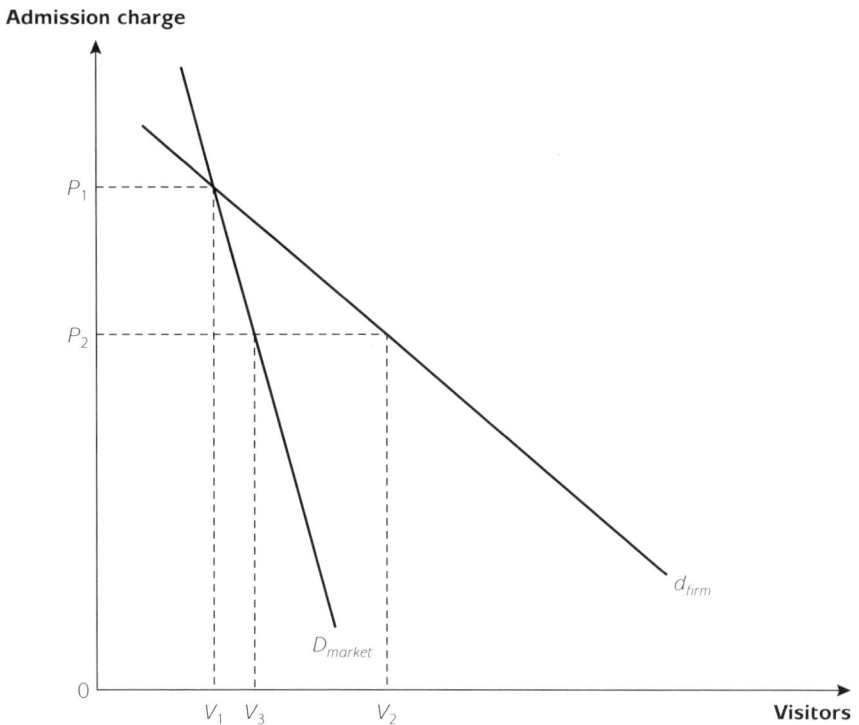

Figure 9.2 Monopolistic competition

Suppose the attraction under consideration has positioned itself with a price panel for different categories of visitors set around a high adult admission charge at P_1, facing a demand schedule d_{firm} (representing willingness to pay, which is the market's perceptions of value for money), and sees an opportunity to increase visitor numbers to V_2 by reducing the adult price to P_2 (and other prices in the panel in a proportionate manner), thereby improving earnings and profitability. However, this action is based solely on the loyalty of the attraction's customers and does not take account of the reactions of competitors. If competitors follow suit with price cuts and new product offers to recapture lost trade, the effect is to erode the short-term market gains made, by driving V_2 backwards towards V_3. The demand schedule D_{market} traces out the market share position of the attraction, when the reactions of competitors to its pricing strategy are taken into account. In Chamberlain's model no one firm will be faced with this situation alone, as there are a multitude of businesses with broadly similar demand and cost functions. With free entry and exit, long-run equilibrium will be achieved when potential gains have been competed away and firms are only making normal profits. If this is at P_2, then the frequency by which price panels change will stabilise, giving the attraction a market share of V_3 visitors, which it will attempt to hold by encouraging brand loyalty through a variety of non-price tactics, say, raising promotional expenditure, augmenting the imagescape by staging events, or price reductions disguised as extra product benefits, such as free rides at certain times, 'two-for-the-price-of-one' offers, local residents' vouchers and temporary concessions for people who are unemployed or students. Where attractions are clustered together, as in cities, thus facing a similar catchment population, they may offer multiple ticketing or an 'all-in-one' pass. The latter are often scheduled in a way that few visitors take up every offer, so it is a way of generating more revenue from a marginal increase in visitor numbers.

Oligopoly and monopoly

Chamberlain was criticised for the myopia of business behaviour in focusing on d_{firm} rather than the market share curve D_{market}, and plainly, the fewer the number of competitors the less likely is it that firms can proceed with a pricing strategy that does not take account of its rivals; thus Robinson (1950), when discussing imperfect competition, took it for granted that a firm's market conduct would be governed by D_{market} rather than d_{firm}. However, on a global scale, the term monopolistic competition has general applicability, since there are many similar attractions, and some 70 per cent of attractions draw in fewer than 200,000 visitors per annum. The evidence from developed tourist destinations has shown that the growth in the number of attractions has exceeded the increase in leisure expenditure, thus diluting market share in the myopic manner indicated by Chamberlain as they compete for both leisure time and spend.

However, there is a further complication, in that commerciality and consumer choice are rather modern concepts for visitor attractions, in the sense that the majority of today's attractions were not originally brought into existence for tourist purposes. At a base level, it is possible to group attractions into those that are gifts of nature and those that are man-made. The former include the landscape, climate, vegetation, forests and wildlife that may require inputs of infrastructure and management in order to use them for tourism purposes, as well as to protect the resource from environmental damage, for example, parks, ski resorts and game reserves. Man-made attractions are principally the products of the historical development of countries and civilisations (Richards, 1994), but also include artificially created popular entertainments, such as wax museums, amusement parks and performing arts venues. Cultural and heritage attractions are constrained by their location and authenticity (Wanhill, 2000), in that the intrinsic value is dissipated in reproductions, and alterations in the cultural capital stock are, in the main, irreversible. By cultural capital stock is meant tangible or intangible assets that hold cultural value, irrespective of any economic value they may possess. The development process in terms of imagescape creation is therefore a gradation from a situation of no adaptation of natural or cultural resources for visitors (but rather controlled management), to visitor attractions that are fashioned for purpose, the latter being in the minority. The bulk of attractions would then be spread out between these two polar cases, which is very different from the normal production economics upon which the classification of markets is based.

From the above, it follows that within the widespread number of permutations of visitor attractions in terms of imagescape, ownership and type, it is possible to layer the attraction market into segments that range from the broad perspective of monopolistic competition arising from many small and similar enterprises, through oligopoly (competition amongst the few) to monopoly generated from attractions that offer a unique selling proposition and limited capacity, making them a tourist 'must see'. Thus, there is only one group of Pyramids at Giza, Taj Mahal, Sydney Opera House, Statue of Liberty, Buckingham Palace, Eiffel Tower and so on. Like national museums, attractions of this kind are capable of drawing in large numbers of visitors and are in a position to elevate admission charges to premium rates, but as many of them are the legacy of the nation, it is morally questionable whether people should pay for access to their own heritage. Over time a consensus emerges in any country about the greatest attractions being national assets and therefore being protected through public ownership through which they are styled as 'public' goods, whereby consumption is considered socially desirable. Publicly owned attractions may receive all or a substantial part of their funds from general taxation, either directly or via grant-in-aid for quasi-public bodies that are given responsibility for their care. But this does necessarily imply an agreement on the amount of money given. Thus an almost continual political debate goes on about the level of charging versus direct funding for national museums, palaces, galleries, churches and cathedrals, and natural resources, such as national/country parks, forests, botanic gardens and designated areas of outstanding landscape value. Recent experience in the UK, with the re-election of a Labour government in 2001, has been to reverse the policy of charging for admission to national museums.

Between the monopoly of publicly owned attractions and the monopolistic competition of the myriad of small ones, lies oligopoly. This is a market structure that holds a small number of sellers and entry of new competitors is not easy because of the sheer size of the enterprises involved. A good example here is the major theme park chains, such as Walt Disney Attractions, Six Flags Inc., Cedar Fair Ltd. and Paramount Parks, where the level of investment required to obtain entry is a deterrent; for example, Universal Studios' Spiderman Ride cost some $200 million. Because there are relatively few sellers, one firm's market strategy in terms of sales and pricing must account for others, particularly when the product is fairly homogeneous. In these circumstances there is a natural tendency for firms to collude over pricing and markets shares. Such practices are made illegal in modern economies as they are seen as exploitative of the consumer. Instead, what may occur is implicit price leadership by which others follow the strategies of the dominant firm.

In the early days of Central Florida at Orlando (Braun et al., 1992; Braun and Sarkin, 2003) Walt Disney World (WDW) was the dominant firm and ruled the market with its own pricing strategy, with a competitive fringe of price followers. Competing parks used price discounting to compensate for Disney's financial advantage and brand name. This was changed in the 1990s when Anheuser Busch carried out a series of acquisitions to complete a successful horizontal merger of WDW's three largest rivals, Busch Gardens, Sea World and Cypress Gardens, and brought in its financial resources to develop the parks. Next, the entry of Universal Studios, with its considerable investment strength and strong imagescapes from its films, enabled it to challenge the WDW premium pricing strategy. The result was that the follower relationship broke down and more collusive parallel pricing behaviour took place, in which the major players matched each other, but not in a price war, but rather in tacit agreement to changing market conditions and cost inflation. This is termed 'barometric' price leadership, as market dominance does not exist, but other parks follow the pricing decision of the one that best reflects market forces, their needs and aspirations. In actions of this kind, businesses are explicitly recognising their interdependence to ensure profitability of the group. The result was that the growth rate in admission prices slowed considerably, price panels converged and the frequency by which they were changed fell. Markets become 'contestable' when potential competition from new entrants forces existing attractions to limit prices and engage in non-price competition.

Theories of pricing strategies under oligopolistic market conditions vary from complete naivety where one firm pursues a strategy without taking into consideration the action of its rivals, to gaming behaviour, whereby the firm assesses a set of possible price options against the reactions of its competitors, choosing that which benefits it the most. What is apparent from the example of the Florida theme parks is that under conditions of rivalry between firms, the price panel tends to steady at a level that meets the collective judgement as to what is appropriate for the market and then stay there. The oligopoly model, which lends weight to this situation, is shown in Figure 9.3.

At the stabilized adult price of P_1 each enterprise faces a kinked demand curve d_{firm}, whereby any attempt by an attraction to lower prices will be matched by competitors, so that both d_{firm} and D_{market} coincide (Hall and Hitch, 1939). Below P_1 the demand schedule is inelastic so that price-cutting, while growing the market, will result in a reduction in overall revenue. On the other hand, a unilateral move by any one attraction to raise prices (without a group consensus as to changes in market conditions or costs) will not be matched by competitors and the business will lose market share. The demand schedule above P_1 is elastic and raising price will cause earnings to fall. This is not to say that price wars will not break out from time to time, but this may only happen when a major innovation gives an enterprise a genuine and sustainable competitive advantage. Such was the case in 1955

Admission charge

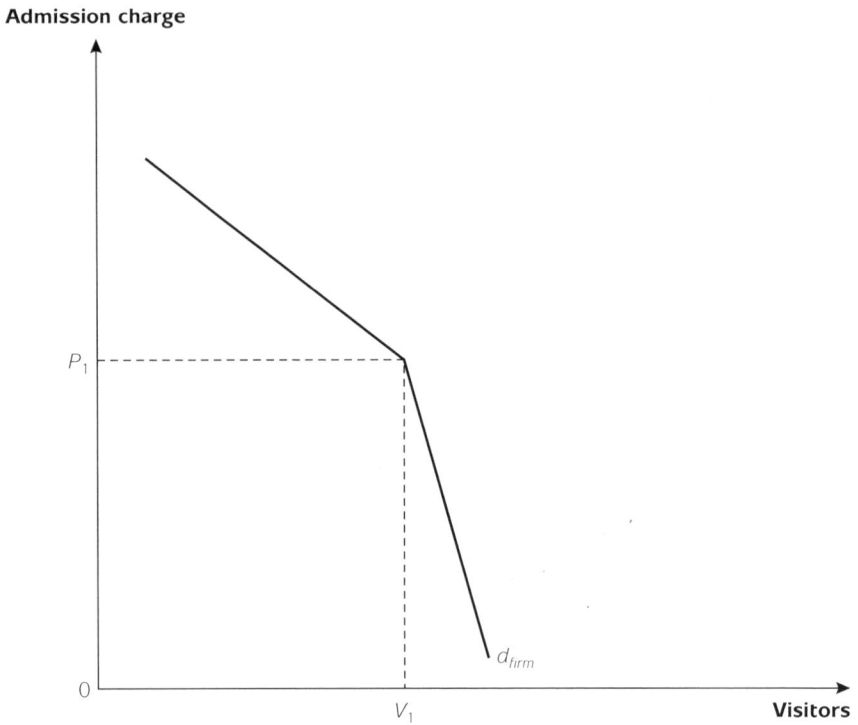

Figure 9.3 Oligopolistic competition

when Disneyland was created in Anaheim, California. Built at a cost of some $17 million, it was the largest park investment that had ever been made. As often happens with new ideas, there were many sceptics who were unable to see how breaking an amusement park tradition going back over sixty years could be successful. For instead of the fairground style of a Midway Plaisance from Chicago's Columbian Exposition of 1893, with numerous concessionaires, Disneyland offered five distinct themed areas (Main Street USA, Adventureland, Frontierland, Fantasyland and Tomorrowland) that provided 'guests' with the fantasy of travel to different lands and times, all designed and managed by one organisation.

Ownership

It should now be apparent that the extent of the attraction sector allows for all the three forms of market structure discussed above to co-exist. The general picture is one of many small attractions, with relatively few large 'aristocratic' attractions that are either owned by the public sector or in the hands of large corporations. The term 'Aristopoly' should reasonably encapsulate this kind of market structure in which price-setting and therefore overall competition is heavily influenced by ownership patterns.

Because of their cultural and historical legacy, a great many visitor attractions are not commercially owned. They belong to central government or quasi-public bodies, which are at an 'arm's length' from the government (in the case of natural resources, collections and monuments of national significance), local authorities and voluntary bodies in the form of charitable trusts, which have to be incorporated, and a variety of clubs and societies that are usually unincorporated. These are generally classified as not-for-profit organisations, as they often have many non-financial objectives that govern market conduct and price-setting. To illustrate this, one of the problems concerning the provision of outdoor areas for leisure purposes on a large scale is that these areas are rarely commercially viable in terms of the investment costs and operating expenditure necessary to establish and maintain them. The reasons for this lie in their periodic use (weekends and holidays) and the political and administrative difficulties of establishing private markets in what are perceived by the public as gifts of nature. Frequently, it is not realistically possible to exclude individuals from consumption once provision has been made. Hence, private markets for these facilities would quickly disintegrate because the optimal strategy for the individual consumer is to wait until someone else pays for the recreation area and then to reap the benefits for nothing.

Yet there are considerable social benefits to be enjoyed by the population from the availability of recreational amenities and in the control of land use to prevent unsightly development spoiling the beauty of the landscape. Economists ascribe the term 'market failure' to situations of this kind and in such circumstances it is common for the state to make the necessary provision of these public or collective goods. Thus some 85 per cent of outdoor recreation areas in the USA are owned by the Federal government, with the object of encouraging consumption and protecting the resource for the enjoyment of future generations. The recognition of this principle in the USA goes back to 1872 with the commissioning of the Yellowstone National Park. In Britain, planning and development for tourism purposes is largely a post-1945 phenomenon, commencing with the National Parks and Access to the Countryside Act in 1949, though it was not until the 1960s that positive action in the field of tourism and recreation provision really got going.

Figure 9.4 examines the normative economics of the appropriate pricing rules that may be followed. As before, d_{firm} is the demand schedule and market economics dictate that private operators should attempt to optimise profitability, which is achieved by equating marginal revenue (MR) to marginal cost (MC), setting an adult admission rate of P_1 and attracting V_1 visitors – pricing according to 'what the market will bear', although, as discussed above, contestable market conditions may give rise to limits on the price level. The public sector, which has the interest of the economy at large, is faced with two economically efficient

Admission charge

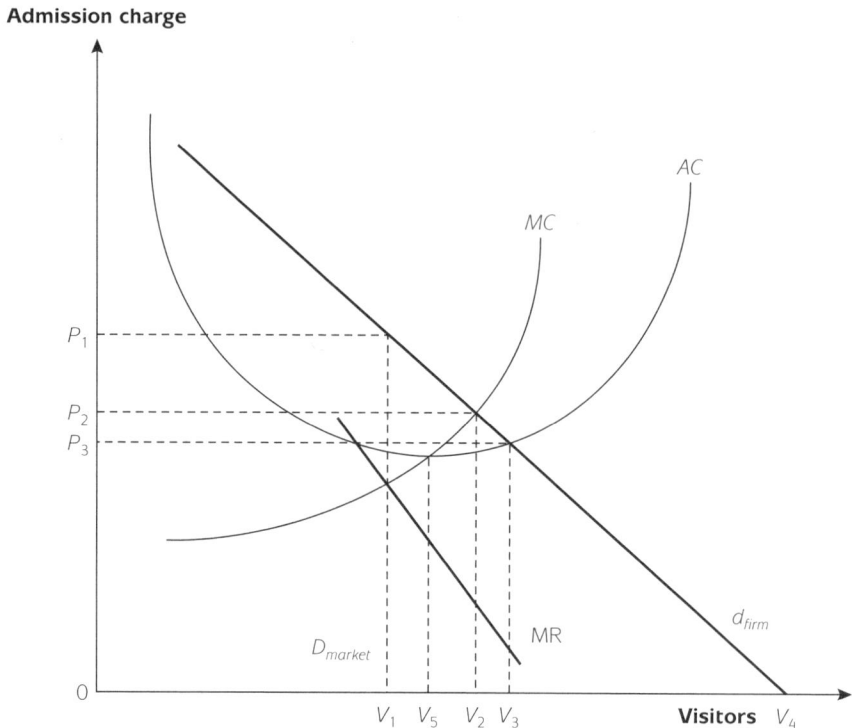

Figure 9.4 Pricing rules by ownership

choices: free at the point of use, which results in a demand level of V_4, or setting admission equal to MC, implying a charge P_2 for V_2 visitors. The former typically applies to outdoor recreation areas or for attractions whose consumption the state wishes to encourage, while the latter is appropriate for state museums, where exclusion from consumption is possible. Equating P_2 to MC is the optimal pricing rule that would be obtained under perfect competition and represents the most efficient use of economic resources, for the price level is both lower and output greater than under monopolistic competition. Figure 9.4 depicts MC lying above AC, but it is common in attractions for MC to be small and lying below AC, which implies that even if governments charge for admission to public museums, they will still have to be subsidised directly from taxation if they are to survive.

On the other hand, many museums and events have arisen out of the collections or interests of a group of enthusiasts who come together to provide for themselves and others collective goods and services which are unlikely to have any widespread commercial appeal (market failure) and are equally unlikely to be of sufficient importance to attract central provision by the state. These organisations are, in economic terms, 'clubs', and because they normally have non-profit aims, they are entitled to claim the status of charities for tax purposes. However, in contrast to the public sector, they are not able to raise funds from taxation and so in the long run must cover their costs out of income. Yet, unlike the private commercial sector, their income is not made up solely from admission charges and visitor spending inside the attraction. Membership fees, gifts, grants from public bodies (both at national and international level) and charities, and bequests often take on a far greater significance in the income statement. As a consequence, recruiting new members to share the collective experience is a priority task for these organisations, and policies may vary from 'members only' to differential charges for admission of members and non-members. The appropriate policy for the voluntary sector, if it wants to distribute maximum benefits to its members, while being mindful of its not-for-profit charitable objectives, is one of average cost-pricing, setting a price P_3 to generate V_3 users. Generally, such operators tend to be 'fix-price' organisations, in that should demand increase in circumstances of limited capacity, they will accumulate waiting lists for membership and extend facilities, rather than seek monopoly rents by raising dues. The optimum-sized club is at the lowest point on the AC curve, so in Figure 9.5 it could be that membership will be restricted to V_5, which is off the demand curve, and so V_3–V_5 will be the waiting list for potential members, who may be allowed to attend as non-members. One of the most well-known examples of an economic club in the UK is the National Trust, which was started in 1895, with the object of protecting places of historic and natural significance for the nation. The Trust maintains a wide range of historic properties, parks and woodlands, and is an institutional model that has been copied elsewhere. Acquisition has normally been via bequests from previous owners together with substantial endowments that provide the economic foundations for the organisation. Given the breadth of its facilities, with the potential of taking on more, it has a policy of expanding membership, since its objective, as any other club, is to encourage consumption amongst like-minded persons. However, it is also careful to hedge the demand risk by receiving income from a variety of sources, namely, admission charges from non-members, shops and catering, grants and donations, sponsorship, events and services rendered, for example, lecture programmes. On the cost side, like other voluntary societies, the Trust benefits from some labour inputs and materials being provided free of charge.

Thus through pricing policy, the pattern of ownership can alter the financial outcomes of an attraction and the nature of competition. A valid criticism of the not-for-profit sector, whether it is public or voluntary, is that it has the inclination to try to do too much, because the management looks to meet perceived needs rather than market demand, the latter being the primary concern of the private sector. To take a simple analogy; if people are asked if they want more of a collective good, then in the absence of a price system, they will surely vote 'Yes', putting the onus of the public sector to meet these needs, as there is a political incentive to do so. As an instance of this, with the establishment of the National Lottery in 1993, the UK government set aside a series of funds to disburse some of the proceeds to the arts, sport and cultural heritage (Heritage Lottery Fund), as these causes are normally under-resourced by any government when faced with the competing demands of health, welfare, education and defence. One aspect that is difficult to guard against where public authorities are involved is the danger of project inflation in response to civic pride and the vainglory of politicians, either nationally or locally. There seems to be an implicit belief that winning in the electoral marketplace translates itself into the economic marketplace. This results in an exaggeration of employment creation to obtain development grants, increased complexity, which boosts consultants' fees, and substantial capital structures to the benefit of the architects. Several Millennium Commission projects in the UK went this way and some had to be closed, for example, the National Centre for Popular Music, Sheffield, the Centre for the Visual Arts, Cardiff and the Earth Centre, Doncaster. Occurrences of this kind rightly raise scorn from commercial operators who argue that if public funding and project inflation results in a situation where there is no relationship between the cost of delivering and what the customer actually pays, then this is a case of predatory pricing (technically defined as the admission charge being below the average variable cost of provision) in an over-supplied market that is likely to harm them commercially. Governments are sensitive to this kind of criticism and, as a rule, avoid trying to compete 'head on' with the private sector.

The lesson for the Heritage Lottery Fund and the Commission from these examples was straightforward: major capital projects should not be undertaken unless their market function is clear, visitor displacement has been considered and a 'proper' viability study has been carried out so that the nature of the risks involved are thoroughly understood and accepted. In defence, it is to be noted that market assessment for such unique attractions is notoriously difficult; for example, the estimates of visitor numbers for the Millennium Dome in London ranged between nine and 17 million (National Audit Office, 2000). Twelve million was the figure that the government was prepared to accept and budget for, on the basis that it was meant to be a public festival, so that everyone who might want to come should be able to do so, but it only realised 6.5 million and was ridiculed by the media because of this. With projects of this kind, there is a need to build up a large database of market trends in different leisure activities, make future change assumptions (predictions) and consider the project in a 'with and without' situation. Developing project scenarios so as to give a thorough understanding of what is being proposed and the risks involved are more important than the actual projections, though the latter are required to give dimensions to the project and to assess its impact on the economy.

Concluding discussion

From the discussion that has taken place, it will be readily appreciated that the ways of classifying and evaluating attractions are immense. Competition in this sector is linked to geographical location, the pattern of ownership and the historical reasons (as most attractions were not originally brought into existence for leisure visitors) and the multiple objectives that beset different ownership structures. The overall situation is one of a whole host of small attractions, with relatively few large 'aristocratic' attractions that are either owned by the public sector or in the hands of large corporations. This permits the co-existence of several market structures at any one time, from monopolistic competition, through oligopoly to monopoly. The term 'Aristopoly' has been used to embrace this phenomenon.

The majority of attractions are in the not-for-profit sector, but once they have been adapted for visitors, then weight builds up to interpret success in terms of the quality of the experience, visitor numbers (to capture the spill-over benefits of visitor expenditure) and, where admission is charged, some level of financial viability, which brings them closer to the workings of commercial operators, for whom economic objectives of profitability are normally paramount. However, with public and voluntary attractions it is important to balance outcomes against the priorities assigned to the various objectives and to eliminate conflicts, as far as possible. Failure to do so is the source of frequent misunderstandings and inappropriate evaluations of such attractions, as in the case of the Millennium Dome cited earlier.

Successful visitor generation requires, in the main, the creation of imagescapes around tangible objects and intangible services, to form experiences that have strong associations with potential customers, enabling value for money to be easily recognised. These may be termed 'reproductive' imagescapes, as they evoke known products or events. They are different, but not too different as to be out of step with fashion and what constitutes 'good taste', and are flexible enough to encourage visitors to return. Their delivery requires clear objectives, proven management skills and knowledge of the target audience. On the other hand, avant-garde or 'anticipatory' imagescapes, which are about evoking expectations, have a high probability of economic failure, both commercially and also in the wider sense of attracting visitor expenditure to an area, particularly if they are not effectively communicated to the general public and allow the media to satirise the project as ersatz and of no substance. History is littered with examples of this kind in one generation that are subsequently judged to have significant cultural value in another. The media critique of the Millennium Dome had echoes in what was said about the construction of the Eiffel Tower for the Paris World's Fair of 1889. This implies that non-market models of resource allocation are needed for many such attraction developments to occur, which is the rationale for the importance of the not-for-profit sector in cultural activities.

References

Braun, B. and M. Soskin, 'Competitive theme park strategies: lessons from Central Florida', in A. Fyall, B. Garrod and A. Leask (eds), Managing Visitor Attractions: New Directions (Oxford, Butterworth-Heinemann, 2003), pp. 220–235.

Braun, B., M. Soskin and M. Cernicky, 'Central Florida theme park pricing: following the mouse', Annals of Tourism Research, 19/1 (1992), pp. 131–135.

Chamberlain, E., The Theory of Monopolistic Competition (Cambridge, MA, Harvard University Press, 1933).

Foley, M. and J. Lennon, 'JFK and dark tourism: heart of darkness', Journal of International Heritage Studies, 2/2 (1996), pp. 195–197.

Hall, R. and C. Hitch, 'Price theory and business behaviour', Oxford Economic Papers, 2/May (1939), pp. 12–45.

Kirsner, S., 'Hack the magic: the exclusive underground tour of Disney World', Wired, March (1988), pp. 162–168 and 186–189.

MacCannell, D., The Tourist. A New Theory of the Leisure Class (2nd ed.) (New York, Schocken Books, 1989).

National Audit Office, The Millennium Dome (London, The Stationery Office, 2000).

Pine II, B., and J. Gilmore, The Experience Economy (Cambridge, MA, Harvard Business School Press, 1999).

Richards, G., 'Cultural tourism in Europe', in C. Cooper and A. Lockwood (eds), Progress in Tourism, Recreation and Hospitality Management (Chichester, Wiley, 1994), pp. 99–115.

Robinson, J., The Economics of Imperfect Competition (London, Macmillan, 1950).

Seaton, A., 'War and thanatourism: Waterloo 1815–1914', Annals of Tourism Research, 26/1 (1999), pp. 130–158.

Smith, V., 'War and tourism: an American ethnography', Annals of Tourism Research, 25/2 (1998), pp. 202–227.

Wanhill, S., 'Mines – a tourist attraction: coal mining in Industrial South Wales', Journal of Travel Research, 39/1 (2000), pp. 60–69.

10

Market definition in the tourism industry

Gunnar Niels and Reinder van Dijk

Introduction

Over the last ten years, competition policy has become more active around the world, and this has not gone unnoticed in the tourism industry. Some high-profile merger investigations have recently taken place in relation to tour operators, e.g. the proposed merger between Airtours and First Choice (Court of First Instance, 2002; European Commission, 1999) and to the provision of cruise holidays, e.g. the mergers involving Royal Caribbean Cruises, P&O Princess Cruises, and Carnival Corporation (European Commission, 2003; UK Competition Commission, 2002; US Federal Trade Commission, 2002). Other parts of the industry have faced competition investigations as well, including hotels and travel agents (European Commission, 2001a and 2001b; UK Competition Commission, 1997).

A central part of any merger or other competition investigation is the definition of the 'relevant market' in which the merger or business conduct in question takes place. This is not an end in itself, but rather a intermediate step, albeit a very important one, in evaluating the competitive constraints faced by the firm or firms under investigation. A relevant market normally has a product and a geographic dimension. It contains all those substitute products and regions which provide a significant competitive constraint on the products and regions of interest – for example, in the Airtours/First Choice decision referred to above the European Commission defined a market for short-haul foreign package holidays sold in the UK and, separately, in Ireland. There may be other dimensions of the market as well, such as the time of consumption (e.g. are holidays in the peak season in the same market as off-peak holidays?) or the type of customer (e.g. leisure versus business travellers). Furthermore, a single investigation may involve multiple relevant markets.

Market definition is often the decisive – and therefore most disputed – stage in competition inquiries. Usually, the broader the relevant market is defined, the less likely it is that the firms investigated are found to have market power. For example, if the market for package holidays is broadly defined as the pan-European or even worldwide market, then a merger between two national suppliers is not likely to reduce competition significantly in that market, since their market share will be relatively low. However, if the market is defined as national, the merger will have a greater negative impact on competition.

The purpose of this chapter is to explain the economic principles of market definition, specifically the so-called SSNIP test and the critical loss test, which were developed by the Department of Justice and Federal Trade Commission (1992) in the USA and have also been accepted by the European Commission (1997) and many other national competition authorities. In essence, the SSNIP test asks whether a hypothetical monopolist of a product (or region) would impose a 'small but significant and non-transitory increase in the price' (hence the abbreviation). If the answer is affirmative, that product (region) is a relevant market; if not, this must be because other products (regions) exert competitive pressure and hence should be included in the relevant market as well. In other words, a market is 'something worth monopolising'.

Before describing these economic tests in more detail, this chapter discusses the reliance on product characteristics to define relevant markets. This used to be the traditional approach to define markets before the SSNIP test was developed, but even nowadays competition authorities still frequently rely on product characteristics. Such an approach may be particularly tempting in the tourism industry, since many operators sell their destination or product as 'unique', and many holidaymakers have very specific preferences – for example, the Côte d'Azur and Costa del Sol are quite different destinations, and some holidaymakers will always prefer one over the other, so does that mean they are in separate markets?

Using the 2000/01 inquiry by the Dutch Competition Authority (Nederlandse Mededingingsautoriteit, NMa) into the merger between Gran Dorado (owned by Pierre & Vacances) and Center Parcs as an example, this chapter illustrates how a market definition exercise focused on product characteristics can lead to misleading, or at best inconclusive, results (NMa, 2001). Oxera provided economic advice to Pierre & Vacances/Gran Dorado during this inquiry. Gran Dorado and Center Parcs both operated self-catering accommodation in holiday parks with a range of facilities (indoor swimming pool, restaurant, playgrounds, etc.), typically used by families for short breaks.

We also show how these problems can be overcome by applying the SSNIP and critical loss tests, as was done at the time by the merging parties. These tests have some clear advantages over an analysis based on the specific characteristics of the products. First, an analysis of product characteristics tends to focus on the preferences of an average consumer, while for market definition the focus should be on the marginal consumer. It is not necessary for all consumers to be willing to switch to render a particular product not worth monopolising, only that enough consumers would switch for it to be unprofitable to increase the price. This is exactly what the SSNIP test measures. Second, the SSNIP test crucially depends on the (own) price elasticity of demand, which can be measured, or at least approximated, empirically. The price elasticity of demand reflects the extent to which demand for a product changes in response to a change in the price and thereby provides a direct measure of consumers' preferences. For example, an own-price elasticity of demand for cruise holidays of –1.5 means that an increase in the price of cruise holidays by 10% reduces demand for such holidays by 15%. The own-price elasticity is normally negative.

Using product characteristics: parks and tropical pools

In February 2001, the NMa approved the joint acquisition of the continental (i.e. non-UK) business of Center Parcs by Pierre & Vacances and DB Capital Partners, though only after the parties had agreed to sell off a substantial number of holiday parks in order to mitigate the competition concerns raised by the NMa. Center Parcs had been owned by Scottish & Newcastle, and operated holiday parks in the Netherlands, Belgium, Germany, France and the UK. Pierre & Vacances is a French company specialising in letting out holiday accommodation and property development. Previously, in April 2000, it had acquired Gran Dorado, a Dutch company that operated holiday parks in the Netherlands, Belgium and Germany as well. Pierre & Vacances became the sole owner of Centre Parcs Europe in 2003. In the same year Center Parcs UK was listed separately on the AIM market in London.

The main overlap in activities between Center Parcs and Pierre & Vacances/ Gran Dorado was in the Netherlands, where five of the 13 holiday parks of Center Parcs, and 35 of the 40 parks of Gran Dorado, were located. There was also overlap in Belgium, where Center Parcs had two parks and Gran Dorado three, and in Germany, where Center Parcs had one park and Gran Dorado two. In France, there was overlap between Center Parcs, which had two parks, and the activities of Pierre & Vacances, but not with Gran Dorado.

The merger was initially notified to the European Commission but subsequently referred to the NMa. Center Parcs and Gran Dorado were the two largest and probably best-known, providers of holiday parks in the Netherlands and surrounding regions where Dutch short-breakers travelled to. Other, smaller players with similar offerings were Landal GreenParks, Zilverberk Parken, Euroase Parcs and Roompot Vakanties. The NMa was concerned with this overlap and assessed whether the combined Center Parcs and Gran Dorado holiday parks would face sufficient competitive constraints to be prevented from obtaining and exploiting market power. Market definition was the first stage in this assessment. The question was whether there is a separate market for self-catering accommodation in holiday parks with a range of facilities, or whether other types of accommodation for short breaks, such as apartments, hotels and camping sites, are considered substitutes by consumers. Furthermore, the geographic scope of the relevant markets needed to be examined, i.e. does the relevant market consist of the Netherlands only or of other destinations as well?

The assessment of the relevant product market undertaken by the NMa mainly emphasised the differences in the characteristics between the different types of holiday accommodation. First, the NMa concluded that it was unlikely that other types of holiday accommodation such as family hotels, hotels for city breaks, hotels close to theme parks and (luxurious) camping sites could be included in the relevant market, given the significant differences between these different types of accommodation. For example, according to the NMa, bungalows (as the holiday homes in the parks are known in the Netherlands) are mainly used by larger groups, in particular families with children, and also offer a park with a range of different facilities for entertainment; in contrast, a hotel primarily offers a place to sleep. The NMa also noted that there were differences in the prices of bungalow and hotel accommodation. In the view of the NMa, camping sites would only be a substitute for holiday parks in specific periods of the year. Furthermore, there could be differences in comfort and luxury between these two different types of accommodation.

Second, the NMa went on to argue that a further distinction could be made between different types of holiday parks in terms of facilities, quality and price. Some of the holiday parks, in particular the larger ones, distinguish themselves from the smaller more basic parks by offering a certain minimum set of facilities, such as a 'tropical' swimming pool and various restaurants. According to the NMa, the presence of a tropical pool may play a role in families' choice of holiday park. Furthermore, the NMa concluded that there are significant differences between the quality and price of the different holiday parks.

On the basis of these considerations, the NMa provisionally narrowed the market down to those holiday parks which can be qualified as four-season holiday villages, which included those operated by Center Parcs and Gran Dorado. These parks are open all year round and offer a wide range of facilities such as a tropical swimming pool, a number of restaurants, several sport/entertainment facilities and outdoor activities. The NMa did not have to come to a definite delineation of the market since it approved the merger after the parties agreed to sell off several parks. In any case, the differences in product characteristics that the NMa emphasised are no doubt of importance to some holidaymakers. However, there are several product features that make the holiday parks arguably more interchangeable in the eyes of other holidaymakers. For example, customer research showed that for many visitors of the Center Parcs and Gran Dorado parks, walking and cycling through the surroundings outside the parks was one of the main activities during their short break there (besides using the pool and other facilities inside the park). Indeed, these holiday parks are typically located in an attractive nature or coastal area, rather than, say, in the middle of an industrial site. Seen from this perspective, other types of accommodation in such areas – including hotels, holiday homes and holiday parks with fewer facilities – arguably compete in the same market.

Moreover, many alternative providers of short-break accommodation in fact also offer access to facilities such as swimming pools and restaurants nearby, even if these facilities are not located within the park itself and/or are operated by third parties. Nor is the self-catering aspect unique to holiday parks. Many hotels now also offer self-catering accommodation (through so-called 'apart-hotels'), and two of Gran Dorado's bigger parks also offered hotel accommodation.

An even broader perspective would be to include all accommodation for short breaks in the same market. Indeed, the parties used to regard Eurodisney as a major competitor. Even if its product offering is quite different – hotel accommodation near a theme park – Eurodisney competes directly to attract families with children for their short breaks, which is inconsistent with the NMa's definition of the market. Indeed, the short-break brochures in which Gran Dorado and Center Parcs advertised themselves also typically included Eurodisney and other options for short breaks. Finally, as to price differences, these were often more marked between holiday parks of a different quality than between a park and, say, hotel, of similar quality – i.e. a short break in a top-range holiday park and a top-range hotel with similar facilities nearby could have a similar price.

Hence, focusing solely on product characteristics potentially leads to a discussion without end. It cannot lead to a conclusive finding. Yet, an even greater shortcoming of this approach is that it fails to address the crucial question for market definition, namely whether a sufficient proportion of consumers consider these products to be substitutes. As noted earlier, products do not need to be perfect substitutes to be in competition with each other; a small overlap of consumers who are willing to switch can be sufficient. This aspect of market definition is captured by the SSNIP test, which is explained in the next section.

SSNIP and critical loss analysis: an economic approach

In the early 1980s, the US antitrust authorities introduced a more economic approach to market definition, the so-called hypothetical monopolist or SSNIP test. According to the US Horizontal Merger Guidelines, referred to above:

A market is defined as a product or group of products and a geographic area in which it is produced or sold such that a hypothetical profit-maximizing firm, not subject to price regulation, that was the only present and future producer or seller of those products in that area likely would impose at least a 'small but significant and non-transitory' increase in price, assuming the terms of sale of all other products are held constant. A relevant market is a group of products and a geographic area that is no bigger than necessary to satisfy this test.

The SSNIP test is used to define both the product and the geographic dimension of the market. A 'small but significant' price increase often means 5–10%, and 'non-transitory' means one or two years. The term 'only present and future producer' implies that only demand-side substitution is considered in this definition – i.e. would consumers switch after a price increase? – although in Europe supply-side substitution may also be considered – i.e. would producers active in neighbouring products or regions switch? It should also be noted that 'not subject to price regulation' means that a hypothetical monopolist would be free to raise prices to maximise profits.

The test follows an iterative process. It starts with the product (or products) and geographic area supplied by the investigated company. The basic logic of the test is that if a hypothetical, profit-maximising monopolist for that product would not raise prices, this can only be because consumers would reduce their demand for the product or because consumers would switch to the next closest substitute product. This other product should therefore be included in the group of products under consideration, and the test should be applied again to the new group. In the next round, the hypothetical monopolist is normally more likely to increase the price of the first product, since most sales would be lost to the second product (the closest substitute), which the monopolist now also controls. If the SSNIP test is still not met, a further substitute product must be included.

The ranking of substitutes requires estimating 'diversion ratios' for each of the possible substitutes (Werden, 1998). This depends in part on the cross-price elasticity of demand, which measures how much demand for one product changes with the price of the other product. For example, if the cross-price elasticity of demand for charter flights with respect to scheduled flights is 0.5, this means a 10% increase in the price of scheduled flights raises demand for charter flights by 5%. For substitute products the cross-price elasticity is positive. For complements (for example, hotel accommodation and flights in the same holiday package) the cross-price elasticity is negative, because if one becomes more expensive demand for the other will also be affected. The products (regions) with the highest diversion ratio are those to which most demand switches after the SSNIP. These are the first to be included in the test if the previous round fails the test. The iterative process continues until the group of products (regions) is such that the hypothetical monopolist supplying that group would indeed raise its price.

It is important to note that the relevant market should be the *smallest* market in which the hypothetical monopolist would raise the price. There may be other, larger, markets that also satisfy the test, but it would be a mistake to consider that larger market as a relevant market. For example, if a hypothetical monopolist of holiday accommodation in the Netherlands were to raise the price, then that is the relevant geographic market. But a hypothetical monopolistic provider of holiday accommodation in the pan-European market could perhaps also raise the price. If, on this basis, the competition authority defined the market as covering the whole of Europe, it would overlook the potential for market power in the Dutch market.

Whether a hypothetical monopolist would impose a SSNIP depends crucially on the price elasticity of demand that he faces. When demand is highly elastic (an elasticity greater than 1 in absolute value), the monopolist loses many sales, and this loss in sales may well outweigh the increase in revenues from remaining customers who pay the higher price. Conversely, if demand is inelastic (elasticity smaller than 1 in absolute terms), the sales loss may not outweigh the revenue gain. The exact cut-off point for the profitability of the price increase can be determined by using critical loss analysis, which is a way to make the SSNIP test operational.

Critical loss analysis essentially considers whether a given price increase – 5% or 10% – is profitable for a monopolist. The monopolist starts from the prevailing price in the market, which is presumably not at the monopoly but rather at some competitive level (but see comment below on the 'cellophane fallacy'). Above a certain percentage sales loss, a 5% or 10% price increase is not profitable. This 'critical' level can be determined using the standard partial-equilibrium monopoly model as commonly used in micro-economic textbook. It depends on the margin between price and marginal cost before the merger and on the type of market demand assumed. The critical sales loss can be expressed as $t/(m+2t)$, where m is the price-cost margin, expressed as a proportion, and t the specified price increase threshold, also expressed as a proportion (Werden, 1998). Another, equivalent, way of performing this analysis is by determining the critical elasticity level. Although deriving critical levels in this way relies on some strong assumptions about demand and supply parameters of the market in question, this use of the standard monopoly model gives a reasonable indication of the order of magnitude of those levels.

For a range of price-cost margins, and with the demand curve assumed to be linear, the critical sales losses for a 5% and 10% price increase are illustrated in Table 10.1 below. An important implication of Table 10.1 is that the critical loss level can be relatively low. For example, in the merger case discussed above it was roughly estimated that the holiday parks had a price-marginal cost margin in the range between 60 and 80% (this is because a large part of their costs are fixed, i.e., do not vary with sales). On this basis, the critical sales loss after a 10% price increase would be in the region of 10–12.5%. This means that even if, say, 80% of visitors to these parks would never switch to other types of short breaks, there can still be sufficient competition from these alternatives – it is switching at the margin that is of relevance to market definition.

Table 10.1 Percentage of critical sales losses (assuming linear demand)

Pre-merger margin between price and marginal costs	0	10	20	30	40	50	60	70	80	90	100
After 5% increase		50.0	25.0	16.6	12.5	10.0	8.3	7.1	6.3	5.6	5.0	4.5
After 10% increase		50.0	33.3	25.0	20.0	16.7	14.3	12.5	11.1	10.0	9.1	8.3

The SSNIP test was originally developed in order to define the relevant market in merger cases. The price increase by the hypothetical monopolist is then applied with respect to the prevailing price level, in order to determine whether a merger would create new market power. The test is also used for market definition analysis in other competition investigations, such as agreements and abuse of dominance cases (under Article 81 and 82 EC Treaty, respectively). However, the so-called 'cellophane fallacy' calls for some caution in applying the SSNIP test to non-merger cases. This is named after the 1956 Du Pont case in the USA (351 US. 377), where the US Supreme Court found that the price of cellophane could not be raised any further without inducing switching toward other wrapping materials. The court overlooked that the cellophane monopolist, Du Pont, was already pricing at monopoly levels. More generally, in a cellophane-type situation the hypothetical monopolist would not increase prices any further since it is already maximising its profits. But this does *not* imply that other products should be included in the market. In abuse of dominance cases, the hypothetical monopolist test should start from a 'competitive' price level. In practice this would come down to a full profitability analysis of the firms in question (Oxera, 2003).

Another phenomenon relevant to market definition in tourism is the so-called chain of substitution. Although two products (or regions) A and B may not be close substitutes, they may still be in the same relevant market if both are substitutes for a third product (or region) C. For example, holiday accommodation providers in the Netherlands may compete for consumers in the Netherlands and Germany while providers in Germany may in turn compete for consumers in Germany and Austria. This means that although providers in the Netherlands do not compete directly with providers in Austria, the former may still be constrained by the latter because both Dutch and Austrian providers compete for German consumers. They may therefore find themselves in the same relevant market. This also depends on the ability of providers to price discriminate between consumers from different countries – if they can discriminate, the chain of substitution breaks down. The same logic may be applicable to the holiday accommodation providers in Austria and providers in other neighbouring countries, potentially putting all providers in Europe in the same relevant market.

Another feature of the SSNIP test relates to the fact that the ability to switch to other products or areas upon a price increase may vary among different types of customers. For example, business travellers are probably more time-sensitive and less price-sensitive than leisure travellers. The former might not switch to, for example, train services if the price of the airline tickets increased, whereas the latter may do so. If a sufficient number of leisure travellers were to switch and the hypothetical monopolist of airlines did not find an increase in price profitable, then the relevant market would include both airlines and train services, despite the fact that, for business customers, airline services are the only option. However, if the hypothetical monopolist could somehow separate the two groups and charge discriminatory prices for the same service (which is what airlines typically do), there would be two different markets: one for business and one for leisure travellers.

The critical sales loss test and the holiday park merger

In the NMa investigation discussed above, the merging parties undertook a consumer survey to identify empirically the level of sales that a hypothetical monopolist would lose as a result of a small but significant increase in price (SSNIP). This type of survey is often the easiest (and fastest) way to obtain some relevant data on switching behaviour, even though it has shortcomings (see also the next section) and the results should always be interpreted with care.

The survey was held among approximately 250 'short-breakers' in the Netherlands, i.e. those who had been on any short break in the past three years – this was considered a representative sample of the whole population of Dutch holidaymakers. In order to focus the minds of the respondents (and hence increase the chance of relevant answers), they were first asked about their current behaviour and preferences in relation to short breaks. Then, before turning to the SSNIP question, respondents were asked which type of short break they were considering for the next two years. Those who (certainly or probably) considered visiting a holiday park with facilities and indoor pool (i.e. of the Center Parcs or Gran Dorado type) were asked whether they would still do so after a 10% price increase lasting for two years, or whether they would switch to an alternative type of short break or not consume a short break anymore at all.

Hence, the survey asked for a non-transitory price increase – two years – by all providers of this type of accommodation (to approximate the hypothetical monopolist and eliminate switching between such parks). To help respondents in interpreting the question, they were not only informed of the 10% increase but were also given a numerical example of what this, on average, would do to the price they would pay. Finally, the survey considered both switching to other products and 'switching' to no short break at all, since both these responses constitute a sales loss from the perspective of the monopolist. In the context of the economic demand system on which the theory of the SSNIP test is based, consuming no short break at all simply means that the consumer in question spends the money on other, completely different products, or saves it.

The results of the survey indicated that the relevant market is broader than just holiday parks with a range of facilities and an indoor swimming pool. This is because 28% of those who considered a short break in such a park said they would switch to another type of short break, or take no short break at all, after a 10% price increase. In other words, a hypothetical monopolist imposing a SSNIP would lose 28% of his customers. This would lie above the critical loss identified above in Table 10.1 (between 10% and 12.5% given the margins of 60% to 80%) and thus the monopolist would be unlikely to impose such a price increase.

Table 10.2 Alternative options considered by holiday park customers after 10% price increase

Option	% who consider this option after a price increase in holiday parks with indoor pool
Bungalow not in park	37%
Apartment	34%
Holiday park with pool and restaurant nearby	26%
Other type of hotel	25%
Family hotel with same facilities as holiday park	24%
Hotel for city break	24%
Luxury camping site with pool and restaurant	22%
Holiday park with range of facilities but no indoor pool	21%
Theme park	18%
Other option	6%
Total respondents (switchers)	68
Total no. of options given	160

The respondents who said they would switch were subsequently asked what options they would switch to. The results are shown in Table 10.2. These respondents on average gave more than two options, illustrating that various different options are considered close substitutes. Stand-alone holiday homes and apartments were clearly seen as close substitutes for holiday parks with facilities and an indoor pool, getting scores of 37% and 34%, respectively. Likewise, the different types of hotels – for city breaks, family hotels, theme park hotels and others – all received high scores as well. The results also show that the different types of holiday parks – those with indoor pool, those without indoor pool, and those with indoor pool nearby – were also regarded as substitutes. Hence, the SSNIP test indicated that the market should be defined more broadly than just holiday parks with facilities and indoor pools, and indeed more broadly than holiday parks.

The survey also shed some light on the geographic scope of the market. Respondents were first asked how far they are willing to travel to their destination for a weekend break (maximum three nights). The question was only asked for weekend breaks because of a potential concern that people are willing to travel less far for this type of holiday – even though the relevant market is that for all short breaks from two days to a week. In fact, 81% of Center Parcs visitors stay for a weekend or mid-week (four nights) break, 17% for a week, and 2% for more than a week (www.centerparcs.com). On average, the maximum travel time for weekend breaks given was 4 hours and the median answer was 3.5 hours. This confirmed the view of the merging parties that people are willing to travel about 3–4 hours for their weekend breaks. A significant proportion of respondents (26%) was even willing to travel 5 hours or more. This travel time determines the catchment area of each park. Drawing circles around each park – with a radius of, say, 200km, which is a conservative distance given the above travel times – gives an indication of the extent of the geographic market.

Respondents were also asked whether they would consider a destination abroad if all prices in the Netherlands for holiday parks with indoor pool were increased by 10% for two years. It turned out that 65% of customers who considered the holiday in question would indeed go abroad. This high percentage sales loss, together with the maximum travel times mentioned above, clearly indicated that the geographic market cannot be limited to the Netherlands only.

A second survey was also undertaken among 227 actual customers of the merging parties themselves, i.e. those who had visited either a Center Parcs or Gran Dorado park in the past three years. These customers were asked whether they considered taking a short break with these operators in the next two years, and how they would react after a 10% price increase lasting for two years. Asking this question made it possible to determine directly the so-called 'unilateral effect' of the merger. That is, if a significant proportion of customers were to switch after a 10% price increase by both Center Parcs and Grand Dorado, then the combined entity would not impose such a price increase after the transaction, implying that the transaction would not create market power. The survey results, not presented here, confirmed that this was likely to be the case.

Following the above analysis, from the perspective of Dutch holidaymakers the geographic market for short breaks covers at least the Netherlands, Belgium and some nearby parts of Germany (in particular the Eifel region) and the north of France. However, Center Parcs and Gran Dorado did not only compete for Dutch custom but also for visitors from neighbouring countries. Indeed, the Dutch currently represent only 43% of customers of Center Parcs Europe, while 28% are German, 18% French and 10% Belgian (www.centerparcs.com). It is therefore relevant to take into account the existence of a 'chain-of-substitution' effect, as discussed in the previous section.

Consider the Center Parcs parks in the Netherlands. These compete for German custom, for example, holidaymakers from Düsseldorf or Hamburg. For those customers, there are other popular short-break destinations within a 3–4 hours drive from where they live, including the Ostsee region, Thüringer Wald or the Schwarzwald. This means that Center Parcs in the Netherlands competes directly with suppliers of accommodation in those other destinations, despite the fact that Dutch holidaymakers are less likely to travel to those destinations. This chain of substitution could in principle be extended, since, for example, the Schwarzwald competes in turn with nearby destinations in France, Switzerland and Austria.

Empirical techniques to assess market definition

A customer survey of the kind undertaken in the above merger case is relatively straightforward, but potentially has a number of shortcomings. It may sometimes be difficult for consumers to assess how they would choose between different types of holidays in response to relative price changes. Careful wording of the questionnaire is important to minimise subjectivity in the answers.

Another approach would be to undertake a conjoint analysis, which is a more sophisticated type of stated-preference survey that asks consumers to choose between a wide range of different (hypothetical) options. Each option has slightly different characteristics and prices. This enables respondents' choices to be analysed in a way that reveals the weight that they attribute to the various factors that underlie their decisions, thereby making it possible to estimate price elasticities. An advantage of conjoint analysis surveys is that it is relatively simple for respondents to undertake, and that the different choices can be designed in such a way that it corresponds closely to real-life decision-making (OFT, 2003).

Competition investigations also increasingly use econometric analysis of historical price and demand data to determine price elasticities (Hausman et al., 1994; Nevo, 2001). An advantage of this approach is that it is likely to be more reliable than survey data since it is based on real transaction and price data which reflect the actual rather than the hypothetical choices made by consumers. The major challenge for this kind of analysis is to obtain appropriate data. If the product concerned is sold by supermarkets or other retailers, point-of-sale scanner data, collated by firms such as AC Nielsen, can be used. In the tourism industry this is less straightforward. However, firms might have developed rich databases of their own prices and volumes, which could still provide useful insight into customer responsiveness to price, and hence be of use to the determination of the relevant market or market power.

Conclusion

Market definition will be critical in any competition investigation in the tourism industry. In this chapter we have explained the basics of the SSNIP and critical loss tests, as commonly used by competition authorities, and illustrated how these can be applied in practice. We also discussed how market definitions based on product characteristics alone can be misleading, or at best inconclusive. Finally, we showed how through the chain of substitution the geographic dimension of a market can turn out to be broader than the actual catchment areas of providers of holiday accommodation.

Empirical evidence on price responsiveness of customers is crucial in most cases. At the least, companies involved in an investigation should seek such evidence through consumer surveys. Economic theory has also developed more sophisticated techniques to measure price elasticities, using econometric analysis of price and demand data. In fact, companies may increasingly find such analysis useful not only for competition investigations – which they presumably do not wish to be involved in too often anyway – but also for more general commercial purposes. After all, understanding who your competitors are and how your customers respond to prices is imperative for any business.

Note

The views expressed in this chapter are those of the authors alone.

References

Court of First Instance 2002. Decision on Airtours – European Commission (Case T-342/99), June.

Department of Justice and Federal Trade Commission, 1992. Horizontal Merger Guidelines, April 2nd (revised in 1997).

European Commission, 1997. Notice on the definition of relevant market for the purposes of Community competition law, OJ C 372/03, December 9th.

European Commission, 1999. Decision on merger between Airtours and First Choice Case No IV/M.1524, September.

European Commission, 2001a. Decision on proposed merger between Hilton and Scandic Case No COMP/M.2451, May.

European Commission, 2001b. Decision on merger between Nomura International and Le Meridien Hotels Case No COMP/M.2464, July.

European Commission, 2003. Decision on merger between Carnival Corporation and P&O Princess, Case No COMP/M.2706, July.

Hausman, J., Leonard, G. and Zona, J., 1994. Competitive analysis with differentiated products. Annales D'Economie et de Statistique, 34, 159–180.

Nevo, A., 2001. Measuring market power in the ready-to-eat cereal industry, Econometrica 69, 307–42.

NMa, 2001. Besluit van de directeur-generaal van de Nederlandse mededingingsautoriteit inzake Zaaknummer 2209/Gran Dorado-Center Parcs, February.

OFT, 2003. Consumer Survey Report – Annexe I. Study Commissioned from OXERA, November.

OXERA, 2003. Assessing Profitability in Competition Policy Analysis. OFT Economic Discussion Paper 6, July.

UK Competition Commission, 1997. Foreign package holidays: A report on the supply in the UK of tour operators' services and travel agents' services in relation to foreign package holidays, December.

UK Competition Commission, 2002. P&O Princess Cruises plc and Royal Caribbean Cruises Ltd – A report on the proposed merger, June.

US Federal Trade Commission, 2002. In the Matter of Royal Caribbean Cruises, Ltd./P&O

Princess Cruises plc and Carnival Corporation/P&O Princess Cruises plc, File No 021 0041, October.

Werden, G., 1998. Demand elasticities in antitrust analysis. Antitrust Law Journal, 66 (2), 363–409.

11

Conclusion
The need for constructive policymaking

Andreas Papatheodorou

A certifier of the book's themes

This book examined issues of corporate rivalry and competition issues in tourism. According to the conventional wisdom, the tourism industries are characterised by the existence of many small and medium enterprises (SMEs) with no strategic behaviour. In reality, however, and following the discussion in Chapter 1, a notable dualism seems to have developed in the tourism marketplace; in addition to the SME, a powerful oligopoly of service providers and intermediaries exists and applies sophisticated techniques of corporate rivalry to enhance position and exercise market power. On these grounds, the study of competition issues is valid; the use of restrictive practices is not unusual and unless spotted, these may harm not only the other producers but more importantly the consumer welfare. Chapters 2 and 3 set the theoretical background of the book while 4 and 5 focused on the air transport industry. Subsequently, Chapters 6 and 7 studied the hospitality sector and the travel distribution system. Chapter 8 analysed the impact of information technology and Chapters 9 and 10 discussed issues related to visitor attractions and holiday parks respectively.

The themes explored in the book may be collectively encapsulated in the context of the cruise sector. This combines elements of transport for tourism and hospitality (lodging and catering) sold as a bundle in an all-inclusive package; to a certain extent, the cruise ship is a visitor attraction itself and acts also as a holiday park. In fact, the cruise industry is characterised by significant scale and scope economies. High utilisation of a ship is crucial, as the income lost because of an unsold berth is much higher than in the case of the airline industry; hence, deep discounting policies and strategic accumulation of spare capacity to deter market entry are inherent in corporate rivalry. To avoid a mutually detrimental price war, cruise liner operators may decide to compete in non-price dimensions such as the configuration of the ship itself, the season of the cruise, the routeing and the methods of booking. Brand awareness and reputation are important in the cruise industry as the product is relatively expensive and its consumers are risk averse, mainly because many are in the older age group. Links with the travel distribution system are strong and disintermediation has not advanced much yet. In fact, vertical integration with tour operators is apparent as is the use of restrictive practices in terms of, e.g., override commissions. Accessibility to the ship market and to port facilities may also constitute significant barriers to new entrants. As a result of a recent wave of mergers and acquisitions, the global cruise industry is now dominated by three major groups accounting jointly for three-quarters of the world market (Papatheodorou, 2006).

Interestingly, the proposed mega-merger between Carnival and POPC was approved by competition authorities in Europe and the USA in 2002 despite the resulting heavy concentration in both product and geographical markets. This may signify the liberal spirits among policymakers and their tendency to move away from structural characteristics and focus their inquiries on conduct and firm performance. It is too early to judge the validity of this approval; in any case, however, an ex post breaking-up of a merger is much more difficult than an ex ante prohibition. In other words, policymakers should be very cautious and alert when dealing with such issues.

Competition policymaking and conflict of interest

An essential issue to address in the case of competition policymaking is territorial jurisdiction. More specifically, the exercise of competition policy is easier in the context of domestic tourism as all service providers act in the same country under the supervision of the same authority. Hence, the notion of public interest, consumer welfare and fair play in the marketplace can be defined and pursued in a clear manner. Nonetheless, the situation is more complicated in the case of international tourism, where service providers from different countries are involved. In fact, a conflict of policy interests may emerge in the case of zero sum games, when the welfare of a tourism origin's stakeholder is achieved to the detriment of the profit made by a service provider based in the tourism destination. Therefore, it is essential to address the various tourism sectors on an individual basis.

Air transport

With respect to the airline industry, the interests of competition authorities in origin and destination countries are aligned. This was not the case in the past, where regulatory constraints prevented origin charter or even scheduled carriers from operating to and from the tourism destination. Nowadays, however, the prevailing spirit is that a competitive airline industry is beneficial for both origin consumers and destination service providers of complementary products (e.g. local transport, lodging and catering): the former may pay lower prices and get a higher service quality while the latter enhance their accessibility in the international marketplace. In this context, the origin policymakers should realise the occasional failure of contestability conditions in the industry and prevent established incumbents from using restrictive practices which deter market entry or induce exit; pricing, network structure and timing of flights, frequent flyer programmes, slot allocation and the use of global distribution systems are some of the important issues to consider, as discussed in Chapter 4. From their perspective, destination planners and policymakers should pursue an active transport portfolio strategy. They might try to boost air competition by providing financial incentives for new routes operated either by incumbent airlines or start-ups in the origins in the destination. Caution, however, is required as the European Commission has severely criticised local authorities in the case of Ryanair subsidies, as discussed in Chapter 5. Moreover, and in collaboration with their colleagues at the origin, the destination policymakers may favour the development of alternative modes of transport as a credible competitive treat. Part of the reason why air fares between London and Paris are kept at relatively low levels is competition from Eurostar; similarly, high-speed ships or catamarans may potentially constitute a good substitute to air transport especially when the sea port is easier to access from the city centre than the airport (Papatheodorou, 2001).

The situation is somewhat more complicated with respect to airports. This is because of the inherent asymmetry in spatial fixity that exists between the operations of airlines and airports; in case of a local business downturn, the former can always redirect their planes to more profitable routes, whereas the latter are condemned to bear the risk of sunk costs in heavy infrastructure of limited alternative functionality. Still, airlines and airports are mutually interdependent and a love-and-hate relationship seems to have developed over time, as argued in Chapter 5. Origin airlines would definitely favour an active rivalry among destination airports, as this could lower airport charges. Competition authorities in the origin country would also be happy if the airlines were then to pass a substantial share of these cost savings to customers as lower prices. On the other hand, policymakers in destination countries would prefer not to experience airport (tax) revenue dilution that would only benefit foreign consumers, unless the increased transport accessibility (due to lower air fares) generated demand complementarities (in terms of expenditure in the other tourism sectors) of sufficient level to outweigh the losses. The argument bears some resemblance to the old rationale behind protectionism of flag carriers; unlike the airline industry, however, public sector interventionism in airports is still very important. While the case of airport subsidies to Ryanair does prove the importance of derived demand in tourism, Bermuda II is an excellent counterexample. This refers to the very restrictive bilateral air agreement between the USA and the UK over access to London Heathrow Airport; despite the liberal spirits prevailing in both countries, the strategic importance of this highly congested airport impedes the liberalisation of the market and denies any potential benefits for leisure and business tourism on both sides of the Atlantic.

Hotels and the travel distribution system

The above argumentation may be also validly applied in the context of the hotel and the travel distribution sectors. We will first assume that the origin tourists travel independently; hence they make their own arrangements with hotels at the destination. If the latter form an oligopoly as part of their affiliation with transnational chains, the interests of competition authorities in both origin and destination countries will not diverge. The former would request the latter to take measures against the abuse of market power by the hotel chains. The latter would probably consent, as high prices render the destination less competitive while any supernormal profits may flow out the country anyway, since shareholders are foreigners; tax revenue may also be low due to internal transfer pricing techniques used by transnational corporations (Dunning and McQueen, 1982). Besides, the international hotel chains may threaten the very existence of locally owned tourism small and medium hotel enterprises. If the headquarters of these transnational hotel chains are located in the tourism origin country, then its competition authorities may take a more active stance by threatening the hotel chains with an investigation in their own home. On the other hand, if the local hotel oligopoly is controlled by shareholders of the destination country, then a situation similar to that involving airports emerges. Nonetheless, the unwillingness of destination competition authorities to deter collusion might be stronger in this case, since tourism consumption (and related tax revenue) beyond transport and hotel activities is limited. This may raise tension between competition authorities in origins and destinations.

This clash of interests may be more intense when the travel distribution system is involved. The origin authorities would favour a competitive oligopsony among the origin tour operators. This would ensure that the latter could exercise their bargaining power over hoteliers and other destination providers to secure reduced prices and cost savings which would be subsequently passed to the consumers. On the other hand, the destination authorities would prefer an overall competitive market among the origin tour operators. In this case, the latter would have only limited market power against destination service providers and would not appropriate their producer surplus; similarly, competition in the sales market would guarantee affordable prices to origin customers and enhance tourism flows in the destination. If an oligopsonistic configuration is inevitable, however, then local policymakers may at best try to reduce its power. This may be done through the creation of a bilateral oligopoly at the destination: for example, local hoteliers may be encouraged to form a consortium to negotiate collectively with the tour operators. Such a decision, however, may be unsuccessful if the tour operators are able to substitute one destination for another easily, as argued in Chapters 6 and 7. Moreover, this strategy would probably raise adverse reactions from the origin competition authorities, especially if it resulted in higher consumer prices. As an alternative, local tourism authorities may pursue a product differentiation strategy to increase the perceived uniqueness of the place and attract niche tour operators. This should be complemented by seeking disintermediation through an integrated platform of destination management information systems and the Internet, as discussed in Chapter 8. The exploration of new origin markets where the travel distribution system is less concentrated may also be used in the context of an active portfolio strategy. Oligopsonist tour operators should also be persuaded to value longer-term corporate relations with local hotels and to pursue service quality rather than lower prices; nonetheless, this very point depends on the nature and the preferences of the origin market's clientele.

Synthesis

It seems, therefore, that the notion of public interest is not always clear; hence and despite the illusory objectivity offered by purely technical approaches, the treatment of corporate rivalry and competition issues is context-dependent. To address any clashes of interests between origin and destination competition authorities, an effort should be made to move beyond a zero-sum game logic and closer to a win-win way of thinking. Origin authorities should understand that the sustainable operation of destination providers in the longer term is a prerequisite for tourist satisfaction and the achievement of consumer welfare. Similarly, destination competition authorities should understand that a 'national champion' mentality and the acceptance of restrictive practices by local oligopolists in the context of a level play with 'foreigners' may subsequently harm and impede the development of domestic tourism. Corporate rivalry should be encouraged; however, co-ordination success is also needed: co-opetition, therefore, may be the way forward.

References

Dunning, J. H. and M. McQueen (1982) Transnational Corporations in International Tourism. United Nations Centre for Transnational Corporations, New York.

Papatheodorou, A. (2001) Tourism, Transport Geography and Industrial Economics: A Synthesis in the Context of Mediterranean Islands. Anatolia, 12(1): 23–34.

Papatheodorou, A. (2006) The Cruise Industry – An Industrial Organisation Perspective. Cruise Tourism: Issues, Impacts, Cases edited by R. Dowling, Wallingford: CABI Publishing.

Index

acquisition: 6, 7, 8, 16, 36, 69, 96, 101, 104, 125, 130, 131, 132, 138, 151, 159, 167, 168, 172, 179, 183, 189, 202 (*see also* merger)
advertising: 11, 20, 21, 22, 26, 27, 65 (*see also* marketing)
aid (state): 15, 60, 86, 87 (*see also* subsidy)
Air France: 7, 63, 67, 70, 160
airline: 6, 7, 11, 13–16, 23–26, 30, 31, 37, 42, 54–72, 76–91, 96–99, 102, 121, 124, 125, 126, 128, 129, 134, 135, 137, 138, 139, 151–162, 164, 165, 167, 194, 201–203
  open skies: 15, 70, 71, 72
airport: 6, 15, 30, 31, 60, 61, 62, 64, 68, 69, 70, 71, 76–91, 135, 157, 203, 204
  handling: 63, 71, 79, 80, 87
  slot: 15, 30, 61, 69, 71, 76, 79, 87–90, 203
alliance: 7, 8, 15, 26, 56, 60–66, 69, 70, 78, 82, 90, 155, 172 (*see also* airline)
  oneworld: 7, 63, 69
  SkyTeam: 7, 63
  Star Alliance: 7, 63, 64
Amadeus: 155, 159, 160, 162
American Airlines: 61, 63, 65, 69, 153, 160
American Express: 130, 131, 133, 139
antitrust: 63–65, 70, 158, 191
attraction: 4, 5, 9, 10, 16, 17, 172–185, 201 (*see also* park)
authorities (public): 17, 37, 44, 67, 76, 79, 158, 181, 184, 188, 191, 192, 198, 202–205 (*see also* policymaking)

BAA: 78, 81, 82, 84, 85
bargaining: 8, 125, 145, 148, 204
barrier (to entry and/or exit): 2, 5, 6, 8, 16, 20, 21, 22, 24, 25, 26, 27, 35, 42, 54, 60, 61, 63, 66, 71, 72, 77, 82, 83, 129, 136, 145, 148, 155, 158, 162, 168, 172, 202

British Airways: 61, 62, 63, 65, 67, 68, 69, 150, 152, 154

C&N: 36, 96
Carlson Wagonlit: 130, 131, 133
Carnival: 7, 187, 202
cartel: 2, 11, 28, 38 (*see also* collusion)
Cendant: 126, 131, 132, 137, 139, 145, 155, 159, 160, 168
China: 102 (*see also* Hong Kong, Taiwan)
collusion: 28, 178, 204 (*see also* cartel)
competitive advantage: 21, 45, 47, 51, 57, 64, 66, 179
consortium: 25, 64, 81, 136, 155, 159, 163, 204
contract: 29, 63, 80, 82, 138, 157, 158, 162
CRS: 24, 65, 125, 127, 153, 155–159 (*see also* GDS)
cruising: 7, 10, 17, 97, 102, 124, 131, 134, 161, 187, 189, 201, 202

Delta Airlines: 58, 63, 134, 160
deregulation: 15, 16, 25, 56, 58, 59, 60, 62, 65, 67, 69, 70, 72, 77, 125, 137, 138, 139, 153, 155, 162 (*see also* liberalisation)
discrete choice: 10, 14, 49, 50, 51
discrimination: 30, 62, 71, 87, 158, 162, 194
disintermediation: 6, 145, 147, 152, 154, 165, 166, 202, 205 (*see also* tour operator, travel agent)
Disneyland: 17, 180
distribution: 4, 6, 7, 15, 16, 21, 24, 25, 26, 62, 68, 94, 98, 100, 101, 102, 111, 119, 120, 121, 124–139, 143, 145, 147, 149–169, 201, 203, 204, 205 (*see also* tour operator, travel agent)
dominance: 2, 7, 15, 67, 90, 96, 129, 165, 179, 194

economies:
  of scale: 3, 6, 7, 9, 13, 16, 25, 26, 36, 58, 80, 81, 83, 130, 155, 162, 201
  of scope: 3, 7, 9, 13, 16, 64, 82, 83, 201
efficiency: 1, 2, 3, 22, 31, 41, 44, 58, 59, 67, 84, 149, 169
elasticity: 22, 24, 44, 46–49, 58, 188, 189, 192, 193, 198, 199
equity partnership: 15, 63, 69, 70, 104
e-tourism: 143, 149
European Commission: 60, 66, 67, 80, 87, 88, 89, 187, 188, 189, 203
Expedia: 99, 128, 131, 133, 136, 139, 145, 150, 151, 155, 164, 166

Federal Trade Commission: 187, 188
France: 49, 87, 94, 96, 97, 101, 102, 103, 108, 109, 114, 119, 189, 197
Fraport: 78, 82, 86
FTI: 36, 96

Galileo: 132, 136, 137, 155, 159, 160
game theory: 14, 20, 21, 27, 32, 54
GDS: 16, 24, 124–128, 132, 136–139, 152, 154–157, 159, 161, 162, 163, 165 (*see also* CRS)
Germany: 11, 36, 50, 79, 94, 96, 97, 99, 101, 102, 103, 108, 109, 114, 115, 117, 120, 127, 128, 129, 159, 164, 175, 189, 194, 197
Gran Dorado: 188–191, 195, 197
Greece: 4, 11, 15, 49, 85, 94–122, 127

Herfindahl-Hirschman Index (HHI): 14, 35, 36, 37, 44, 51 (*see also* market concentration)
Hilton: 164
Hong Kong: 78
hospitality: 9, 15, 16, 37, 94, 132, 163, 201
hotel: 3, 4, 6, 7, 8, 10, 11, 13, 14, 15, 23, 24, 25, 26, 28, 29, 31, 44, 79, 82, 94–122, 124, 125, 129, 132, 133, 134, 136, 137, 139, 145, 146, 150, 151, 152, 154, 155, 161, 163–168, 187, 189–192, 196, 204, 205

International Air Transport Association (IATA): 55, 56, 57, 63, 66, 67, 70, 88
Information Communication Technologies (ICT): 16, 143–147, 149, 150, 151, 153, 157, 163–167, 169, 201
industrial organisation: 4, 14, 20, 21, 32, 72
innovation: 1, 3, 16, 21, 22, 26, 27, 136, 172, 179
integration: 63, 64, 166
  horizontal: 25, 26, 54, 139, 167
  vertical: 16, 22, 26, 96, 167, 168, 169, 202
interdependence: 11, 23, 27, 28, 32, 40, 48, 179
intermediation: 147, 150, 152, 164, 165, 167
Italy: 36, 49, 94, 99, 103, 114

KLM: 7, 69, 70

Lastminute.com: 99, 150, 151, 164, 166, 167, 168
liberalisation: 31, 62, 67, 71, 72, 80, 83, 203 (*see also* deregulation)
loyalty: 64, 65, 66, 67, 152, 172, 176, 177
LTU: 36, 96, 114
Lufthansa: 7, 61, 63, 66, 67, 69, 97, 160

market:
  concentration: 7, 14, 17, 25, 35, 36, 40, 43, 44, 96, 128, 129, 130, 138
  definition: 1, 17, 187–199 (*see also* SSNIP test)
  entry: 2, 6, 7, 8, 21, 24, 25, 28, 42, 175, 176, 201, 203 (*see also* barrier)
  exit: 2, 6, 7, 21, 24, 25, 28, 63, 175, 176, 203 (*see also* barrier)
  power abuse: 2, 3, 6, 7, 9, 11, 13, 28, 45, 72, 83, 86, 172, 194, 204
  structure: 1, 2, 3, 7, 8, 14, 16, 20–24, 31, 32, 35, 43, 44, 98, 127, 172, 178, 180, 181, 185 (*see also* monopolistic competition, monopoly, oligopoly, oligopsony, perfect competition)
marketing: 25, 26, 27, 49, 51, 54, 61–65, 67, 70, 76, 87, 101, 119, 120, 121, 125, 126, 149, 150, 154, 156, 159, 163, 165 (*see also* advertising)
merger: 2, 3, 7, 8, 16, 17, 21, 36, 37, 43, 58, 64, 69, 70, 88, 96, 101, 130, 138, 151, 159, 167, 172, 179, 187, 188, 189, 190, 191, 193, 194, 195, 197, 198, 202 (*see also* acquisition)
monopolistic competition: 1, 2, 9, 11, 16, 175–178, 182, 185, 187, 188 (*see also* market structure)
monopoly: 2, 6, 8, 9, 15, 21, 28, 30, 31, 35, 43, 45, 46, 59, 76, 79, 80, 83, 84, 156, 172, 177, 178, 183, 185, 188, 191–195 (*see also* market structure)
MyTravel (formerly Airtours): 26, 96, 97, 110, 112–117, 127, 187

Netherlands: 17, 70, 96, 97, 101, 103, 114, 189, 190, 192, 194, 195, 197
network: 5, 8, 25, 60–62, 65, 67–70, 72, 78, 83, 97, 99, 102, 104, 144, 165, 168, 203

oligopoly: 1, 2, 3, 6, 7, 8, 9, 11, 14, 16, 27, 28, 44, 54, 98, 127, 128, 137, 177–180, 185, 201, 204, 205 (*see also* market structure)
oligopsony: 6, 11, 98, 103, 104, 121, 204, 205 (*see also* market structure)
Opodo: 150, 155, 166
Orbitz: 131, 132, 133, 145, 150, 155, 166, 168
ownership: 17, 59, 61, 62, 64, 69, 70, 71, 76, 80, 81, 85, 88, 90, 102, 144, 155, 159, 160, 178, 180, 183, 185

park: 4, 14, 17, 147, 174, 175, 177–181, 183, 188–191, 193, 195, 196, 197, 201
P&O Princess Cruises: 7, 187, 202
perfect competition: 1, 2, 37, 175, 177, 182 (*see also* market structure)
policymaking: 14, 17, 201–205 (*see also* authorities)
Portugal: 49, 87, 94, 95
price war: 2, 6, 11, 13, 27, 28, 101, 155, 179, 201
privatisation: 15, 76, 82, 84
profitability: 8, 13, 16, 22, 24, 28, 31, 32, 43, 44, 56, 57, 89, 118, 145, 149, 150, 153, 154, 162, 163, 164, 167, 175, 176, 179, 181, 185, 193, 194

quality: 2, 3, 5, 6, 11, 13, 14, 23, 25, 26, 32, 38, 45, 46, 60, 64, 71, 79, 80, 85, 111, 113, 118, 121, 129, 185, 190, 191, 202, 205

research and development: 1, 27
regulation: 14, 15, 20, 22, 25, 26, 58, 59, 63, 70, 76, 83–86, 88, 90, 156, 158, 191, 192
restructuring: 8, 68, 144
retail: 6, 15, 26, 79, 83, 95, 97, 98, 100, 101, 102, 120, 124–140, 164, 165, 166, 173, 174, 198 (*see also* travel agent)
Rewe Touristik: 96, 97, 110, 112–117, 129
risk: 6, 8, 25, 61, 82, 86, 158, 167, 183, 184, 201, 203
Royal Caribbean Cruises: 7, 187

Sabre: 126, 136, 138, 153, 159, 160, 161
Structure–Conduct–Performance (SCP) paradigm: 14, 20–23, 31, 32
Small and Medium Enterprise (SME): 125, 164, 201, 204

Spain: 49, 58, 87, 94, 95, 96, 99, 103, 160
SSNIP test: 17, 188, 191–196, 198 (*see also* market definition)
Starwood: 164
subsidy: 13, 20, 22, 59, 61, 71, 82, 86, 87, 182, 203
substitution: 1, 14, 22, 24, 46–49, 54, 83, 125, 145, 148, 149, 187, 189–192, 194, 196, 198, 203, 204
sunk cost: 1, 3, 6, 17, 25, 26, 31, 203

Taiwan: 37, 44
Thomas Cook: 26, 96, 97, 110, 112–117, 127, 128
Thomson: 7, 26, 96, 97, 101, 102, 111, 114, 127, 128
tour operator: 2, 6–11, 13–16, 24–28, 31, 36, 45, 82, 94–122, 124, 125, 127–130, 132, 136, 152, 161, 164–167, 187, 202, 204, 205 (*see also* distribution, wholesale)
transnational: 7, 8, 13, 17, 24, 25, 26, 70, 168, 204
travel agent: 6, 7, 15, 16, 24, 26, 31, 62, 65, 82, 95, 97, 98, 99, 101, 102, 105–108, 110, 120, 124–140, 150–159, 161, 162, 164–168, 187 (*see also* distribution, retail)
    commission: 16, 65, 98, 134, 135, 136, 139, 153, 154, 155, 157, 162, 164, 165–168, 202
Travelocity: 99, 131, 132, 133, 136, 139, 150, 155, 160, 166
TUI: 7, 11, 15, 36, 96–99, 101–104, 110–117, 127, 128, 129, 165
Turkey: 94, 95, 96, 103, 119

uncertainty: 17, 30, 85, 87, 89
United Airlines: 61, 63, 89
United Kingdom: 11, 26, 28, 31, 37, 38, 41, 42, 43, 47, 49, 68, 81, 82, 84–87, 89, 94, 96–99, 102, 103, 114, 115, 127, 132, 164, 167, 175, 178, 183, 184, 187, 189, 203
United States: 7, 15, 16, 24, 25, 31, 37, 58, 59, 60, 62, 66, 67–72, 77, 79, 81, 86, 88, 89, 90, 97, 124–140, 151, 155, 159, 160, 180, 181, 188, 191, 194, 202, 203

welfare: 1, 2, 13, 184, 201, 202, 205
wholesale: 6, 95, 100, 124–128, 131, 132, 136, 137, 168 (*see also* tour operator)